Family Law

Edited by

Professor Joel Wm. Friedman

Tulane University Law School
Jack M. Gordon Professor of Procedural Law & Jurisdiction

D1605138

Wolters Kluwer
Law & Business

Wolters Kluwer Law & Business
Attn: Order Department
PO Box 990
Frederick, MD 21705

Printed in the United States of America.

1 2 3 4 5 6 7 8 9 0

ISBN 978-0-7355-9796-9

About Wolters Kluwer Law & Business

Wolters Kluwer Law & Business is a leading global provider of intelligent information and digital solutions for legal and business professionals in key specialty areas, and respected educational resources for professors and law students. Wolters Kluwer Law & Business connects legal and business professionals as well as those in the education market with timely, specialized authoritative content and information-enabled solutions to support success through productivity, accuracy and mobility.

Serving customers worldwide, Wolters Kluwer Law & Business products include those under the Aspen Publishers, CCH, Kluwer Law International, Loislaw, Best Case, ftwilliam.com and MediRegs family of products.

CCH products have been a trusted resource since 1913, and are highly regarded resources for legal, securities, antitrust and trade regulation, government contracting, banking, pension, payroll, employment and labor, and healthcare reimbursement and compliance professionals.

Aspen Publishers products provide essential information to attorneys, business professionals and law students. Written by preeminent authorities, the product line offers analytical and practical information in a range of specialty practice areas from securities law and intellectual property to mergers and acquisitions and pension/benefits. Aspen's trusted legal education resources provide professors and students with high-quality, up-to-date and effective resources for successful instruction and study in all areas of the law.

Kluwer Law International products provide the global business community with reliable international legal information in English. Legal practitioners, corporate counsel and business executives around the world rely on Kluwer Law journals, looseleafs, books, and electronic products for comprehensive information in many areas of international legal practice.

Loislaw is a comprehensive online legal research product providing legal content to law firm practitioners of various specializations. Loislaw provides attorneys with the ability to quickly and efficiently find the necessary legal information they need, when and where they need it, by facilitating access to primary law as well as state-specific law, records, forms and treatises.

Best Case Solutions is the leading bankruptcy software product to the bankruptcy industry. It provides software and workflow tools to flawlessly streamline petition preparation and the electronic filing process, while timely incorporating ever-changing court requirements.

ftwilliam.com offers employee benefits professionals the highest quality plan documents (retirement, welfare and non-qualified) and government forms (5500/PBGC, 1099 and IRS) software at highly competitive prices.

MediRegs products provide integrated health care compliance content and software solutions for professionals in healthcare, higher education and life sciences, including professionals in accounting, law and consulting.

Wolters Kluwer Law & Business, a division of Wolters Kluwer, is headquartered in New York. Wolters Kluwer is a market-leading global information services company focused on professionals.

CHECK OUT THESE OTHER GREAT TITLES:

Friedman's Practice Series

Outlining Is Important But PRACTICE MAKES PERFECT!

All Content Written By *Top Professors* • 100 Multiple Choice Questions • Comprehensive *Professor* Answers and Analysis for Multiple Choice Questions • *Real Law School* Essay Exams • Comprehensive *Professor* Answers for Essay Exams

Available titles in this series include:

Friedman's Administrative Law

Friedman's Bankruptcy

Friedman's Civil Procedure

Friedman's Constitutional Law

Friedman's Contracts

Friedman's Criminal Law

Friedman's Criminal Procedure

Friedman's Evidence

Friedman's Family Law

Friedman's Property

Friedman's Sales

Friedman's Torts

Friedman's Wills, Trusts, and Estates

ASK FOR THEM AT YOUR LOCAL BOOKSTORE
IF UNAVAILABLE, PURCHASE ONLINE AT *http://lawschool.aspenpublishers.com*

About the Editor

Joel Wm. Friedman
Tulane Law School
Jack M. Gordon Professor of Procedural Law & Jurisdiction,
 Director of Technology
BS, 1972, Cornell University; JD, 1975, Yale University

Professor Joel Wm. Friedman, the Jack M. Gordon Professor of
Procedural Law & Jurisdiction at Tulane Law School, is the lead
author of two highly regarded casebooks — "The Law of Civil
Procedure: Cases and Materials" (published by Thomson/West)
and "The Law of Employment Discrimination" (published by
Foundation Press). His many law review articles have been
published in, among others, the Cornell, Texas, Iowa, Tulane,
Vanderbilt, and Washington & Lee Law Reviews.

Professor Friedman is an expert in computer-assisted legal instruction who has lectured throughout
the country on how law schools can integrate developing technologies into legal education. He is a past
recipient of the Felix Frankfurter Teaching Award and the Sumpter Marks Award for Scholarly
Achievement.

CONTENTS

FAMILY LAW
ESSAY EXAMINATION
QUESTIONS

INSTRUCTIONS

Unless otherwise indicated, all events in the hypotheticals take place in Commonalia, the 51st state of the United States. It is a common law jurisdiction. Unless otherwise stated, all causes of action available in the other states are available in Commonalia to the extent that they are compatible with one another. To the extent that they are not, unless otherwise indicated, every issue in Commonalia is de novo, to be decided by consulting the relevant rules of the other states to determine the best answer. Unless otherwise indicated, any principles or procedures of law provided in a question are to be treated as law for the purposes of that question only; they are not to be treated as applicable in other questions on this or any of the other examinations in this book.

FAMILY LAW ESSAY EXAM #1

QUESTION #1

Harry and Wanda married ten years ago, when Harry was 30 and Wanda was 27. Neither had been married before. They have three children, Dorothy (age 3), Deirdre (age 6), and Scott (age 8). Harry is the family breadwinner, and Wanda stays home with the children. Harry is a lifelong Catholic; Wanda was raised as a Baptist. They married in the Catholic Church. At the time of their engagement, they agreed that any children they had together would be raised and educated as Catholics because, whereas Harry has always been a devout practitioner of his faith, Wanda at that time had no religious beliefs and had not engaged in religious practices since her teenage years. Before the wedding, the couple memorialized this agreement in a writing that, in terms of its form, meets the legal requirements for a contract. It contains no other provisions.

Since her mother's death two years ago, Wanda has returned to the Baptist church. She is now deeply disturbed about the religious views her children have learned from the teachers at their Catholic school, from their pastor's sermons, and from Harry; these differ radically from Baptist teachings. She has told Harry that she wants the children to attend the local public school and Sunday Bible classes at the Baptist church that she has joined. Harry adamantly opposes changing the children's religious upbringing. Both parents are sincerely concerned for their children's welfare.

Harry has discovered that Wanda reviews the children's assignments for religion class each day. When Catholic beliefs covered in them differ from Baptist ones, she tells the children that the Catholic beliefs are false. She then teaches them the Baptist beliefs on the same subject. Wanda has repeatedly refused to stop this practice when Harry requested that she do so. She now refuses to cooperate in the children's attendance at the Catholic school or at Catholic religious services. Until this dispute concerning the religious upbringing of the children, the couple had been happily married.

Assume that Commonalia has a mixed fault and no-fault divorce statute, and that its fault statute preserves the possibility of receiving a judicial separation from bed and board. Harry does not want a divorce because it is contrary to his religious beliefs. He is seeking to have the marriage declared void, and in the alternative, a judicial separation on grounds of cruelty. He is also seeking sole custody of the children, and asking the court to enforce the premarital agreement in the custody determination. Wanda has counterclaimed for divorce on the state's no-fault ground of irretrievable breakdown. That statute requires only that one of the parties state under oath that the marriage is irretrievably broken. The court then evaluates the marriage; it can order a "cooling-off" period of up to 60 days. It can find irretrievable breakdown if there is no reasonable prospect of reconciliation. Wanda also has asked for sole custody of the children, and is seeking to have the prenuptial agreement declared null and void as a violation of her fundamental right to freedom of religion under the First Amendment of the U.S. Constitution. Assume that Commonalia's child custody statute contains a preference for joint custody over sole custody, but that the preference does not control if the court finds that sole custody is in the best interest of the children. Advise Harry as to the likely outcome of his case.

QUESTION #2

Ben and Jerry, a same-sex couple, and Sam, their 16-year-old adopted son, moved to Commonalia a year ago when Jerry's employer transferred him there. Prior to the move, they were domiciled in California for twelve years. Beginning nine years ago, Jerry and Ben acted as foster parents to Sam, an orphan with no family. California law permits joint adoption of a child by two parents of the same sex. Two years after beginning to foster Sam, Jerry and Ben sought and received a state court judgment of adoption decreeing that they were Sam's legal parents. In May 2008, the Supreme Court of California struck down the state's statutory limitation of marriage to opposite-sex couples, and refused to issue a stay on same-sex couples' marriages. Ben and Jerry married during that month. In November 2008, a majority of Californians voted in favor of a referendum that amended the state Constitution to ban same-sex marriages in the state. The amendment was challenged in court, but the Supreme Court of California upheld the ban in May 2009. California's attorney general has issued an opinion that the same-sex marriages already contracted remain valid. Thus far, a few court challenges to the validity of those marriages have been filed, but were dismissed for lack of standing.

On November 12, 2009, Jerry was critically injured in an automobile accident in Commonalia. Jerry is in the hospital's intensive care unit (ICU) in a coma, in critical condition. Members of patient's immediate family age 15 and older have a right under state law to visit him for a ten-minute period every hour unless a visit has directly caused deterioration of the patient's condition. Either Ben or Sam or both have been at Jerry's side every time he is permitted to have visitors.

Jerry has never executed a power of attorney appointing someone to make decisions for him if he became incompetent to make them himself. Jerry's parents, notified by Ben, have arrived; they have asserted the right to make decisions for Jerry under Commonalia's statute on Substituted Decision-Making for Incompetent Individuals. According to that statute, in the absence of a power of attorney duly executed prior to incompetence, the spouse not estranged from the incompetent has the right to make decisions for the incompetent; if no spouse exists or is available, the adult child or children of the incompetent have that right; if no adult child exists or is available, the parent or parents of the incompetent have that right. The hospital agrees with Jerry's parents. Jerry's parents' first decision is to exclude Ben and Sam from the ICU.

On the basis of his California marriage to Jerry, Ben wants to challenge the choice of the parents as substituted decision-makers. He also wants to challenge the exclusion of Sam from the room. Assume that your state has never recognized same-sex marriage either judicially or legislatively. However, it has no legislation, court decisions, or constitutional measures that explicitly ban such marriages. Advise Ben.

QUESTION #3

Mona and Frank were married for six years when Mona had an affair with Ed, who was unmarried. Mona became pregnant. She and Frank no longer had sexual relations because he had found out about the affair with Ed; Mona told Ed this, and that he was the only possible father of the child. Ed asked her to marry him. Mona told Frank that she wanted a divorce so that she could marry Ed. Frank told her that under the circumstances, he wanted to end the marriage as quickly as possible. He said that he had seen on the Internet an advertisement for an attorney in Alabama who said that she could obtain a quick divorce for couples there, provided it was consensual and based on a no-fault ground. Frank contacted the attorney, Ima Fraud. After describing the situation, he made an appointment for himself and Mona with Ms. Fraud. The two of them flew to Alabama, where Fraud was located. There, Frank and Mona signed what appeared to be a divorce petition and supporting documentation. They paid Fraud $500. Six weeks later, they received copies of what appeared to be a judgment of divorce.

Mona showed Ed her judgment of divorce from Frank. Mona and Ed's wedding took place before a justice of the peace two weeks later, two months prior to the child's birth. Ed's name was entered as father on the child's birth certificate. Mona and Ed named her Gina. They raised her together for eight years, by which point Mona had become bored with Ed. Taking Gina with her, she moved in with Frank, with whom she had begun an affair.

Mona asked Frank whether, if she divorced Ed, he would marry her again. Frank said yes, and so the two of them searched for Ima Fraud's phone number on the Internet. They discovered that Fraud was serving a sentence in the federal penitentiary in Alabama, having been convicted of running a phony divorce racket across state lines for 12 years. Thousands of people all over the United States who believed themselves to be divorced were not. Frank called an information hotline set up by the Alabama judicial system to answer inquiries from possible victims, and discovered that he and Mona had not received a divorce. Frank and Mona let Ed know that he had never been validly married to Mona. Mona and Frank answered Ed's suit for custody of Gina, alleging that she is Frank's child because Mona was married to Frank at the time of Gina's birth and thereafter. Ed, seeking to level the playing field for the custody action, filed a paternity action to establish that he was Gina's biological father. The trial court dismissed Ed's suit for lack of standing.

Commonalia is the state where all the parties live. It has a statute on the establishment of paternity that adopts the common law marital presumption that the husband of the mother is the father of a child conceived or born during the marriage or within 300 days of its termination. A man entitled to the marital presumption has standing to bring the action for recognition of his paternity. The statute also declares that "[i]f two or more presumptions conflict with each other, the presumption which on the facts is founded on the weightier considerations of policy and logic controls." Under the statute, a man not entitled to the marital presumption has standing to bring a paternity action with regard to a child who is entitled to it with respect to a different man in two situations. First, the statute provides that if an expert conducts a blood test and concludes that "the alleged parent is not excluded and that the probability of paternity is ninety-eight percent or higher . . . and the paternity action is brought within five years of the child's birth," the alleged father has the requisite standing. Second, if the alleged father with the consent of the child's mother formally acknowledged the child and the paternity action is commenced within five years of the child's birth, he has standing to bring it. Gina is 8 years old, and Ed has done neither of these.

Commonalia, the domicile of Mona, Ed, Frank, and Gina, has adopted the putative marriage doctrine (also known as the putative spouse doctrine) by a state statute. This doctrine protects a party who attempted in good faith to enter a valid marriage, if the marriage was in fact void, by giving that party the rights conferred on a legal spouse. Ed has fired his original attorney and wants you to advise him whether he has any likelihood of winning if he appeals the dismissal of his paternity action. Advise Ed.

QUESTION #4

Liz and Tim married in 1996 and divorced in 2000. They had one child, Judy, who was 3 years old at the time of the divorce. The original divorce decree granted Tim and Liz joint legal and physical custody of Judy. The divorce was not un-friendly, and neither was the joint custody arrangement during the first ten years following the divorce. Tim purchased a house within walking distance of Liz's home. The parenting time arrangements were as close to equally shared as Tim and Liz could make them. Judy, now 13, alternates between her father's house and her mother's on a weekly basis. Judy attends a nearby Montessori school and is doing well academically and socially.

However, since Judy has become a teenager, the co-parenting has become difficult because Judy wants to dress in certain ways and engage in certain behaviors of which Tim strongly disapproves, but Liz regards as normal teenage development. Tim and Liz have argued over whether Liz permits Judy to wear her skirts too short and her necklines too plunging for a 13-year-old. Liz thinks that Judy could start dating at 15, but Tim thinks it's inappropriate until she is 17. Tim reacted in a heated negative fashion when Liz allowed Judy to take a dance class held in a town 20 miles away because Judy and her friends had to be dropped off by a friend's mother after school. They were unsupervised for three hours prior to the 7:30 p.m. class. The class itself required them to be out until 9:30 p.m. on a school night.

Liz has filed a petition seeking to modify the parents' joint custody to her sole custody. Liz cited as factual grounds for the modification the recent development of hostility between the parents because of a breakdown of communication. Tim opposes the change, arguing that the communication difficulties between him and Liz are not serious enough to justify it. They are not permanent, and merely reflect occasional divergent opinions about appropriate dress and social activities. Tim also alleged that Liz should not be the sole custodian because she spent money frivolously; in the year following her mother's death, Liz spent $40,000 of her $500,000 inher-itance on psychic hotlines. She thus lacked the maturity to guide Judy to adulthood.

Liz countered by demonstrating that she had invested $200,000 of the inheritance in a fund for Judy's higher education.

The judge interviewed Judy, who was mature enough for her wishes to be taken into account under Commonalia's custody law. Judy told the judge that she preferred her mother's sole custody. She said that she had a close, loving relationship with her father, but was uncomfortable sharing personal feelings with him lately because he had started to react badly if she and he disagreed. On the other hand, she could talk to her mother about anything. How should the court rule?

FAMILY LAW ESSAY EXAM #2

QUESTION #1

Chuck and Di were married for 12 years; they have two children, Will, aged 11, and Harry, aged 8. Di obtained a divorce from Chuck for adultery because she discovered that he had, before and during their marriage, a long-term and continuing affair with a married woman, on whom he has spent large sums. Di received sole custody of the children. In the hearing on child support, the following information as to the parents' income and assets emerged. Chuck is an architect at a large firm, where his salary is $120,000 per annum. After deductions, which are mostly mandatory but partially voluntary, his take-home pay is $6,000 per month. The firm makes contributions to a retirement account for each of its employees in the amount of 10 percent of salary. Chuck is voluntarily contributing another 5 percent per month from his income to that account. The firm also provides, and partially pays for, group health insurance for its employees and their families; Chuck's contribution for coverage for his family is now $500 per month because Di has been dropped from his policy. Health insurance for Chuck alone would cost him $200 per month. In addition, throughout his marriage, Chuck had taught one architecture course each year in the architecture school at a local university, for which he received a lump-sum payment; from that, he had a net annual income of $5,000. Chuck has stopped teaching this course since the divorce. It was not included in his income when Di's alimony was calculated. This year, Chuck's wealthy parents provided him with cash gifts in the amount of $50,000, which are not treated as his taxable income by the IRS. His alimony payments to Di are deductible from his income for tax purposes.

Di received a postdivorce alimony award of $1,000 per month for ten years. She was a caregiver for children at a daycare center when she married Chuck. She earned minimum wage at that time because she had no college degree or vocational training; she has not obtained either during the marriage. If she returned to employment in that field, she could earn $12.00 per hour. However, she would like to continue her role as homemaker for her children after the divorce, rather than seek employment. Di has received no gifts or other income. Aside from Chuck's retirement account, of which Di will receive a share based on the length of their marriage once Chuck reaches retirement age, the marital property has very little value, and does not consist of income-producing assets; each party's share amounted to $20,000. The home in which they lived while married, and in which Di is presently residing with their sons, belongs to Chuck's parents. They will not permit Di to continue to live there once a child support order is entered.

Commonalia, like the majority of U.S. jurisdictions, has a statute prescribing the method of calculating parents' incomes for purposes of child support. Like most jurisdictions, it provides that *income* includes "income from any source, broadly defined." It then provides for the same deductions from gross income as the majority of states. What is likely to be included as gross income for each parent in the calculation, what will likely be included as net income, and why?

QUESTION #2

Will Sanger has consulted you about divorcing his wife of two years, Traci. Will and Traci met as freshmen in high school. They did not become romantically involved until they renewed their acquaintance four years later as freshmen in college, where both of them frequently performed in musical theater productions produced by the college's theater and music departments. They became engaged after college graduation four years later, but didn't marry. Will and Traci moved to New York City, rented a tiny apartment, and pursued careers in musical theater while working part-time at menial jobs to do so. Six years later, still engaged, somewhat better off financially owing to an inheritance received by Will, but with any hope of full-time theatrical careers dashed, Will and Traci learned that their former high school in the small town of French Green, Commonalia was advertising for a music and drama teacher. It seemed like a perfect fit for Will, who had gotten certified to teach when he got his BA in theater. Will had come to the realization that what he wanted was a traditional family life: a marriage with Will as the breadwinner and Traci as the homemaker, and three children. Traci was happy to support Will's changed plans. Will applied for the teaching job and was hired; he and Traci decided that in honor of their fresh start, they would marry in Commonalia, which had passed a statute creating "covenant marriage." It seemed like a commitment to the traditional type of marriage their parents had had. To enter it, the couple had to agree to a state-authored declaration that marriage was "for life," and that if either of them considered divorce, they would first seek counseling. In addition, by obtaining a covenant marriage license, the couple gave up the option for either of them to use Commonalia's no-fault divorce statute. Instead, they were confined to Commonalia's fault grounds for divorce, which read as follows:

> **Com.R.S. 103.7.** Notwithstanding any law to the contrary, and subsequent to the parties obtaining counseling, a spouse in a covenant marriage may obtain a judgment of divorce only upon proof of any of the following:
>
> (1) The other spouse has committed adultery.
> (2) The other spouse has abandoned the matrimonial domicile for a period of one year and had constantly refused to return.
> (3) The other spouse has been convicted of a felony and sentenced to death or to more than four years in prison.
> (4) The other spouse has engaged in habitual intemperance or cruel treatment that renders living together insupportable, and the spouses have been living separate and apart continuously and without reconciliation for a period of two years.

Will and Traci bought a house and Will began teaching, at which he excelled. However, Traci was having difficulty conceiving a child. After a year, the couple turned to assisted reproduction. Another year went by, and the couple began to feel increasing tension and stress. Traci became jealous of the women Will worked with; Will became resentful because he felt that his second dream, being a dad, was slipping away. They bickered and snapped at one another continually. Finally, Traci came home from the fertility clinic and announced that she was pregnant.

After a couple of months, Traci no longer wanted to have sex with Will; she said her increasing girth made her uncomfortable. She also avoided letting Will see her undressed. One day, Traci started to slip; Will grabbed her around the waist to steady her and realized that she had a pillow under her maternity dress. Traci broke down and confessed that she realized some time ago that Will wanted so badly to be a father that their marriage was going to end if she did not get pregnant. Her doctor had told her half a year earlier that it was unlikely that she would ever become pregnant. Desperate to save her marriage, she came up with the idea of pretending to be pregnant for Will's benefit. She had arranged to privately adopt the as-yet-unborn baby of a pregnant teen at the high school and pass the child off as her biological child. She announced her pregnancy so that her due date would coincide with the baby's birth.

Initially, Will and Traci saw a marriage counselor and tried to give their marriage another chance. However, Will has no trust left in Traci because of her deception. He suffers nightmares of having a child who Traci kills, and is clinically depressed because Traci lied to him. In addition, Traci has become more jealous than ever of Will's relations with female co-workers, and is constantly monitoring Will's movements. He finds her frighteningly possessive and cannot stand to be around her anymore. He has decided that it would be better for them to go their separate ways as quickly as possible. However, the problem is that the covenant marriage license that they obtained at the time of their marriage means that he cannot obtain a quick no-fault divorce.

Will has several ideas about ways to obtain a divorce that does not require a long period of separation. He believes that Traci has treated him with cruelty that makes living together intolerable by deceiving him about being pregnant, given how important having children is to him. However, divorcing her for cruelty would require a two-year separation. He has considered bribing Traci to say that they were living apart, but she probably would not cooperate because she'd be afraid that it might reduce her alimony if she's found to have been cruel. It's unlikely that she'd agree to testify falsely that she had an affair if he offered her money to do so, for the same reason. He considered staging a fake affair with the help of the high school's guidance counselor, who is crazy about him and would do it if he asked. He would arouse Traci's suspicions and then let her catch them in a hotel bedroom. Traci would thus have a ground for divorce that doesn't require prior separation. But he is concerned about the impact on his and the guidance counselor's positions at the high school; besides, Traci might not sue for the divorce, or might be distraught enough to attack the guidance counselor. Alternatively, he could offer Traci money to testify that he abandoned her over a year earlier. He has a good friend on the faculty who would be willing to say that Will had been living with him for a year. Will would like to know whether any of these, or any other means, exist for him to get a quick divorce from his unstable, deceptive wife. Advise Will.

QUESTION #3

George and Martha became engaged in college and married after graduation, when both were 21 years old. George, who had been a premed student throughout college, had been accepted to Commonalia State University medical school. Prior to their marriage, the two had had many discussions of their future; the two assumed that Martha would work to support the two of them while George attended medical school, which does not allow time for a student to hold a part-time job. They wanted to avoid piling up student loan debts. Martha, who had majored in drama and education, had obtained a teaching certificate, qualifying her to teach in the Commonalia public schools. However, because of budget cutbacks in arts education, she was unable to find a full-time position in her field. She took the best-paid job that she could find, as an office assistant, and worked all the overtime she could to maximize the family's income. Much of the family's money went to pay for George's tuition, books, and medical equipment, such as a microscope; what was left went to pay for household expenses, such as rent for their apartment, utilities payments, medical insurance and care, food, clothing, and gasoline and upkeep for their two older cars.

After four years, George completed medical school and accepted a residency in surgery in a different town; he intended to specialize in cardiac surgery. Such residencies are relatively well-paid. Martha has already resigned her office assistant position and accepted a position as a part-time drama teacher in the town where George's residency is located. She was looking forward to working in her field, ultimately having children, and staying home to raise them as she and George had discussed years earlier. Seven days after George's graduation from medical school, he informed Martha that he wanted a divorce. He and a nurse that he had met while he was a medical student had been having an affair for two years and wanted to marry. Martha is shattered. George has made it clear that he is determined to divorce her under the state's no-fault statute, without making any attempt to save their marriage. She and George have not acquired property that is income-producing or has much value. Martha has consulted you, wanting to know what financial assistance, such as alimony, she might have rights to from George. Commonalia's statute providing for alimony reads in pertinent part as follows:

C.R. 9. (a) In a proceeding for dissolution of marriage . . . the court may grant an alimony order for either spouse only if it finds that the spouse seeking alimony:

(1) lacks sufficient property to provide for his reasonable needs, and

(2) is unable to support himself through appropriate employment. . . .

(b) The alimony order shall be in amounts and for periods of time the court deems just, without regard to marital fault, and after considering all relevant factors, including:

(1) the financial resources of the party seeking alimony, including marital property apportioned to him and his ability to meet his needs independently. . . .

(2) the time necessary to acquire sufficient education or training to enable the party seeking alimony to find appropriate employment,

(3) the standard of living during the marriage,

(4) the duration of the marriage,

(5) the age and the physical and mental condition of the spouse seeking alimony,

(6) the ability of the spouse from whom alimony is sought to meet his needs while meeting those of the spouse seeking maintenance.

Advise Martha.

QUESTION #4

Elly has come to your office for advice concerning the validity of her marriage to Josh, who died a month ago. Elly and Josh were first cousins who grew up in Commonalia's largest city. Elly's mother was the sister of Josh's dad. The cousins knew each other casually from family events such as birthday parties and weddings. For his higher education, Josh, who was a year older than Elly, chose to attend a college in a small town in Vermont. A year later, Elly, partially because of Josh's description of the place and partially because she was offered a scholarship, began attending the same college. There the cousins saw one another frequently. They were among a handful of students of their ethnic and religious heritage, and would meet at religious services at a more populous town several miles away. They also frequently went to an ethnic restaurant in that town, with each other or with groups of friends; the food, both claimed, tasted like their mothers'. When Josh was a junior, the two began dating and a year later became engaged.

When he graduated, Josh returned to their hometown to work in the family's food business. He and Elly began making wedding plans with their parents. However, they discovered that Commonalia law prohibited marriage between first cousins. Consulting an attorney, Elly, Josh, and their parents learned that almost half the states in the United States, including Vermont, did not prohibit first cousins from marrying one another. Their parents decided to hold the wedding ceremony during the week of Elly's graduation in the small Vermont town where Josh and Elly attended college. The parents and engaged couple made all the necessary arrangements for a marriage there, such as hiring a celebrant licensed in the state and obtaining a marriage license. The wedding took place in the college chapel. Many family members were there, along with many of the couple's closest friends. After Elly's graduation and a two-week honeymoon on the Maine coast, the couple returned to Commonalia to live. Elly and Josh had four children together; neither had any other children. Under Josh's leadership, the family food business grew and made him and Elly very wealthy. Josh and Elly celebrated their 50th wedding anniversary. Three years later, Josh died of a heart attack.

To the surprise of everyone but Josh's lawyer, who had repeatedly advised Josh to make a will, Josh left no will. Under the inheritance law of Commonalia, the estate of one who dies intestate passes in its entirety to his or her surviving spouse if all the children of the deceased person are also the children of the surviving spouse, and the surviving spouse has no other children. If there is no surviving spouse, the estate passes to the descendants of the deceased in equal shares. Two of Elly's children, Goneril and Regan, petitioned to challenge the distribution of the estate to Elly, whom they believed had always favored their siblings, and would do so again in her will. The disgruntled pair introduced evidence of the first-cousin relationship between Elly and Josh and petitioned for their marriage in Vermont to be declared void, an absolute nullity under Commonalia law. Goneril and Regan also requested that Josh's estate be distributed in equal shares to his four children as Josh's heirs. Most of the income-producing property accumulated during Elly's marriage to Josh was titled in Josh's name; Elly would be destitute if her daughters' suit is successful. Advise Elly.

FAMILY LAW ESSAY EXAM #3

QUESTION #1

Ann and Belinda were unmarried same-sex partners living in Commonalia, a jurisdiction that does not permit same-sex marriages. They purchased a home together and lived together as a committed couple for ten years. In the sixth year of their relationship, they decided that they wanted to be parents. Because Ann's family has a history of Tay-Sachs disease, they decided that Belinda would be the genetic mother and carry the child, who would be conceived by means of artificial insemination using an anonymous donor. The two women chose the donor together, deciding on one who had the same ethnic and religious heritage as Ann, and who shared the interests of both of them. During Belinda's pregnancy, Ann actively participated in planning for the child's birth. She accompanied Belinda on her prenatal visits to the doctor and to childbirth classes and prenatal exercise programs. When Belinda was five months pregnant, the two women learned that Commonalia's adoption law would not permit adoption by a second parent of the same sex, so they created a written agreement that they titled "Agreement to Raise Our Child Jointly." The document purported to "set out our rights and obligations with regard to our child, whom Belinda is carrying." In it, they said they would "jointly and equally parent," and would have "equal power to make decisions" concerning the child's upbringing. They also agreed that both would "be responsible for the child's support and education" until the child reached the age of 25. They further agreed to participate in a jointly agreed-on program of counseling if either considered separating due to "the possible trauma to the child" that might be caused if they separated. In the document, they agreed that if they separated, "[W]e will do our best to see that our child maintains a close and loving relationship with each of us," "will share in our child's upbringing and support," "will make a good-faith effort to jointly make all major decisions affecting our child's health and welfare," and "will base all decisions upon the best interests of our child." They further agreed that in the event of a separation, "the person who has actual physical custody will take all steps necessary to afford the other equal parenting time." The two signed the document.

Ann was present when Belinda gave birth to a baby girl, Mary Ruth. Her first and middle names were the names of Ann's and Belinda's late maternal grandmothers. They used a hyphenated version of their two last names as her last name. The state of Commonalia would not allow this name to be entered on the birth certificate, or enter Ann's name as a parent. Belinda refused to sign the birth certificate because of the omissions. However, both women were recognized as parents by many third parties, such as friends, teachers, doctors, and Ann's health insurance carrier; and Belinda referred to Ann as Mary Ruth's "other parent" or "other mother" in conversations. Mary Ruth called Belinda "Mama" and Ann

"Mummy," and in conversation with third parties refers to both of them as her mothers.

During the next three years, the women continued to be committed partners, raising Mary Ruth together. They shared parental duties, including the physical care and companionship of the little girl, furnishing her financial support, participation in her social activities, and involvement in her education. When Mary Ruth was three years old, Ann and Belinda separated. However, the separation was cordial. Ann purchased a home within a few blocks of the one she had shared with Belinda and Mary Ruth, and they fully cooperated with each other on child support, decision-making, and avoiding conflict, in accordance with their agreement. They had equal parenting time and responsibility for care in alternating weeks, shared major life events like Mary Ruth's birthday parties, and alternated or shared major holidays. Each was flexible about her schedule if the other had a conflict that required a change in their schedules with regard to Mary Ruth.

When Mary Ruth was nine, Belinda began a heterosexual relationship with Charlie, who had two preteen sons from his marriage. Charlie utterly opposed continuing contact between Ann and Mary Ruth and between Belinda and Ann. He did not want his sons to interact with Ann at all. After a few months with Charlie, Belinda e-mailed Ann saying that they would have to make "adjustments" because Belinda and Mary Ruth were now in a new family. She limited Ann's time with Mary Ruth and refused to allow Ann the parenting responsibilities she had exercised up to this time. When Ann is with Mary Ruth, the child repeatedly asks why they can't be together as much as they used to. When Belinda comes to take the child home, Mary Ruth clings to Ann, crying, and often struggles with Belinda. After two months of limited visits, Ann filed a motion requesting joint custody and designation as primary physical custodian of Mary Ruth.

Belinda opposes Ann's motion. She points to Commonalia's custody statute, which expressly prohibits joint custody by a parent and a nonparent because the two do not have equal rights to the company and upbringing of the child. In addition, although the courts of Commonalia have adopted the doctrine of equitable parenthood and applied it frequently to heterosexual couples, they have never been faced with a request from someone claiming to be a same-sex equitable parent. Belinda argues that if it were applied to Ann, it would violate the Marriage Protection Amendment of the Commonalia state constitution. That passage reads:

§11. Definition of marriage
Only a union between one man and one woman may be a marriage valid in or recognized by this state and its political subdivisions. This state and its political subdivisions shall not create or recognize a legal status for relationships of same-sex individuals that intends to approximate the design, qualities, significance or effect of marriage.

Analyze and evaluate the arguments for and against Ann's motion, indicating how you think a court would rule.

QUESTION #2

Dennis and Candy were married in 1999. They have three children, Xena, aged 10; Yvette, aged 8; and Zach, aged 5. Dennis works at an auto repair shop, earning $30,000 per year; Candy worked half-time as a caregiver at a nursing home, earning $10,000 per year. She also managed the household and has principal responsibility for the children. Each party has a separate checking account into which each deposits his or her paycheck. They maintain a joint account from which Candy could pay the household expenses. They contributed to it on a proportional basis: Dennis contributed three quarters of the budgeted figure for each month, and Candy contributed one quarter.

Candy has been fired by the nursing home after she was arrested for stealing controlled pain medications such as Vicodin and Oxycontin from its pharmacy. She is presently incarcerated while awaiting trial for theft, drug dealing, and drug use. Her bond is set at $100,000. Dennis has discovered that his and Candy's joint checking account and Candy's checking account contain only the minimum amount required to keep them open. Candy had no longer been using the funds that she withdrew from the joint account to pay for household expenses; their utility and telephone bills have not been paid in three months. Candy has admitted to Dennis that she used funds from the joint checking account to purchase drugs.

Because of the family's income, Candy does not qualify as indigent, so no public defender will be appointed for her. The attorney that Candy hired to represent her, Elvis, has told Dennis that the prosecution has no evidence to support the drug-dealing charge. Candy took the drugs because she has a drug addiction. She began taking the painkillers by doctor's prescription when she was suffering severe back pain from a slipped disk six months earlier. When the doctor would no longer prescribe them after two months, she turned first to the illegal drug market to suppress the back pain so that she could keep working, and then to the one theft that led to her arrest. Elvis is confident that he can get the charges reduced if Candy agrees to go into a treatment program and reimburses the nursing home for her theft. If she successfully completes the treatment program, she would be released on probation because this is her first offense. There is an excellent private inpatient drug-treatment facility with a record of success in a larger town 25 miles away. The treatment used in cases like Candy's takes six weeks and costs about $12,000. The facility is willing to arrange financing for Candy. Elvis has arranged for her to go to this treatment facility on her release from jail; her location would be electronically monitored by the local sheriff.

Candy's check to Elvis in payment of his retainer has been returned for insufficient funds. She has asked Dennis to pay it, and he has refused. She has also asked him to put up her bail. For a $5,000 payment to a bail bondsman, Candy would be released on bond. She knows Dennis has more than that amount in his personal checking account. Again he refused.

Elvis has advanced Candy the funds for her bail. Elvis has told Candy that he intends to sue Dennis to recover payment for his work so far. In addition, after representing Candy, he plans to bring a suit for payment for his legal work and for reimbursement of any and all of his expenses connected with the litigation because as a spouse, Dennis owes Candy support.

Dennis was shocked and enraged to learn of Candy's drug use and her expenditure of funds in the joint account. He has consulted you because he wants a divorce as fast as possible, and to sue to recover from her the funds that she spent on drugs. He does not want to pay for Candy's bail, her attorney, the reimbursement she owes the nursing home, or her treatment for addiction.

The grounds for divorce in Commonalia are the traditional fault grounds of adultery, abandonment for over a year, conviction of a felony resulting in a prison sentence of death or more than four years, and cruelty or habitual intemperance such that living together is intolerable, which requires in addition a continuous separation of at least a year. In addition, the statute provides a ground of living separate and apart for more than two years without the need to show any of the above faults. Advise Dennis.

QUESTION #3

Martha has come to your office to ask advice on litigation she is pursuing against her husband, George. George married Martha 28 years ago. George, a multimillionaire, was 46 at the time; he had been previously married and divorced. He had lived his entire life in Commonalia. Leonie, his 25-year-old daughter by his first wife, objected strenuously to his marriage to Martha, who was 23 at that time and earned $7,000 a year. The night before their wedding, at George's insistence, Martha and George signed a prenuptial agreement that George presented to her for the first time. In it, each waived any claims for marital property or postdivorce alimony from the other upon divorce. For the purposes of this question only, assume that Commonalia has no special legislation governing the validity of prenuptial agreements, and that the issue is de novo in its courts.

George and Martha had no children together. They resided together in the state of Commonalia, with George supporting Martha, who was a traditional homemaker spouse, not only managing their household, but also hosting numerous parties for George's business associates and important clients, for 26 years. At that time, George, whose physical health and mental acuity had been failing, disappeared from their home without any notice to Martha. After two years of frantically searching hospitals, nursing homes, and reports of unidentified persons' deaths with the aid of the Commonalia police and a private detective, Martha located the 74-year-old George in the 52nd state of the United States, Caltex, where he had been living with Leonie in a house that she owned. She had spirited him away from his home in Commonalia. George's only explanation to Martha for leaving was that "Leonie told me to." When Martha asked George if he'd like to come home with her, he said yes, and that Leonie kept promising they could go home to Commonalia, but she was taking a long time.

Martha has filed suit in state court in Commonalia, where spouses can sue one another in contract, for a declaratory judgment that the prenuptial agreement was void due to fraud and unconscionability. George's lawyer is seeking to remove the action to federal court on the basis of diversity jurisdiction. Martha wants to oppose the move from state court. No other litigation has been filed between these parties. Martha has told you that she does not want a divorce from George. She would like to know what considerations will govern removing the action from state to federal court, and what the likelihood of success is.

QUESTION #4

Six years ago, Dell and his wife Edith obtained a no-fault divorce in Commonalia, where they had lived for ten years. Their child, Frank, was 5 years old at the time of that divorce; he had been living with Edith between the spouse's separation and the child custody hearing. Edith had been a full-time homemaker, and Dell is a highly successful trial attorney. In the custody adjudication, the two were awarded joint custody of Frank, with Edith as domiciliary (also known as "residential" or "primary physical") custodian. Dell had not objected to Edith receiving domiciliary parent status because Dell felt that Edith would be able to spend more time and attention on Frank. Dell's work was so demanding that he often did not arrive home until late at night, and worked a full day most Saturdays. Dell has specified periods of physical custody totaling approximately four months each year. Except for a four-week period during the summer, Dell's custody consists of long weekend or week-long periods of time at his new home, which is 15 minutes by automobile from Edith's and Frank's home. Dell reduced his workload to be able to be home during Frank's visits.

Both Dell and Edith remarried. Dell's wife, Bitsy, is a traditional homemaker spouse who seems to love Frank. Dell has such confidence in her that he has returned to his former workload, leaving Frank with Bitsy for much of the shorter visitation periods. Edith's new husband, Gordon, an executive with an energy company, has been transferred from Commonalia to Jackson, Mississippi, a three-hour drive from the town where Edith and Frank lived when she was married to Dell. Edith and Frank relocated to Jackson with Gordon; Edith remains a full-time homemaker. This move means that when Dell has weekend custody, Frank and Dell must take one six-hour round trip and Dell must take two if he wants to bring Frank home himself. Even during the summer, when Dell has Frank for a week at a time, Dell believes that the amount of time that Frank must spend traveling to spend time at Dell's house is physically and psychologically disruptive for the child. Frank is tired when he arrives, and the lengthy trips reduce the amount of time that Dell and Frank can spend doing "father and son" things, Dell says. Dell wants to secure a change in the custody decree. He still wants joint custody, but wants to be named domiciliary parent. Dell acknowledges that Frank would have to travel to visit Edith in Jackson, but points out that because Edith does not have to work, she would be able to spend much more time with the child during her periods of physical custody than he can. He has come to you to learn whether he has to go to Mississippi and hire a lawyer there to pursue a change in the child custody order, whether he is likely to obtain the change to domiciliary parent, and if not, what you would recommend that he do to increase his quality time with his son. Advise Dell.

FAMILY LAW ESSAY EXAM #4

QUESTION #1

Dan, a successful author of humorous newspaper columns and nonfiction books, has consulted you because he is considering a divorce from his wife, Beth. Dan and Beth were high school sweethearts; they have been married for 20 years and have one son, Ron, who is now away at college. Dan says that Beth has changed a lot in the past few years. When they were first married, she supported the family as a clinical social worker while he wrote at home. Whereas Beth used to support and encourage him, since he has become successful, she seems to disapprove of his work. Most of his writing consists of humorous depictions of family life, particularly of the very different reactions that Dan and Beth have to ordinary events, such as Ron wanting to dress as a Goth when he was 11 years old, Dan's decision to acquire a Harley, and Beth's attempt to lose weight for their high-school reunion. Dan transforms these events into hilarious moments from which he generalizes about the differences between men and women. The public loves it.

Beth, on the other hand, has informed Dan on numerous occasions in recent years that she is hurt by his revelations of her personal life in his columns and books. She was furious with him a few years ago when Dan wrote a column describing how he and Ron sabotaged her attempt to return to full-time work because they would have missed her at home. She told Dan that she feels that she can no longer confide in him, or even do things with him, without risking being subjected to public humiliation. She also has lost her sense of humor about other topics, Dan said. For example, several weeks earlier, as they ate at a restaurant with friends, he was making jokes about two other diners who wore hideous toupees; Beth told him to stop, and she walked out when he would not. When they were younger, according to Dan, she would have joined in the laughter.

Beth has repeatedly "nagged him," according to Dan, to go with her to marriage counseling, but Dan has refused to participate. Their last discussion of this topic ended in an argument, which Dan turned into a very funny column called "How to Fight Like a Girl." Dan has tried to talk to Beth since, but she replies that she's not willing to discuss anything with him unless he goes with her to marriage counseling. Besides this ban on discussion, they have not had sex for over a month.

Dan thinks that he knows the cause of Beth's alienation from him. Some time ago he examined her computer while she was away from home, and found that Beth has been visiting chat rooms on the Internet, where she has been corresponding for over a year with someone named Charles. Beth tells Charles the things that she used to talk about with Dan, from her political opinions to her personal feelings about Ron going away to college to her relationship with Dan. Beth and Charles have also exchanged photos of themselves online. Although the online conversations contained nothing of a sexual nature, Dan thought Beth and Charles might be having an affair. He confronted Beth about the online relationship, and said he wanted her to end it. Beth said that although she had never met Charles, they were good friends and she would not stop corresponding with him. As usual, she demanded that Dan go with her to marriage counseling. She also changed her computer password. A private detective who Dan hired has not been able to find any evidence that Beth and Charles have ever met. The advice columnist at Dan's newspaper, however, has told Dan that Beth is having an "emotional affair" with Charles, which is just as much a breach of loyalty to Dan as a sexual affair.

Dan would rather stay married to Beth if she could be the supportive spouse she was in years past. He is also afraid of the effect of a divorce on his book sales, given the subject matter of his writing. He is thinking of moving out and telling her he'll return when she stops communicating with Charles. If Dan and Beth are to get a divorce, he'd prefer to divorce her, both because of the publicity and because he believes that the problems that they are having are her fault. He wants to know whether he has grounds to divorce Beth for adultery or for some other reason, and whether there's any basis on which Beth could divorce him.

Commonalia has a divorce statute typical of many U.S. jurisdictions, containing both traditional fault grounds for divorce and a modern no-fault ground. The fault grounds are adultery, abandonment for over a year without cause and with a refusal to return, and physical cruelty, mental cruelty, or both, such that living together is intolerable or insupportable. The no-fault ground is irretrievable breakdown of the marriage, and requires that the couple live separate and apart continuously for 12 months. The usual common-law defenses to these grounds exist in the jurisdiction. Advise Dan.

QUESTION #2

Rob met Laura while he was a private in the U.S. Army. He was stationed at Fort Despair, Commonalia; she was a dancer with a troupe of entertainers from nearby Point Claire in the same state, who often performed on the base. After a whirlwind romance, Rob and Laura married. Because Laura's parents had objected to her marrying Rob so quickly after meeting him, the young couple drove to the next county in Commonalia to obtain their marriage license, and again to marry, without telling anyone about their plans until after the ceremony. Once Rob was discharged from the Army, they decided to settle in Point Claire to be close to her family, who had now accepted Rob. The two had one child, Richie, now an electrical engineer.

Thirty years later, while Rob was helping Laura clean out her late mother's home, he came across a copy of Laura's birth certificate. He noticed that the certificate was dated a year later than the birth certificate she had submitted to the clerk to obtain their marriage license. Laura confessed that she had forged a copy of the birth certificate, dating it a year earlier so that she wouldn't have to get her parents' consent to marry. She was, in fact, only 17 at that time. Commonalia's statute on the age at which one can enter marriage, both at that time and in the present, requires that both parties have attained the age of 18 to marry without parental consent. Rob has consulted you because he is troubled by this discovery. First, Rob thinks that he and Laura must go through another wedding ceremony for their marriage to be valid. However, Rob is not certain that he wants to do so. A very serious, law-abiding person himself, Rob was horrified to discover Laura's deception. She showed disregard for the state law of marriage; moreover, because the license application took the form of an affidavit, she broke state laws concerning perjury and filing falsehoods in the public records. Even worse, because he was 22 and she was 17 at the time of the marriage, she put him in danger of being charged with statutory rape. He would like to know, first, whether he is legally married to Laura; and second, if he is, whether he can have the marriage declared void because of her deception. Because of his religious beliefs, he does not want a divorce under these circumstances.

QUESTION #3

Jessica, a 24-year-old single mother, has come to you for advice concerning a suit by her great-aunts for visitation with her son, David, now 7 years old. When David was 2 years old, Jessica was admitted as a freshman to Commonalia State University and granted a scholarship that covered her tuition and fees, and provided her with a part-time job in the school's work-study program. Despite this benefit, Jessica still required additional income for living expenses, books, transportation, baby supplies, and child care for David, who was then 2 years old. David's father had deserted her when he found out that she was pregnant, and the state department of social services had not been able to locate him to compel him to pay child support. Jessica did not think that she would earn enough to attend the university.

Jessica's two great-aunts, Bea and Ethel, live in the town where Commonalia State University is located. They invited Jessica and David to live rent-free in the spare room of their home. They also volunteered to babysit David, also without charge, while Jessica was at the university and at work if Jessica would contribute to household expenses such as food and utilities, which she agreed to do. Without the expenses of rent and child care, Jessica was able to support herself and attend the university, where she majored in nursing. From 7 a.m. to 5:30 p.m., Jessica was at the university, attending class and working. During this time, her aunts took David on outings to the local park, fed him lunch, entertained him with children's games, and watched television and read with him. In the evenings, Jessica would help Bea and Ethel prepare dinner for the four of them, then played with David, bathed him, and read or sang him to sleep. Then she studied. During summers, Jessica worked full-time.

After three years of this arrangement, David started kindergarten. Bea and Ethel took him to and from school, and continued to be his sitter between school and Jessica's return. Jessica took days off from work and study on special occasions, such as his performance in a holiday pageant, to be present with Bea and Ethel to encourage him.

When Jessica received notice of the first parent–teacher conference concerning David, she had to insist to Bea and Ethel that they could not attend with her. David's teacher told Jessica that although David was a bright boy, he lagged behind his peers

in initiative, cooperation in activities, self-control, respecting others, and toilet training. This lack of age-appropriate development made him unpopular and the victim
of teasing, which his teacher feared would damage his self-confidence. At school,
David interacted mainly with his teacher; he demanded to be the center of her
attention and for her to entertain him continually. If he was not interested in an
activity, he refused to engage in it; and if he wanted to continue with an activity, he
would not stop when the class moved on to another. The school guidance counselor
had not found any indications of a learning disorder. She and his teacher thought that
David needed to learn to handle social responsibilities commensurate with his age.

Jessica took charge of David's toilet training in the evenings and mornings. She
scheduled playdates for him with the children of her fellow nursing students and co-
workers, and tried to guide him both in initiating games and projects and in
cooperative behavior, such as leaving an interesting activity when he needed to
use the toilet. At the next parent–teacher conference, the teacher congratulated
Jessica on David's progress. Bea and Ethel both thought she was expecting too
much of David, given his age.

After graduating from nursing school with honors, Jessica got a well-paid
position at a medical products firm in Commonalia, assisting in testing and presenting
new products. She and David moved out of Bea and Ethel's house, although she
insisted on continuing to help them with grocery and utility costs. She and David saw
Bea and Ethel frequently. They often came to dinner at Jessica's house. Bea and Ethel
continued to transport David, who was now in first grade, to and from school. Jessica
would pick him up at her aunts' home on her way home after work. When Jessica
had to travel out of town, David stayed with his aunts. He also occasionally spent
"overnighters" with them at their invitation.

Jessica noticed that when David came back from spending a day or more with
his aunts, his toilet training would regress. He would once again demand attention
and entertainment, and had no interest in doing things for himself, such as getting a
cup of water, putting on his shoes, or amusing himself. When she would insist that he
do so, he would protest that Aunt Bea and Aunt Ethel didn't make him do that.
When she tried to get David to dress himself in the morning, he told her that Bea and
Ethel had said that she was mean to make him do so. Jessica talked with her aunts
about making David take responsibility, but they insisted that David was too young
to understand, and continued to indulge him. Jessica ended the overnight visits so
that David would have to dress himself every morning. When Jessica was with David,
Bea, and Ethel, the latter pair would spend much of the visit contradicting what she
told David to do, and arguing with her about it. Jessica then enrolled David in an
after-school activities program of Pee-Wee League sports and supervised play so that
he had care other than Bea and Ethel. David says he hates this program because he has
to run around, and wants to be with Bea and Ethel after school. He has also frequently
asked her to let him go to Bea and Ethel's house for an overnighter; and Jessica has
heard Bea and Ethel instigate these requests during visits. Jessica now picks him up at
5:30 from school, and limits Bea and Ethel's time with David to one two-hour visit a
week, in Jessica's presence.

Bea and Ethel have filed suit in Commonalia court for unsupervised visitation
with David, who is now 7 years old. They are seeking to have three hours with him

two afternoons a week, and overnight visits on alternating weekends. Commonalia's visitation statute contains the following provision for court-ordered third-party visitation:

Com.R.S. 152 Sec. 4. On petition to the court, a relative of the child with whom the child has previously lived in a stable relationship may be granted visitation by the court if the court finds after a hearing that the preexisting relationship with the non-parent has engendered a bond such that visitation is in the best interest of the child.

Jessica is willing for Bea and Ethel to see David, but is opposed to any unsupervised visitation for them, especially overnight visitation, because she is of the opinion that they undermine her decisions regarding his upbringing. Advise Jessica.

QUESTION #4

World-famous operatic soprano Nelia Naturno and her husband, Oliver Opus, a professional voice coach, are in the process of obtaining a no-fault divorce in Commonalia after ten years of marriage. When Oliver and Nelia first married, she was an unknown. Oliver gave up two of his high-paying clients to concentrate on training Nelia's voice, which he recognized as potentially great. He supported Nelia and himself through his earnings for the first two years of marriage. After six years spent advancing from minor to major roles, Nelia became a lead soprano at the Metropolitan Opera. After two more years, she was an internationally known diva commanding top dollar for performing, recording, and endorsements. During all this time, she had continued to study with Oliver. Because of the demands of her career, Oliver also was the primary caretaker for their two minor children.

After ten years of marriage, Oliver and Nelia separated by mutual agreement and sought a divorce. Both are domiciled in Commonalia. Commonalia has adopted the economic partnership theory of marital property and its principles of division. In the property distribution, Oliver has requested distribution of a property interest in Nelia's present and future earnings based on her celebrity status on the basis of his contributions to her through financial support and training. Nelia's future career has been valued by actuarial experts at $50 million. The issue is de novo in Commonalia. However, the Commonalia statute on equitable distribution includes in marital property "all things of value acquired by either or both spouses during the marriage and before the commencement of the dissolution action, regardless of the form in which the title is held." Nelia and Oliver are in settlement negotiations. She wants to know what possible basis there is for Oliver to claim that her voice is marital property, and if there is one, what type of remedies are available, before deciding what to offer him.

FAMILY LAW ESSAY EXAM #5

QUESTION #1

Inez, who was 27, and Jerry, who was 53, were married in June 1998, after having lived together in Jerry's home in Commonalia's Capital City for three years. Jerry, a developer of commercial real estate, had accumulated, for the most part, real-estate holdings, as well as other property worth approximately $5 million at the time of the parties' marriage. Inez, an exotic dancer who had not finished high school and had no skills training other than in dance, had approximately $15,000 worth of personal property at that time. A month before their wedding, Jerry presented Inez with an prenuptial agreement, drawn up by his attorney, that he insisted that she agree to before he would marry her.

The agreement provided that in the event of a divorce, neither party would have any claim to any property that the other owned before the marriage, and that any property that they accumulated during the marriage would be divided at divorce in accordance with its title. Property titled jointly would be divided between the parties in lots of approximately equal value. The agreement provided that if the parties had been married at least ten years at the time of divorce, Inez would receive $50,000 and would waive all other rights to property and alimony.

The prenuptial agreement also contained a provision titled "Financial Disclosure" that read: "The parties have revealed to each other full financial information regarding their respective net worth, assets, holdings, income, and liabilities. They have made full disclosure to each other, with full explanations of their respective financial statements and summaries that have been supplied to one another." The agreement contained lists of some of the husband's assets; however, it did not include their values. No further financial information, such as Jerry's tax records, was attached. Inez received a copy of the agreement on April 9, 1997, and retained independent counsel to review it. One month later, she signed the agreement.

Inez did not work outside the home during the marriage because Jerry did not want her to continue with her exotic dancing career. She was homemaker, companion, and hostess for his parties. Jerry worked from his home office in a loft on the second floor of their home. He kept the office locked when he was not present. When Inez asked about his finances, he would brush her off, telling her not to bother her head about such matters and that he hated to see a pretty woman worry about business. This had been his practice during the three years that they lived together prior to their marriage.

In October 2006, Jerry filed a petition for a no-fault divorce from Inez. Inez's answer and cross-claim asked that the prenuptial agreement be declared invalid. At the time of the divorce, all of the parties' real property was still titled in Jerry's name. Inez's attorney submitted evidence that her net worth had increased from $15,000 at the time of the marriage to $60,000, principally in the form of personal property given to her by Jerry.

At the trial concerning the prenuptial agreement, Jerry's lawyer introduced into evidence a copy of the agreement; attached to it were exhibits detailing Jerry's assets and their value. These established that Jerry's net worth had been $5 million at the time of the marriage. Inez's attorney entered the copy of the agreement that Jerry had given to her. It had included none of the exhibits. Further exhibits showed that Jerry's assets had increased to $15 million at the time he asked for the divorce.

The prenuptial agreements statute in Commonalia, where Inez and Jerry executed the agreement and have always been domiciled, contains the following relevant language:

> **C.R.S. 9:6. Enforcement**. (a) A prenuptial agreement is not enforceable if the party against whom enforcement is sought proves that:
>   (1) The party did not execute the agreement voluntarily; or
>   (2) The agreement was unreasonable when it was executed and, before execution of the agreement, the party:
>   (i) was not provided a fair and reasonable independent disclosure of the property or financial obligations of the other party;
>   (ii) did not voluntarily and expressly waive, in writing, any right to disclosure of the property or financial obligations of the other party beyond the disclosure provided; and
>   (iii) did not have, or reasonably could not have had, an adequate knowledge of the property or financial obligations of the other party.
>   (b) An issue of unreasonableness of a prenuptial agreement shall be decided by the court as a matter of law.

Courts in Commonalia had found in past cases that (1) a prenuptial agreement is "unreasonable" if it does not adequately provide for the spouse who seeks to avoid enforcement, and (2) to evaluate the agreement as not adequately providing for the spouse, the court must find that the agreement is "disproportionate to the means" of the spouse requesting enforcement. How should the court rule on the enforceability of the prenuptial agreement between Inez and Jerry?

QUESTION #2

Maria and Quentin, a divorced couple, have been engaged in a long and bitter custody struggle over their daughter. Quentin is an American citizen, and Maria is a citizen of Italy. The couple met in 1999 when Quentin, a film producer, was visiting his Italian relatives in Milan after attending an international film festival. Quentin, who is fluent in Italian, invited Maria to visit him in the United States that year, and she did so. They married in 2000, and resided together in Commonalia. Their daughter, Rosa, was born there in 2001. In 2003, the couple separated. At the time of the separation, the two entered into a custody stipulation that was the basis for a custody order by the Commonalia court. It provided that the two parents would have joint custody of Rosa. Maria would have primary physical (a.k.a.

residential or domiciliary) custody. Rosa and Maria would live in Italy. Quentin would have regular visitation rights, to take place in Italy. Maria, with Quentin's consent, took Rosa with her to live in Milan, Italy. On arrival there, she registered the custody with the Italian court in Milan, as was required to give it the effect of Italian law.

Quentin, whose business required frequent trips to Italy, visited Maria and the child monthly. Quentin purchased an apartment in Milan to provide a convenient place to entertain Rosa during their visits. Rosa learned Italian as her primary language, and began attending school in Italy at the age of 5. Most of her friends are Italian. She socializes with both her father's and her mother's relatives in Milan. In 2007, the couple divorced.

Once the divorce was final, Maria began to interfere with Quentin's visitation. In 2007, she changed her address in Milan, and would not give Quentin her location or telephone number. She would instead arrange to bring Rosa to Quentin at his apartment. Sometimes she arrived with Rosa as planned; sometimes she did not come. If she did bring Rosa, she would often return to collect the child after only a couple of hours, rather than permitting her to stay for an afternoon or overnight, as she had in the past. In late 2008, Quentin filed a petition for sole custody in Commonalia, in the court that had issued the initial custody order. The Commonalia court's decision, handed down in 2009, modified Rosa's custody. Because of Maria's interference with Quentin's visitation, Quentin was granted sole custody of Rosa. The order provided Maria with monthly visitation rights in Commonalia, and determined that she was in civil contempt for her violation of the prior court order. Maria appealed, but the Commonalia appellate court affirmed the judgment and the state Supreme Court denied writs.

Because Quentin was afraid that Maria would hide the child if asked to comply with the custody order, he flew to Milan without notifying her. Without registering the new custody order, he seized Rosa outside of her school with the help of one of his relatives, who had rented a car. They drove with Rosa to France. From France Quentin and Rosa flew to Dubai, and from Dubai to the United States, ending their trip in Commonalia, where they have lived since.

The Italian court that had registered the original custody order learned of the child's kidnapping from the authorities in Milan. The court ruled that at the time of Rosa's removal, Quentin and Maria had joint custody under the original order, which had the effect of Italian law. It found that Quentin had acted unlawfully in removing the child without Maria's agreement or a registered court order permitting him to do so. It ordered Quentin to return the child immediately to Maria. Quentin has refused to comply with the Italian court's order. Maria immediately filed a petition in federal district court in Commonalia requesting Rosa's return, basing her claim on the Hague Convention on the Civil Aspects of International Child Abduction, codified in the United States as federal law, the International Child Abduction Remedies Act (ICARA). Maria alleges that Quentin wrongfully removed their daughter from Italy to the United States, and that the child's immediate return is mandated by the convention. How should the federal court rule, and why?

QUESTION #3

Hank and Wilma went through the official state ceremony of marriage 29 years ago in Commonalia. They were of opposite sexes, no relation to one another, and neither had been married before, and were both competent adults. Their wedding ceremony contained every element required for marriage. Hank and Wilma had no children. After seven years, Wilma left Hank and moved to Caltex, the 52nd state of the United States; she did not return to Commonalia as long as Hank lived there. In Caltex, she went through the official state ceremony of marriage with Sam, whom Wilma never informed of her earlier marriage to Hank. Wilma and Sam have lived together in Caltex since that ceremony, holding themselves out as husband and wife, and regarded as such by all their acquaintances in Caltex. Sam has proved to be a dreamer who has never been very financially successful. Wilma did not work during her marriage to Sam. Hank had no long-term intimate relationships after Wilma left him; he dedicated himself to his business, and became extremely wealthy.

Four years ago, Hank, who had resided in Commonalia for the remainder of his life, died there without a will. Under Commonalia's estates law, when a deceased person leaves no will, his surviving spouse inherits his property. If there is no surviving spouse, his closest surviving relative inherits his property. Wilma, hearing of Hank's death, has claimed Hank's property as his surviving spouse. She says she is his surviving spouse because she never divorced Hank, and their marriage was never, and indeed could not be, annulled. The lawyer administering the estate opposes her claim; he says that Buddy, Hank's brother and closest surviving relative, should inherit because Wilma and Hank were no longer married when Hank died. Wilma has come to you seeking advice as to whether she is entitled to Hank's estate, and what she must do to recover it. In addition, she would like to know if she has any financial responsibility to Sam for the benefits ordinarily awarded to a former spouse, such as alimony and a share of the property they acquired since their marriage ceremony. Sam has now left Wilma and filed for a divorce and, in the alternative, an annulment on learning for the first time of her earlier marriage. Advise Wilma.

QUESTION #4

Paul, a businessman, was married to Olivia for 20 years; they had two children, Melanie and Niles. At the age of 40, Paul decided his real calling was to be an artist. He left his disapproving family to cohabit with an artist's model, Leda, in New Paris, Commonalia. Paul and Leda had rejected the notion that a piece of paper issued by the state created a family, so Paul did not divorce Olivia and marry Leda. Leda and Paul were completely faithful to one another, and had cohabited without marriage for ten years when Leda became pregnant with their only child. Paul had developed an inoperable brain cancer. When Leda was four months pregnant, he became comatose, and remained in the coma for three months. He died without regaining consciousness two months before their child's birth. The child, a daughter whom Leda named Thea, is now three months old.

Paul left no will. As a result, his entire estate, which includes substantial and financially complex business holdings, is to be distributed under Commonalia's law of intestacy. That statute provides that if the deceased person is survived by a spouse and children, half of his estate passes to the surviving spouse, and the other half to his surviving children, divided in equal shares among them. The administrator of Paul's estate is his brother Sylvester. Leda approached Sylvester shortly after Thea's birth and asked about her child's rights. Sylvester has refused to include Thea as an heir because she is not recognized at law as Paul's child.

Under the paternity statute of Commonalia, there are three ways that the paternity of a child not entitled to the marital presumption of paternity may be established for the child to take in a deceased's estate: (1) if the father had later married the mother of the child and held the child out to be his own; (2) if the father had acknowledged the child by following a statutory procedure for written acknowledgment of the child; and (3) if, during the father's life or within a reasonable period thereafter, to be determined by the court in accordance with the just and orderly distribution of the intestate's estate, the child brought an action through which she obtained a judgment of paternity identifying her as the deceased's child. The first two of these have not occurred in this case. Leda filed suit a month after Thea's birth seeking a judgment that Thea is Paul's child. Leda has the results of a DNA analysis that establishes Paul and Thea's relationship with a 99.99 percent degree of certainty, higher than the result required under state law. However, the trial court dismissed the case for Leda's failure to bring it within a reasonable period after Paul's death. Leda, who has begun to appreciate the value of pieces of paper issued by the state in creating a family, has come to you because she still hopes to obtain a one-sixth share of Paul's estate for Thea as one of Paul's three surviving children once the estate is distributed. She asks your advice as to whether, if she appeals the case, it is likely that she can do so. Advise Leda.

FAMILY LAW
ESSAY EXAMINATION
ANSWERS

FAMILY LAW ESSAY EXAM #1

QUESTION #1

I. Harry v. Wanda: Annulment of the marriage

The facts do not suggest any basis for the marriage to be void *ab initio*; Harry and Wanda had no prior marriages and no kindred relationship between them is suggested. Harry would have to establish that the marriage is voidable because of some defect in capacity or consent. However, both parties were of age, and there is no suggestion of mental impairment or duress. Harry's only basis for obtaining an annulment of the marriage would be fraud. He would allege that Wanda misrepresented her willingness to rear their children in the Catholic faith. Under the Massachusetts objective test (*Reynolds v. Reynolds*, 85 Mass. 65 (1862)), the fraud must be material (that is, a serious reason why Harry would not have married Wanda but for the misrepresentation). It must also be related directly to the essentials of the marriage, which were narrowly defined as sexual intercourse and procreation. A more recent test is subjective: It considers material fraud to be sufficient to obtain a declaration of nullity, without regard to whether it was related to the traditional procreative essentials of marriage.

If Wanda had in fact deceived Harry as to her intent at the time of the marriage, Harry might have succeeded under the subjective test. However, Wanda did not misrepresent her intentions to induce Harry to marry her. The facts indicate that Wanda cooperated in the plan to raise and educate their children as Catholic in accordance with the agreement until two years ago, after her mother's death. This cooperation is evidence that Wanda intended to and did comply with the agreement; she has only departed from it because of a serious life event.

II. Fault-based judicial separation for cruelty

1. Nature of fault-based action for separation and divorce   Fault-based divorce grounds require a showing that the innocent, injured spouse was the victim of a fault committed by the guilty spouse; the fault must be one recognized in the state's divorce statute. A number of states retain the possibility, under their fault systems of divorce, for a spouse to obtain a judicial separation either as a first step in obtaining a fault-based divorce, or without pursuing the divorce further. A judicial separation is an artifact of the ancient divorce *a mensa et thoro*, from bed and board, that relieved the spouses from the obligation to live with one another without dissolving the marriage. The grounds for this type of "divorce" are generally the same as those for fault-based absolute divorce *a vinculo matrimonii*, which ended the bond of marriage. They are interpreted in the same way. An apparent fault can be ineffective if the allegedly guilty spouse can provide a defense.

2. Cruelty and mental cruelty   The cruelty that provides a ground for divorce is an intentional course of conduct by the defendant that is so harmful to the plaintiff's physical or mental health that it makes continued cohabitation unsafe, improper, or intolerable. The conduct must be seriously harmful; it cannot be mere incompatibility, or nagging and bickering.

In this case, to obtain his judgment of separation, Harry must produce evidence of cruelty by Wanda. There is no suggestion of physical cruelty on Wanda's part. Harry must establish mental cruelty. Mental cruelty could be in the form of words directed at the innocent spouse (e.g., fault-finding, quarreling, mocking), or in the form of actions (e.g., tricks that victimize the spouse). It must be serious enough to destroy the mental well-being of the innocent spouse. Harry can allege that Wanda's refusal to abide by the agreement that they made prior to marriage through her present refusal to participate in raising the children as Catholic and her interference with their religious education constitute mental cruelty. He would demonstrate his own practice of and belief in his faith; her behavior causes him anxiety concerning the children's spiritual welfare. In addition, he would allege that she is causing him anxiety about their temporal welfare. She is undermining the children's ability to trust their caretakers by confusing them when they are too young to make independent religious choices. Harry could allege as well that Wanda's breach of their agreement has destroyed his trust in her because she knew how important he thought his religion was to family life at the time that they married. Harry would have to demonstrate that this concern was serious enough to destroy his peace of mind, endanger his health, or both. The most convincing evidence would be medical evidence of physical symptoms associated with mental health disorders, such as depression or anxiety.

3. Wanda's defense to Harry's separation action   If Harry succeeds in establishing sufficiently severe mental suffering, the traditional defenses to fault-based divorce grounds (connivance, mutual fault (also known as unclean hands), condonation, recrimination, insanity and collusion) would not supply a defense for Wanda. Instead, Wanda would maintain that the ground itself is not met because her acts and words to Harry were not cruel. They amount only to incompatibility because of religious differences. Although a court has found a spouse's language concerning religion to be cruel (see *Hybertson v. Hybertson*, 582 N.W.2d 402 (S.D. 1998)), it was because the religious language was used to attack the other spouse directly and to prevent communication with the other spouse. However, if she knew of the effect on Harry's peace of mind or his concerns for the children, and continued to proselytize them anyway, a finding of mental cruelty is possible.

III. No-fault divorce action

The modern no-fault divorce means that the state recognizes a ground for divorce in which a finding of guilt plays no role. The ground of irretrievable breakdown does not create the need or opportunity for the plaintiff spouse to demonstrate that the other spouse caused the breakdown, or for the defendant spouse to present proof of any defense. The breakdown of the marriage is determined by reference to the subjective state of mind of the spouses. If one spouse declares under oath that the marriage is irretrievably broken, the other spouse's insistence that it is not (and even offers of reconciliation, if not accepted) cannot prevent the divorce. Harry, therefore, cannot prevent Wanda from divorcing him. She can obtain a divorce from Harry easily and probably quickly, waiting at most the two-month cooling-off period in the state statute if it is ordered.

IV. Custody of the children

1. Basis for child custody awards   In the United States, the universal basis for an award of child custody is the best interest of the child. Child custody awards to parents generally take the form of either joint physical and legal custody or sole custody with visitation. Joint custody leaves the authority to make legally enforceable decisions concerning the child in the hands of both parents; both usually have physical custody of the child at times as well. Sole custody assigns the decision-making authority to one parent, who also has physical custody of the child, and the other parent has an award of visitation with the child. The decision as to *who* receives child custody and *in which form* is based on factors related to the best interest of the child. Relevant factors for this question include the ability to provide a stable home life and continuity for the child, each parent's willingness to cooperate with the other, each parent's prior caretaking responsibility, each parent's ability and willingness to foster an ongoing relationship with the other parent, and each parent's ability to provide moral guidance and ethical upbringing for the child.

2. Joint or sole custody and the factors indicating the best interest of the children   Joint custody is preferred in Harry's state, and the devotion of both parents to their children's welfare would normally cut in favor of it. However, in this instance, both parents have exhibited uncompromising attitudes concerning religious upbringing in what each regards to be the children's best interest. Harry insists that it requires that the children be raised in the Catholic faith, attend Catholic school, and participate in Catholic religious ceremonies. Wanda's attempt to introduce them to her Baptist faith arises out of her belief that that faith would serve their best interests. The parents are thus unlikely to be able to make joint decisions on a childrearing issue that both consider extremely important. Their requests for sole custody indicate their unwillingness to cooperate with one another. Thus, sole custody in one parent is most likely to result. That sole custodian, having the authority to make legally enforceable decisions regarding the children, would have the power to choose the children's religion and schooling unless the court provided otherwise.

The choice of sole custodian depends on applying the relevant factors to determine best interest. The factors of stable home life and of prior caretaking responsibility favor Wanda. She has been the traditional homemaker and caretaker of the children. However, she is less likely to provide continuity in the older children's education — she wants to remove them from their current Catholic school — and in their religious and moral upbringing, as she is making a dedicated attempt to change their religious beliefs and practice. Harry, on the other hand, would encourage continuity in their religious practice and education; however, his adopting the traditional breadwinner role means that he has not got Wanda's experience and well-established relationship with the children as caretaker. His sole custody would create instability because it would present very young children with an unfamiliar home life. Harry might argue further that Wanda's abandonment of her commitment under the prenuptial agreement indicates that she has a deficient ethical sense; she deserts her commitments when her opinions change. This conduct could negatively impact the children.

3. The enforceability of the prenuptial agreement   The prenuptial agreement that the children be raised in the Catholic faith implicates, as Wanda has indicated, the First Amendment of the U.S. Constitution. Wanda would argue that enforcement of such an agreement would interfere with her First Amendment right to practice her religion. She would be prohibited from passing her faith on to her children. Harry would argue that (1) Wanda contracted away her right to raise her children as Baptists; and (2) he relied on her having done so in the prenuptial agreement; without it, he would not have married her. Therefore the agreement concerning the children's religion should be treated as a private contract, not a constitutional issue.

Jurisdictions differ on the outcomes of attempts to enforce such a prenuptial agreement. Some jurisdictions, especially in older cases, have enforced the agreement, utilizing Harry's reliance argument. Ordinarily, though, the contract to raise the children in a particular religion, where it has been acted on, is treated as related to the continuity and stability factors in best interest, not as independently controlling. The most common result is for the court to refuse to enforce the agreement because doing so would excessively entangle the state with religion. The court then decides custody on nonreligious grounds using the factors, and the custodian has the authority to determine the children's religion. If the factors are inconclusive, and the children are old enough to be strongly attached to one religion, their preference could be decisive. Some jurisdictions have imposed restrictions (e.g., limitations on taking the children to church) on either the custodian, the noncustodial parent, or both. These are intended to protect the children from confusion as a result of parental conflict over religion.

4. Result   The court is likely to refuse to enforce the prenuptial agreement and to award sole custody to Wanda on the basis of her role as primary caretaker. However, it might restrict her authority in the realms of religion and school choice to preserve continuity in the children's education and religious practice.

QUESTION #2

I. Recognition of Ben as Jerry's spouse

1. Comity as the basis for recognition of out-of-state marriages   Ben would first attempt to obtain recognition of his marriage to Jerry, which would give him, as Jerry's spouse, superior claim to make decisions for Jerry, including who may visit him in the hospital. The first sentence of Article IV, Section 1 of the U.S. Constitution, known as the Full Faith and Credit clause, reads, "Full Faith and Credit shall be given in each State to the public Acts, Records, and judicial Proceedings of every other state." Despite this sentence, states have historically not been considered compelled to recognize marriages celebrated in other states as valid. Instead, the nonbinding principle of comity—deference to the acts of another sovereign—is the basis for recognition of out-of-state marriages of couples domiciled or residing in the state. The requirements for securing such deference are found in conflicts of laws rules regarding marriage. Section 283 of Restatement (Second) of Conflicts of Laws provides two steps for determining an out-of-state marriage's validity. First, it looks to the local law of the state with the most significant relationship to the spouses and the marriage, generally agreed to be the state where the spouses were domiciled when the marriage took place. In the case of Ben and Jerry's marriage, California would be the state whose law would govern. Then, it provides that a marriage that satisfies the requirements of the state where the marriage was contracted will everywhere be recognized as valid unless it violates the strong public policy of another state that has the most significant relationship to the spouses and the marriage at the time of the marriage. Because no state had a more significant relationship to the couple when they married than California did, then California law governs.

2. Effect of a change in the law   However, two additional issues must be addressed. First, what is the effect of California's reversing its decision to permit same-sex marriages to be confected in the state? That reversal took place after Ben and Jerry's marriage. Under California state law at the time of the accident, Ben and Jerry no longer could enter into marriage in that state. This reversal undermines recognition under the Restatement, which uses the present tense. Ben's argument would be that once parties have entered into the marital relationship under the state's regime, the state cannot divest them of it and its privileges retroactively. California's Attorney General supports the interpretation that the validity of California marriages that occurred before the November 2008 ban is unaffected by it. No courts have found otherwise. To permit the marital status to change after the fact would not only damage the individuals involved and their families, but the reliability of the public records. On the other hand, the California Attorney General's opinion is not a judicial ruling or a legislative act. The court could find that marriage cannot be treated in the same way as a property right or an ordinary contract. Because it is more than either of these, in the past its regime has been subjected to change without the need for the state to preserve past laws' applicability to those who had already contracted it. *Maynard v. Hill*, 125 U.S. 190 (1888). That case, though, concerned the availability of a new type of divorce, not the ability to enter marriage, a far more significant privilege. The attorney general's position could well be accepted.

3. Effect of the Defense of Marriage Act   Second, the Defense of Marriage Act, codified at 28 U.S.C. 1738C, declares that "[n]o State . . . shall be required to give effect to any public act, record, or judicial proceeding of any other State . . . respecting a relationship between persons of the same sex that is treated as a marriage under the laws of such other State . . . or a right or claim arising from such relationship." Thus, if Full Faith and Credit had been extended to recognition of marriages, your state could refuse to give Ben and Jerry's marriage such recognition. However, although the language of the Full Faith and Credit clause is echoed, the statute does not confine its reach to arguments under that clause. It simply exempts states from having to recognize out-of-state same-sex marriages, without additional requirements. Because of the lack of state-court guidance on recognition, the court could invoke this statute to refuse recognition of Ben as Jerry's spouse.

The absence of any authoritative legal source rejecting same-sex marriage or its recognition is a hopeful sign that the court might be open to Ben's argument. This issue has been addressed in numerous state legislatures and in state constitutional amendments for over 15 years. The fact that your state has not taken action could indicate that it does not regard these marriages as so offensive to public policy that they should not be permitted. Moreover, even if your state does not want to permit a type of marriage to be entered into within its borders, a state can recognize such marriages when confected elsewhere under the principle of *favor matrimonii*. (*Estate of May*, 114 N.E.2d 4 (N.Y. 1953)). Thus the court could recognize Ben as Jerry's spouse not estranged, and transfer to him the substituted decision-making power for the incompetent Jerry.

II. Sam's status as Jerry's child by adoption

Even if Jerry's parents succeed in retaining decision-making power, they will not be able to prevent Sam from visiting Jerry in the ICU unless they devise a way to make Jerry's condition deteriorate from his presence. Your state's law provides a right to immediate family members to visit a patient for ten minutes every hour. Excluding them is only provided for if their visits directly cause the patient's condition to deteriorate. First, Sam, as Jerry's adopted son, is member of Jerry's immediate family. Ben and Jerry obtained a California court judgment of adoption. Your state is required to recognize that adoption under the Full Faith and Credit clause of the U.S. Constitution because it is a judgment, the result of a judicial proceeding in another state. Adoption places the adopted child in the same standing as a biological child. The Full Faith and Credit clause has historically been applied to out-of-state judgments, and no federal statute excuses states from recognizing them. Only if Sam's presence caused Jerry's condition to deteriorate would his visits be precluded. Because he had not been excluded prior to the arrival of Jerry's parents, it appears that his visits do not have this effect. He would therefore be permitted to visit his father in the ICU.

QUESTION #3

I. Mona v. Ed and Ed v. Frank

You should advise Ed to pursue the appeal. It is true that the discovery that Ed and Mona were not married at the time Gina was born, but that in fact Mona was still married to Frank, gives Frank the advantage of the common law presumption that the husband of the mother is the father of a child born during the marriage. In most states, the presumption becomes conclusive when a specified period of time — here, five years — since the child's birth has passed, and others asserting paternity are foreclosed from bringing suit because they lack standing. This denial of standing has been held by the U.S. Supreme Court to be constitutional in *Michael H. v. Gerald D*. However, because the state adheres to the putative marriage doctrine for those who in good faith attempt a marriage that is in fact void, Ed can argue that he, too, is entitled to the marital presumption, and that its policies are better served by permitting him to establish his paternity. In addition, he has a more tenuous argument under the less well-established doctrine of equitable parenthood in favor of being recognized as Gina's parent. If either of these is accepted, he would stand on an equal footing with Mona in the ultimate contest for custody.

II. The putative marriage doctrine creates conflicting presumptions of paternity

Because his state has adopted the putative marriage doctrine, Ed can claim the status of a putative spouse provided he can demonstrate that he in good faith attempted to enter a valid marriage that was void because of an impediment of which he had no knowledge. If he demonstrates that he merits that status, he would receive the rights conferred on a legal spouse. The presumption in favor of a spouse's paternity of a child born during the marriage is one such right. Establishment of his putative marriage to Mona would place Ed on the same footing as Frank; each would have the same presumption in his favor. Thus, Ed must establish that he attempted to marry Mona, that the attempt failed, and that he was in good faith at the time that he made the attempt.

Ed and Mona went through a wedding ceremony before a justice of the peace two weeks after Mona showed Ed her "divorce judgment." The attempt to marry failed because of an impediment, Mona's prior undissolved marriage, which results in a marriage void *ab initio*. Ed must establish that he was in good faith at that time to receive the benefit of putative spouse status. Good faith in this instance requires that the participant in the failed attempt at marriage neither knew, nor should have known, of the defect in the marriage. There is evidence that Ed was in good faith at the time of the attempted marriage. He had seen Mona's judgment of divorce. The purveyor of these fraudulent documents had crafted them well enough to fool thousands of individuals over a period of 12 years. Thus, their fraudulent nature was not apparent on the face of the documents. Ed himself had nothing to do with selecting the lawyer for the divorce; that was done by Frank and Mona. Thus Ed would not have seen any questionable material that might have been on Ima Fraud's advertisement. Even if Ima Fraud had offered genuine divorce services, lack of an Alabama domicile for an Alabama divorce would make it a nullity. However, nothing in the facts suggests that Ed would have the legal sophistication to know that. Moreover, if the "reasonable person" standard is used, the number of people scammed by Ima Fraud and the number of years that she perpetrated this fraud suggest that the domicile requirement for divorce is not widely known among the general public.

Thus, Ed can make a strong case for application of the putative marriage doctrine, which would confer a husband's rights on him — in this case, the right to be presumed the father of a child who was born during his putative marriage. His standing to bring the action on the basis of the presumption should be recognized. However, Frank is still entitled to the presumption of paternity because Gina was born during the existence of his actual marriage to Mona. Thus, the court would have to resolve the conflict between the two presumptions to determine who is to be legally identified as Gina's father.

III. Resolving the conflicting presumptions of paternity

The paternity statute provides a method by which the court could resolve the conflicting presumptions of Ed's and Frank's paternity; it states that where two or more presumptions of paternity conflict with each other, the court's decision is controlled by the presumption "which on the facts is founded on the weightier considerations of policy and logic." The court's determination of the policies and logic underlying the presumptions and their relative weight might favor Frank if the court determines that the purpose of the statute is to protect an intact, legally recognized marital family against disruption by an outsider. Frank and Mona are husband and wife; Gina is Mona's child and under the law presumptively Frank's as well. This logic won the day for the defendant legal father against the biological father in *Michael H.* However, *Michael H.* can be distinguished because the defendant in that case did not enjoy putative spouse status; he had no presumption of his own paternity with which to counter his status as an outsider. In this case, Ed can make the argument that the family unit consisted of himself, Mona, and Gina, born during his putative marriage. He, not Frank, has a long-established psychological and emotional relationship with Gina, who was cared for by himself and Mona for eight years until Mona's desertion in collusion with Frank. The disruption of the marital family has already occurred, and Frank, not Ed, is the outsider. In addition, Ed can argue that the marital presumption to which he is entitled came into existence in common law before scientific methods of identifying the father were available. Its underlying policy was not just to protect a marital family, but to filiate the child to the person most likely to be the parent, protecting both the child's interest and the parent's right in the care, custody, and control of the child. This policy would be served by applying the presumption in his favor because he is Gina's biological father. To support this argument, Ed should request a court order for DNA testing comparing blood samples from Gina and himself. This test, Mona's testimony that she told Ed that she no longer had sexual relations with Frank, and evidence of Ed's years of paternal care for Gina would supply underlying facts supporting Ed's interpretation of the policy.

It is possible that the court would say that based on the context of the statement concerning conflict resolution, this solution was only to be used when two men who had both validly married the mother were both entitled to the marital presumption, that is, the child was born within 300 days of the dissolution of the marriage to the first husband, and during the marriage to the second. However, the statute refers to conflict between two "or more" presumptions, suggesting that paternity presumptions arising from other legal doctrines, such as his as a putative spouse, would also be resolved in this fashion.

IV. Equitable parenthood

Should the court reject Ed's argument for allowing him the marital presumption and refuse to recognize him as having standing to establish his paternity, he could request that the court apply the equitable parenthood doctrine to recognize his parental rights with regard to Gina. The doctrine permits an individual to assume the rights and responsibilities of a natural parent through a judicial determination. It requires that the mother of the child cooperated in the development of such a relationship over a period of time, that the petitioner desires to have the rights afforded to a parent, and that the petitioner is willing to take on the responsibilities of a parent, such as child support. Here, Mona, by attempting to marry Ed and treating him as her husband and Gina's father for eight years, cooperated in establishing the parent–child relationship. Ed desires to have parental rights and to shoulder parental responsibilities. However, the doctrine has been rejected by some states. Where it is used, it has been restricted to recognizing a husband's right to parent a child who is not his biological offspring after the husband and the child's mother divorce. If it has been accepted in the state where the action is taking place, Ed could again point to his status as putative spouse to claim the rights conferred on a validly married spouse.

QUESTION #4

The court should modify the original joint custody decree and award sole custody to Liz, who has met the legal requirements for such a change.

I. The standard for modifying a decree of child custody

The usual rule for modifying the custodial terms of a divorce decree is that custody will be modified only on a showing of a substantial change in circumstances since the time of the decree that (1) was not contemplated by the court when the decree was entered, (2) is of permanent duration, and (3) relates to the welfare of the child.

II. Breakdown of communication between the parents as a substantial change in circumstances for custody modification purposes

Liz could argue as changed circumstances the development of hostility between the parents because of a breakdown of communication. The failure of communication between the parents is a change in circumstances; prior to Judy's becoming an adolescent, Liz and Tim had cooperated in their child's upbringing. The onset of their disagreements coincided with that of Judy's adolescence. The change, Liz would claim, is substantial both because of the difference from the harmonious co-parenting that had characterized their custody before this point, and because of the importance to Judy's future of her development during adolescence. Tim could respond that disagreement between the parents is not a sufficient change of circumstances to justify disrupting Judy's life by changing custody from joint to sole. Moreover, the fact that Judy would become an adolescent must have been contemplated by the court at the time of the original decree; it is the normal course of a child's life. The disagreement is not permanent, as it is triggered by a passing phase of life, and is merely a reflection of occasional divergent opinions about appropriate dress and social activities rather that related to the welfare of the child.

Liz's request appears to meet the standard for modification. Although the fact that Judy (barring some tragic occurrence) would mature into a teenager was no doubt foreseen, the conflict it would trigger between these parents is not likely to have been, given the congeniality that had characterized their relationship until then. The requirement that the change be permanent does not require that it literally last forever. The change is "permanent" because it is indefinite in length, and because Judy's adolescence will last until her attaining the majority age of 18, it would be a permanent characteristic of the rest of her parents' custody of her.

As to the requirement that the change relates to the welfare of the child, Liz's argument is likely to prevail. The two parents' differences are rooted in divergent views of what is appropriate everyday behavior for their child. When Tim's opinion differs from Liz's on such matters as when Judy can begin to date, the length of Judy's skirts, whether she can stay out on a school night, and whether she and her friends can spend three hours unsupervised, it is because he favors postponing Judy's transition to adulthood for a few more years. Liz is willing to let Judy make decisions on these matters. A court is unlikely to label either point of view as the sole correct approach. However, because, until Judy is an adult, the conflict is likely to continue, and parental conflict is considered damaging to a child's best interests, the change is related to the welfare of the child. Therefore, the "substantial change in circumstances" requirement has been met.

III. The child's preference

The conflict between Judy's parents as to her upbringing could be resolved by awarding sole custody to either parent. However, Judy expressed a preference for her mother's custody. Her reason for doing so indicates that she is mature enough for her preference to be given weight: She can communicate freely with her mother, but not with her father. Because parent–child communication is considered important to a child's welfare, it is appropriate for the court to award sole custody to Liz.

IV. Effect of Liz's frivolous spending on Judy's best interest

Liz's large expenditures on psychic hotlines in the year after her mother's death, according to Tim, indicate that she lacks the maturity to give Judy proper guidance, and therefore she should not receive sole custody. However, Liz does not appear to be consistently irresponsible in her spending; she also invested $200,000 in a college fund for Judy. The fact that Liz spent the money following her mother's death suggests that she might have been suffering from that loss, and seeking comfort. The spending appears to have been a transient occurrence, and should not outweigh Liz's superior ability to communicate with her daughter and her daughter's preference.

FAMILY LAW ESSAY EXAM #2

QUESTION #1

I. Determining net income of the parents

The most important factor in determination of the amount of child support in U.S. jurisdictions is the net income of the parents. Net income is determined by subtracting deductions permitted by the child support statute from each parent's gross income to determine how much income the parties have access to. Fewer deductions are permitted under this statute than under state and federal tax law. They usually include federal and state taxes, social security and Medicare contributions, and health insurance for the parent. In most jurisdictions, employer contributions to a parent's retirement account are not considered to be his or her income for child support purposes. Therefore, Chuck's income for child support purposes would include the $6,000 per month of his take-home pay, amounting to $72,000 per year. The 5 percent of his gross income that he contributes to his retirement account as a voluntary deduction, $6,000 per year, would probably also be included. Chuck has chosen to defer his present income to provide for his future security; given the employer contribution, a court would probably not consider Chuck's own contribution to be deductible from the amount on which it bases his child support obligation. The $3,600 in deductions for his children's health insurance is also not deductible at this point. This is not because Chuck will not get credit for it; it is because part of that cost should be paid by Di. It is necessary to break out the figure to calculate separately her share of the cost. Chuck's child support payment would ultimately be reduced by what he pays for the children's health insurance, including the part owed by Di. In addition, Chuck has $20,000 in assets from the division of the marital property. Because this property does not produce income that would in the long run help support the children, the court would consider it available for liquidation to pay child support.

II. Voluntarily foregone income

There is less consensus on the foregone income from teaching the architecture course at the local university, the gifts from his parents, and Di's alimony. Most states include all usual sources of earned income in the calculation. They also provide for imputation of income if a parent is voluntarily unemployed or underemployed. If Chuck reduces his employment and thus his income, the court might consider him voluntarily underemployed, and impute to him the amount of income he would have netted had he continued his usual practice. In that case, an additional $5,000 would be added to his net income. In addition, the gifts from his parents, although not taxable and not necessarily recurring, are in most jurisdictions treated as income for child support calculations, adding $50,000 to his income. If his parents do not provide him with a similar gift in future years, Chuck can petition for a modification of the child support award on that basis. Finally, Di's alimony might be deductible from

Chuck's net income, depending on the jurisdiction. If it is considered as income in determining Di's child support obligation, to count it as Chuck's net income as well would add $12,000 that does not exist to the amount the two parents have available for child support. If it is not considered as income to Di, it would no doubt be considered as part of Chuck's net income, although the fairness of this is highly questionable.

III. Imputation of income to unemployed parent

Di's net income for child support purposes may include the $12,000 in alimony paid to her by Chuck, as previously noted. Like Chuck, she has $20,000 in assets from the division of the marital property. She has no source of regular earned income. She wants to continue in her role of homemaker to her children, but if she does so, she is likely to have the income she has foregone imputed to her for child support purposes. Most jurisdictions permit the parent who is caretaker of the parties' children to remain unemployed while the children are preschool age without imputing income to him or her, but after that time, in the absence of special circumstances affecting the children or the caregiver, income will be imputed to the voluntarily unemployed caregiver. Because Will and Harry are well beyond preschool age, Di must return to work to avoid having income imputed to her because she is voluntarily unemployed. The income that would be imputed would be the equivalent of the wage that Di could earn, in this case, $12 per hour, or $480 per 40-hour work week. This would amount to $24,000 per 50-week working year. If Di takes a job that pays less, she risks being found to be voluntarily underemployed, and having the difference between what she could have earned and what she actually earned imputed to her. If she cannot find a job, or a job paid at least the expected wage, she can petition the court for a modification of the child support award.

QUESTION #2

Will should be advised first and foremost that all his suggestions involve someone lying under oath to a court of law, also known as perjury, a criminal offense. No lawyer who values his or her license will knowingly permit a client to commit perjury himself, or to suborn perjury from another. Historically, the more liberal courts winked at such actions in the past because of the desperate situation that husbands and wives found themselves in prior to the widespread adoption of quick no-fault divorce in the second half of the twentieth century. However, divorce courts did not care for being labeled "Courts of Perjury," and in the present era, they are unlikely to want to return to that status—especially for the sake of married couples who, like Will and Traci, freely chose to give up the divorce option that would have solved Will's problem. He must not pursue any of these schemes if you are to represent him.

I. Commonalia's covenant marriage divorce options

Will has no evidence on which to bring a divorce action for Traci's adultery, or for her conviction of a felony; he also has not provided her with such grounds, should she be willing to cooperate. He has two options for ending his marriage under the covenant marriage divorce regime.

1. Abandonment   First, he could provide Traci with the ground of abandonment. Abandonment requires, first, that he voluntarily leave the matrimonial domicile. Courts have required that the departure be shown to be made with the intention of ending the marriage. Will would therefore move out of his house to a different domicile. Second, fulfilling the fault ground requires that Will remain outside of the domicile for a period of a year. This requirement has been judicially interpreted to mean that the spouses live continually separate and apart. Any move back into the matrimonial domicile or even sharing living arrangements with Traci elsewhere could be interpreted as reconciliation. Reconciliation, the resumption of the marital life together, wipes out any fault ground in existence and the time accumulated toward divorce. Will would have to recommence accumulating the year of living separately and apart from Traci, slowing the process of divorce. Finally, Will must constantly refuse to return to the matrimonial domicile if Traci asks him to.

The difficulty that Will faces if he attempts to use this divorce ground is that it requires Traci's cooperation. The abandonment would be Will's fault; thus, Traci must bring the divorce action against Will. For his departure to constitute abandonment, she must ask him to return for him to refuse to do so. She might do so willingly, given her possessive behavior; or she might not. She must also initiate the divorce action. If she is possessive of Will, she might prefer to remain separated rather than to divorce him. Given her apparent lack of regard for truth in important matters, Will would not be wise to trust her even if she said she would bring the suit.

However, a second form of abandonment, constructive abandonment, might be available to Will, and allow him to file suit against Traci. The doctrine of constructive abandonment was created by judicial interpretation. Under it, Will would have a ground of abandonment to bring the divorce action against Traci if he can demonstrate that she drove him from the matrimonial domicile by engaging in conduct that made continuance of the marital relationship unendurable or dangerous to life, health, or safety. This cause of action requires that spouses remain continuously separate and apart for the same time period required for conventional abandonment, so the strictures against conduct suggesting reconciliation apply to it as well. He can bring the action if he can show the departure and the continuous separation for a year, and he must also show that Traci's conduct meets the standard of making the marital relationship unendurable or dangerous. Will can bring evidence of Traci's deception concerning her pregnancy and her plan to pass a student's child by another man off as Will's and Traci's biological offspring. He could contend that her outrageous scheming has made living with her unendurable because she has demonstrated her untrustworthiness concerning a fundamental feature of married life. Living with someone he cannot trust caused serious psychological and mental illness, his clinical depression and fearful dreams. Her possessive behavior added to his fears. Thus, Traci's conduct made continuing the marital relationship not only unendurable, but also dangerous to his mental health. Although this cause of action does not provide for a faster divorce than abandonment, it has the advantage that the fault is Traci's, and therefore Will is not dependent on Traci's cooperation to get into court.

2. Cruelty   Will also has a cause of action for divorce based on Traci's cruelty. Cruelty has been expansively interpreted for purposes of divorce. It includes physical and mental cruelty. Mental cruelty does not require a showing of bodily harm or a threat or fear of such harm. It is defined by its effect: It consists of words or acts that destroy the peace of mind of the victimized spouse, or the legitimate objects of marriage. It has also been said to destroy the injured spouse's peace of mind and happiness so as to endanger his or her health. Traci's words and conduct with respect to her pregnancy, and the possessive conduct that followed Will's discovery of her lies, appears to fit this ground. This behavior destroyed Will's peace of mind, and also destroyed one of the legitimate objects of marriage, familial trust. Will's clinical depression, frightening dreams, and fear of Traci indicate that she has caused severe mental trauma. Thus, he finds living with her insupportable.

This ground, although it appears to fit Will's situation well, contains a provision that makes it less attractive than constructive abandonment. Like constructive abandonment, it requires that the couple live separate and apart without reconciliation for a period of time before a divorce can be granted. Will must again move out and resist taking action that might suggest that he and Traci have resumed the marital life. Unfortunately for Will, the period of time required is twice as long as that required for the constructive abandonment ground for divorce. Thus, constructive abandonment appears to be the more attractive ground.

3. Traci's defense of insanity   The common law created a defense of insanity against the fault grounds for divorce. It was frequently used against claims of cruel treatment, including mental cruelty, because the underlying theory that the offending spouse was at fault was vitiated by lack of responsibility for the offensive acts or words. A causal relationship between the mental illness and the cruelty is required: The cruelty must be attributable to the spouse's insanity and not to her willful choice. Such a defense would be equally applicable to the fault of constructive abandonment if the conduct that drove the victimized spouse out of the matrimonial domicile was caused by the other spouse's insanity rather than that spouse's will. Traci might try to advance an argument that mental illness caused her to pretend to be pregnant. There is a psychological condition referred to by laypersons as "false pregnancy"; however, Traci was not suffering from it. False pregnancy occurs when a woman has the delusion that she is pregnant when she is not. Sometimes the delusion is strong enough to produce physical changes resembling pregnancy. However, Traci knew that she was not pregnant, as her negotiations to adopt a newborn, her use of the pillow, and her unwillingness to let Will see her undressed indicate. The facts do not indicate that Traci suffers from any other mental condition that could relieve her of responsibility for the deception, such as schizophrenia, paranoia, or major clinical depression, although this possibility would have to be investigated before trial. At present, her deception appears to be a product of her choice rather than irrational compulsion.

II. Migratory divorce

Another option for divorce exists that would enable Will to obtain a divorce more quickly. However, it requires that Will move to a jurisdiction that does not recognize covenant marriage, and has both a short period of physical residence required for one to become domiciled there and a quick, easy procedure for divorce.

A spouse seeking a divorce is not required to obtain it in the state of matrimonial domicile; he or she can obtain a divorce in any state. Moreover, the court need not have personal jurisdiction over the other spouse for the divorce to be valid; a divorce can be granted *ex parte*. In the case of *Williams v. North Carolina*, 317 U.S. 287 (1942) (*Williams I*), the U.S. Supreme ruled that an *ex parte* divorce judgment granted by a state must be recognized in other U.S. jurisdictions under the Full Faith and Credit clause of the U.S. Constitution provided at least one of the spouses was legally domiciled in the divorce-granting state at the time the divorce was granted. Domicile was held to be both necessary and sufficient for that state to have judicial power to pronounce the party's divorce. The other party must be notified of the impending divorce, but need not appear for the divorce to dissolve the marriage.

Even before the *Williams I* decision, some states — most notably Nevada — had used their *ex parte* divorce powers, liberal interpretation of divorce grounds, and quick divorce procedures to attract residents, tourists, and business. *Williams I* articulated what was required to guarantee recognition of these divorces throughout the United States. Of course, if such a state offered covenant marriage, it might require that Will, having entered such a marriage, was confined to using its divorce grounds; however, it is unlikely that a state in the quick-and-easy divorce business would adopt covenant marriage, the goal of which is to make divorce difficult and slow. Thus far none has.

Establishment of domicile in a state has two prerequisites: (1) physical presence within the state for a period of time determined by that state (2) with the intent to make it one's primary residence for an indefinite period of time (sometimes phrased as "one's permanent home"). Will could move to a state such as Nevada that requires a short period of physical residence to qualify as domiciliary and engage in activities indicative of his intent to make it his home indefinitely, such as renting an apartment, transferring his bank accounts, changing his mailing address to the new state, registering his automobile in that state, inquiring about voter registration, applying for jobs, and looking at homes that are on the market. He would also consult a divorce lawyer there to learn the grounds required to obtain a no-fault divorce in the state and begin divorce proceedings. For example, a state might have a six-week residence requirement for domicile, require six weeks of living separate and apart from one's spouse for an *ex parte* no-fault divorce, and permit the six weeks spent in the state prior to acquiring domicile to be counted toward the period of living separate and apart. Upon finding that domicile was established so that subject-matter jurisdiction exists, the court will determine whether the separation requirement has been met, and hand down the judgment of divorce if it has. Thus the entire process of getting the divorce would take a little more than six weeks. Moreover, although the intent to make the divorcing state one's home is required for the judgment to be valid, if circumstances change, the divorcing party might relocate, perhaps to his or her original domicile.

Will should be made aware of several pitfalls to avoid if he decides to move to a different jurisdiction to obtain a divorce. First, another state, such as the original domicile of the divorcing party, can readjudicate the determination of domicile by the divorcing state. In the subsequent case of *Williams v. North Carolina*, 325 U.S. 226 (1945) (*Williams II*), the Supreme Court upheld North Carolina's readjudication of

Williams's domicile and its finding that he was, in fact, still a domiciliary of North Carolina at the time Nevada granted his divorce. Thus his divorce judgment was not entitled to full faith and credit. Therefore, Will should avoid behavior that makes his satisfaction of the residence requirement questionable, or that casts doubt on his intention; for example, he should actually reside in the apartment that he rents for the full amount of time required, and should not leave the state immediately after the divorce is granted. If, however, he moves to the state in early June, receives the divorce in the third week of July, and spends another six weeks looking for appropriate work in his new state of domicile before giving up and returning to Commonalia around Labor Day, his domicile would be difficult to defeat because the one challenging the decree bears a heavy burden of proving its invalidity owing to lack of jurisdiction (see *Williams II, supra*). Additionally, although the divorce may be validly granted *ex parte*, the financial incidents of divorce such as division of marital property and alimony cannot be. Adjudications that deprive the nondomiciliary spouse of rights or impose obligations on her cannot be *ex parte*; under the U.S. Supreme Court's doctrine of "divisible divorce," such adjudications would deprive the absent spouse of due process. See *Vanderbilt v. Vanderbilt*, 354 U.S. 416 (1957). Will must deal with such matters in a state with personal jurisdiction over Traci. Finally, some foreign jurisdictions also offer migratory divorces to U.S. citizens, and usually have shorter time periods for establishing domicile and quicker no-fault divorce requirements, such as 24 hours for both. Migratory divorces in these jurisdictions are not entitled to full faith and credit in the United States to begin with. U.S. jurisdictions may choose to grant them deference under the principle of comity. However, such deference will not be accorded to a divorce if it violates constitutionally mandated due process and the requirement of domicile for subject-matter jurisdiction. A 24-hour residence period for establishing domicile appears too short to demonstrate the intent to remain in a country indefinitely. Will should avoid such a divorce because it is likely to be treated as a nullity in the United States, and he would find himself still married to Traci.

Will's best option for a speedy divorce appears to be a migratory one. Given the length of time and complexity of proof required for a covenant marriage divorce in Commonalia, migratory divorce might be the less expensive option as well.

QUESTION #3

I. Criteria for awarding permanent periodic alimony

Martha does not have many of the characteristics that entitle spouses to conventional "permanent periodic" postdivorce alimony. The availability of alimony to a spouse is based on his or her need. The court determines whether the party seeking alimony has sufficient property to provide for his or her reasonable needs, and whether he or she is able to be self-supporting through appropriate employment. Martha meets the first criterion; she does not have sufficient property to provide for her needs, as the parties acquired little property of value during the marriage. However, she is able to support herself. Nothing in the facts suggests that she is unhealthy. She is 25 years old. She has a degree and a position, albeit half-time, in her field. She has supported herself and George for four years, and earned enough to pay for his medical schooling as well.

The question, then, is whether she can support herself through *appropriate* employment. Courts interpreting this statute have defined appropriate as suited to the individual and reflecting the expectations and intentions established during the marriage. Under this test, the court may order alimony for Martha while she searches for a full-time position in teaching drama. Martha and George expected her career as an office assistant to end once he graduated from medical school, for her to work teaching drama, and ultimately for her to stay home with their children.

II. Amount and duration of alimony

If the court determines that Martha is entitled to alimony, the next step is for the court to determine its amount and duration. Most of the factors that courts use in making this determination cut against Martha's receiving a large or long-term award. The factors include the petitioner's abilities, education, physical condition, age, access to income-producing property, standard of living during the marriage, length of the marriage, and the disparity in the parties' earning capacities or incomes. Martha, as we have seen, is young, educated, apparently healthy, and in a short-term marriage in which the standard of living was not high. However, she does not have access to income-producing property and she might be found not to have appropriate employment, as the position she has accepted is only part-time, and requires her to shoulder the expense of moving. Additionally, her husband's earning capacity greatly exceeds hers. Given his standard of living during the marriage, he should have no difficulty meeting his needs, although perhaps not all his wants, while meeting Martha's. Thus, alimony for a limited duration while she seeks a full-time position as a drama teacher would be appropriate.

III. Reimbursement and property division solutions

A number of jurisdictions, driven by equitable considerations, have devised methods for compensating a spouse in a career-threshold divorce who has worked to enable the other spouse to secure an advanced degree or professional license with the intent of increasing both parties' future standard of living. The first of these is reimbursement, sometimes termed "reimbursement alimony." For examples, see Cal. Fam. Code sec. 2641 and Ind. Code sec. 31-15-7-6. If the court considers Martha's sacrifices to have reduced her standard of living while enhancing George's in the future, and to have been made in the parties' mutual expectation that both would benefit materially from them, it could order reimbursement. Martha's monetary contributions to George's education from her income reduced her standard of living at the time. In addition, any money beyond what was needed for their support went to George's tuition, books, and medical equipment, rather than being invested or saved for her future. Therefore, Martha's contributions to George's education would entitle her to reimbursement for these monetary contributions. In addition, some state courts have included the financial contributions made to meet the living expenses of the student spouse (see *De La Rosa v. De La Rosa*, 309 N.W. 2d 755 (Minn. 1981) and *Reiss v. Reiss*, 478 A.2d 441 (N.J. Ch. Div. 1984)), despite the marital obligation of support.

In addition, one state, New York, has adopted the unique approach of treating the degree or license acquired by the student spouse as marital property, and subjecting it to equitable distribution. See *O'Brien v. O'Brien*, 489 N.E.2d 712 (N.Y. 1985). Although a professional license does not fit within the traditional common law view of property, it resembles other new forms of property recognized at present, such as entitlements. Although it cannot be distributed in the traditional manner, an award can be made of the monetary value of the earner spouse's share. This share is calculated as a share of the present value of the student spouse's future earnings. This approach is less likely to succeed in securing an award for Martha than the reimbursement approach. It has not been adopted in any state other than New York; objections to it include the speculative nature of calculating future earnings and the fact that the earnings themselves, as opposed to the degree, would be acquired after the marriage is over.

QUESTION #4

The two questions raised in this problem are the validity of first-cousin marriages, and the recognition of marriages that are valid in the state where confected in jurisdictions where such marriages would be void. If Elly and Josh's marriage is an absolute nullity, then she was not his spouse and could not inherit his estate.

I. The principles for determining whether a state will recognize a marriage from a different jurisdiction that does not comply with state requirements

The validity of Josh and Elly's marriage in Vermont depends on its compliance with the marriage laws of that state, not those of Commonalia. In Commonalia, first-cousin marriages are permitted. Nothing in the facts suggests that either party had a prior undissolved marriage or that they were the same sex, or that any marriage formalities were omitted. Thus, the Vermont marriage was valid where confected.

Under Conflicts of Laws rules concerning marriage recognition by other jurisdictions, the principle is usually stated as, "A marriage that is valid where contracted is valid everywhere." This is, however, an overstatement. States have long refused to recognize marriages that were valid in the jurisdiction where confected, but violated a strong public policy of the state. Thus, even before the Defense of Marriage Act was passed, states that prohibited same-sex marriage could refuse to give effect to those validly confected elsewhere under principles by which conflicts of law are decided by establishing that a strong public policy was responsible for the refusal. The validity is decided by the law of the state that, with respect to the particular issue, has the most significant relationship to the spouses and the marriage. See Restatement (2d) of Conflicts of Laws, Section 283.

II. Arguments of the parties

Goneril and Regan would claim, first, that Commonalia has a strong public policy against first-cousin marriages because the prohibition on those marriages is a public health statute, a very strong policy basis. The prohibition reduces the occurrence of birth defects caused by recessive genes in offspring of couples who are closely related to one another. Thus the strong public policy requirement is fulfilled. Second, Commonalia, they would maintain, has the most significant relationship to the parties and the marriage. Both spouses were domiciled in Commonalia at the time that they married. Residing in a different state does not change an individual's domicile unless he or she intends to make the new state of residence his or her permanent home. Attending college in Vermont did not change Elly's and Josh's domiciles because they gave no indication that they intended to move to Vermont permanently. Of course, individuals can marry in a state other than the one of domicile, but that does not change the fact that the domiciliary state has the closest relationship with the parties to the marriage, both at the time of the marriage and ever since. Josh and Elly's Vermont marriage was a fugitive marriage, confected there expressly to avoid Commonalia's marriage laws, but the two then returned to Commonalia after a mere two weeks, and have lived there for the rest of their lives. Its laws on the validity of marriage should prevail.

Against these arguments, Elly can argue that first, no strong public policy of Commonalia permits it to deny recognition to a marriage validly confected between first cousins in another state. Prohibitions of first cousin marriages do not rise to that level. In the United States, marriages between first cousins — or consanguineous kin generally — are unusual because their reproduction is regarded as risky in Western culture. Although dangers of inbreeding exist, in a largely outbreeding population with periodic first-cousin marriages, the risk of them is not great. Moreover, Western medical technology provides mechanisms for avoiding reproduction, either in individual cases or entirely, if the risk exists. Many U.S. jurisdictions permit first-cousin marriages, indicating that they do not consider them a grave enough danger to public health to interfere with people's marital choices. Other U.S. jurisdictions with prohibitions on first-cousin marriages have not consistently treated them as void when they are challenged, especially in the present era; see *Ghassemi v. Ghassemi*, 998 So. 2d 731 (La. App. 2008). First-cousin marriages, unlike marriages between closer kin, are not criminalized. Therefore, their prohibition does not rest on a public policy strong enough to overcome the policy of interstate recognition of marriage. Second, with regard to the particular issue of recognition of the validity of Elly's marriage, Vermont has the strongest relationship to the parties and the marriage. The integrity of Vermont's marriage law and the free movement of citizens and their families within the United States could both be impaired by denying recognition to these marriages. Comity between states with respect to marriage recognition is the norm; the weak public policy leading to prohibitions on first-cousin marriages is insufficient justification for denying it.

Given the weakness of the policy underlying prohibition on first-cousin marriages, even in states that prohibit it, in comparison to that underlying marriages between closer relations, it is likely that the court will find Josh and Elly's marriage to be valid.

FAMILY LAW ESSAY EXAM #3

QUESTION #1

Commonalia's joint custody statute prohibits its courts from granting joint custody to a parent and a nonparent to privilege the child's parent over nonparents when it comes to the care, custody, and nurture of the child. Thus, for Ann to succeed with her joint custody request, she must establish that she, like Belinda, is Mary Ruth's parent, despite the absence of a biological or adoptive relationship between Ann and the child. Commonalia recognizes the doctrine of equitable parenthood (sometimes termed by courts "de facto parenthood"), under which Ann, if recognized as a parent, could be awarded joint custody with Belinda, and receive court-ordered parenting time with Mary Ruth. However, if the jurisdiction limits the doctrine's application to heterosexual couples, Ann would be unable to obtain joint custody with Belinda because of the state statute prohibiting a parent and a nonparent from sharing that custodial arrangement.

I. The doctrine of equitable parenthood

A minority of U.S. jurisdictions have adopted the doctrine of equitable parenthood. The purpose of the doctrine is to give effect to the expectations and reliance interests resulting when a nonparent develops a parent-like relationship with a child with the agreement and cooperation of the child's legally recognized parent. Under it, one who is not considered to be a parent of a child in law may be deemed in equity to have that status. He or she can be awarded the benefits (such as custody or visitation) of parenthood, as well as its obligations (such as child care or child support). The doctrine thus can be used not only to fulfill the nonparent's expectations, but also the parent's, and to secure both psychological and material benefits for the child.

Three requirements for recognition as an equitable parent exist. First, both the legally recognized parent and the child must have acknowledged the parent–child relationship between the nonparent and the child. Second, the legally recognized parent must have cooperated in the development of the relationship between the child and the nonparent. Third, the nonparent must have agreed to take on parental rights and responsibilities (e.g., support of the child).

In some jurisdictions, the second element is characterized as a voluntary intent and agreement, express or through conduct, by the legally recognized parent to relinquish custody to the nonparent. Intent and agreement to a partial rather than to a full relinquishment of custody have been recognized as fulfilling this requirement for establishing equitable parenthood; see *In re Bonfield*, 780 N.E.2d 241 (Ohio 2002). Whether characterized as intent and agreement, or merely as cooperation in the development of the relationship, the legally recognized parent's voluntary encouragement of the relationship of the nonparent with the child, combined with the other two elements, estops that parent from denying the parental status of the nonparent. Equitable parenthood is therefore also termed "parenthood by estoppel."

II. Application of the doctrine to a second parent of the same sex

Courts in many states do not accept the doctrine of equitable parenthood at all; the facts, though, indicate that Commonalia courts have accepted it. Therefore, although Belinda has pointed to a state statute that would prevent joint custody in a nonparent and a parent, if Ann can demonstrate that she is an equitable parent, the statute would not apply to her. The underlying purpose of the doctrine is to give parental status in equity to one who is not entitled to that status in law. However, Belinda cites the state constitution's Marriage Protection Amendment as an objection to Ann's receiving this status, which prohibits "creat[ing] or recognize[ing] a legal status for relationships of same-sex individuals that intends to approximate the design, qualities, significance or effect of marriage." Belinda appears to be suggesting that equitable parenthood has the significance or effect of marriage by granting parental status on the basis of a relationship. Therefore, for the doctrine to be constitutional, it must be limited to nonparents of a different sex from the legally recognized parent to accord with the state constitution.

In some states, courts have limited the applicability of equitable parenthood, only extending the status to the legally recognized parent's former spouse. However, the facts indicate that Commonalia courts have applied it to both formerly married and never-married heterosexual couples. Thus, this state's use of the doctrine is unrelated to marriage. The constitutional amendment is irrelevant.

Moreover, even if the doctrine had thus far only been applied to formerly married couples, its underlying policies argue for an extension to former nonmarital partners of the same sex, as well as nonmarital partners generally. The doctrine seeks to prevent unfairness to either party in the relationship who has been led by the other's agreement and cooperation to act as a parent toward the child by holding the other party to their original understanding. It also protects the interests of the child. Unfairness and disregard for the child's interests do not occur only through marriage to the legally recognized parent. Thus, it is more consistent with the court's use of the doctrine to extend its protection to Ann in this case.

III. Application of the doctrine to Ann's relationship with Mary Ruth

In the case of Ann's relationship with Mary Ruth, many facts favor an argument that the first requirement is fulfilled. The child acknowledged the parent–child relationship. Mary Ruth addresses Ann as "Mummy." In referring to Ann as her mother in conversation with third parties, Mary Ruth has again shown that she considers Ann as in the same parental relationship with her as Belinda, that of mother. The facts also indicate that the legally recognized parent Belinda acknowledged Ann's parent–child relationship with Mary Ruth as well. Prior to the child's birth, Belinda signed a document stating that she and Ann would equally parent Mary Ruth, who the agreement referred to as "our" child. Belinda gave the name of Ann's late grandmother to the child. She referred to Ann to third parties as "the other parent" and "the other mother" of Mary Ruth. Belinda had refused to sign a birth certificate that did not include Ann's name as one of Mary Ruth's parents and Ann's last name as part of the child's last name, which further support her intention that Ann be Mary Ruth's parent. Belinda's abiding by the co-parenting agreement for six years after the break-up of the women's partnership is a continuing acknowledgment that

Ann and Mary Ruth's parent–child relationship exists. Only when Belinda's new partner insisted on her severing ties with Ann did Belinda refuse to give Ann equal parenting time.

In voluntarily permitting Ann to have a significant role in Mary Ruth's life, Belinda fulfilled another requirement establishing Ann's equitable parenthood: She cooperated in the development of the parent–child relationship between Ann and Mary Ruth. Belinda's cooperation began before Mary Ruth was conceived. Belinda consulted with Ann in choosing the sperm donor, agreeing to one with a heritage similar to Ann's. She allowed Ann to be present when Mary Ruth was born. Belinda also allowed Ann, despite the absence of biological or legal relationship, to support the child, to care for her, to be called "Mummy" by her, and, in short, to be involved in every aspect of Mary Ruth's life in the way that a parent is involved. Moreover, after the breakup, Belinda continued to encourage the parent–child relationship between Ann and Mary Ruth by cooperating in carrying out the terms of the agreement that she entered during her pregnancy. Belinda assisted the continued development of Ann and Mary Ruth's relationship as parent and child by accepting Ann's role as Mary Ruth's parent, allowing Ann to support the child financially and to have input into decisions affecting Mary Ruth. Belinda's cooperation with regard to equal physical care and parenting time furthered the relationship between Ann and Mary Ruth for six more years.

The nature of Belinda's cooperation in the relationship allows it to be characterized as a voluntary intent and agreement, express or through conduct, by the legally recognized parent to relinquish custody to the nonparent, should the jurisdiction require that. The intent and agreement are demonstrated both expressly, through the Agreement to Jointly Parent Our Child, and through Belinda's conduct. Belinda encouraged and permitted Ann to exercise a parent's rights and duties: support, physical care, education, companionship, supervision, and decision-making. Belinda also exercised these herself as well, but under the equitable parent doctrine, it is not necessary for her to give up her own parental role; her intent and agreement were to partially rather than fully relinquish custody to Ann. This has been recognized as fulfilling the requirement of cooperation of the legally recognized parent for establishing equitable parenthood.

Finally, the third requirement, Ann's agreement to take on the role of parent to Mary Ruth, is also evidenced expressly and through conduct. Ann signed the same agreement that Belinda did, demonstrating by her explicit statement her consent to parent the child. Until Belinda limited her parenting time, Ann's actions likewise evidenced her agreement to be Mary Ruth's parent. She paid support, made decisions jointly with Belinda, and physically cared for the child. If the jurisdiction recognizes the equitable parenthood doctrine, it is most likely that Ann would be recognized as having parental status with respect to Mary Ruth.

IV. Effect on Ann's motion for joint custody of recognition as equitable parent

The effect of the equitable parenthood doctrine is to award parental rights to an individual who, with the acknowledgment of the legally recognized parent and of the child, and with the assent of the legally recognized parent, agreed to and did develop a parent–child relationship with the child. Thus, if Ann were deemed to be the equitable parent of Mary Ruth, her request for joint custody would not be prohibited by Commonalia's joint custody statute. Additionally, the higher standard that courts employ in custody contests between a nonparent and a parent, requiring that harm to the child would likely result from parental custody, would not apply. Ann and Belinda would enjoy equal status before the court with regard to the right of custody. The court would decide whether joint custody of Mary Ruth would be granted to Belinda and Ann with one of them as primary physical custodian, or sole custody (assuming she asks for it) to Belinda, employing the standard for determining parental custody, the best interest of the child. Because the custody of Mary Ruth has not been previously adjudicated, but was based on a private arrangement, Ann would not have to demonstrate a substantial change in circumstances to have her request considered.

V. Application of the best interests of the child standard

The factors that courts consider in determining best interest vary in some respects in different states, but certain constants are present in all of them. Those concerning parental inclination and competence to provide for the child's physical well-being do not arise on these facts. However, two factors related to the psychological well-being of the child are issues here. Stability and continuity in caregiving is commonly viewed as in the child's best interest. A second relevant factor is the willingness of each custodial parent to facilitate the child's relationship with the other parent because a continuing relationship with both parents is considered optimum for the child.

Ann's request for joint custody with Belinda is supported by these factors, although her request to be primary physical custodian is not. Stability and continuity in caregiving have been interrupted by Belinda's de facto exercise of sole custody. Until Belinda began limiting Ann's time with Mary Ruth, the two women had followed an established pattern of equal caregiving since Mary Ruth was born, even after their breakup. Belinda's disruption of this pattern has produced the negative psychological effects on Mary Ruth that are apparent in her reaction to separating from Ann after their visits. In addition, Belinda appears unwilling to foster a continued relationship with Ann; her "adjustments" to Ann's parenting of Mary Ruth interfere with the child's continued relationship with Ann. An award of joint custody to the two women would enable Ann to exercise some decision-making power, and to obtain parenting time similar to that which she had before Belinda curtailed it.

These factors do not favor Ann's request to be the primary physical custodian of Mary Ruth. Mary Ruth has been in the sole physical custody of Belinda since the latter's relationship with Ann ended, a total of six years. Continuity and stability in caregiving strongly favor Belinda's continued physical custody despite her recent change in attitude toward Ann's parenting; Mary Ruth's reaction to Ann's curtailed parenting time has shown her distress at the changes that have occurred in her family, and changing her primary caregiver would risk further distress. The court could fashion a visitation order for Mary Ruth and Ann that would approximate the schedule observed voluntarily for the prior six years.

QUESTION #2

I. Dennis's divorce action against Candy

Dennis's desire for a quick divorce means that he will not want to wait through two years of separation before obtaining one. He could seek a divorce on a fault ground, but his choices are limited because Candy's actions do not fulfill the requirements of the faults. There are no facts that suggest Candy committed adultery. Her departure from the home owing to her arrest cannot constitute abandonment because it was involuntary, and there are no facts suggesting constructive abandonment, that is, one party's cessation of sexual relations with the other.

Cruelty as a fault basis for divorce in Commonalia includes habitual substance abuse, in which Candy has engaged. Two questions arise as to whether she was at fault: whether the effect of Candy's drug use has been to make living together intolerable, as the fault requires, and whether Candy has an affirmative defense to this fault, mental impairment. As to the first, Candy could argue that her misuse of drugs was insufficiently noticeable for Dennis to realize that she was using them at all; if Dennis couldn't even tell that Candy was taking illegal drugs, it cannot have made living with her intolerable to him. However, it would not be stretching the cruelty ground for a court to find that one spouse's illicit drug use is intolerably cruel even without producing perceptible behavioral effects. It places the whole family in jeopardy of the disruption that Dennis's family is now suffering, and thus is cruel. As to the second, in some jurisdictions addictions such as alcoholism and drug abuse have been found to be mental illnesses that can be subject to the "insanity" defense. Candy could argue that she began taking the medication on a doctor's advice to cope with a health problem. She did not intentionally addict herself to the drugs or continue to use them; the addiction was an inadvertent and uncontrollable result of her use of the medication as the doctor prescribed. She might succeed with this defense, given the way that her addiction developed.

Of course, Candy could be convicted of a felony and sentenced to prison for more than four years. Dennis would then be able to divorce Candy for fault. Dennis refuses to pay for Candy's lawyer, treatment, and reimbursement of the nursing home, all of which might make her conviction and sentencing more likely. However, Dennis will have to wait until the trial is over to procure the divorce. There is no guarantee that Candy will be convicted, even if she must rely on the public defender, and if her suit succeeds, she might not have to. Although Dennis can include these two faults in his suit for divorce, they are neither reliable nor quick.

Dennis's most reliable divorce option is the two-year separate and apart ground. It requires that at least one of the parties to the marriage voluntarily separates from the other with the intent to terminate the marriage, and that the separation lasts the requisite period of time. Candy's removal by the police is involuntary, and so will not start the time period running. To establish to third parties that he is separating from Candy with the intention of ending their marriage, Dennis should move from the marital home and let Candy and reliable witnesses know his purpose in doing so.

If Candy remains incarcerated, he could probably move back to the home after a short period of time; see *Adams v. Adams*, 408 So. 2d 1322 (La. 1982), in which the wife's return to the marital home on the same day that the police removed the husband who tried to kill her did not interrupt the running of the separation period that began when she left and told several third parties, including her husband's parole officer, that she was doing so to end her marriage. If Candy makes bail, Dennis would have to find someplace else to live for the duration of the two years, unless conditions (such as Candy's conviction and a sufficiently long sentence) make another ground for divorce available.

II. The obligation of support and the doctrine of necessaries

One of the obligations of marriage is support for the spouse. However, as the classic case of *McGuire v. McGuire*, 59 N.W.2d 336 (Neb. 1953), made clear, courts are unwilling to enforce the spousal support obligation within an existing marriage. Only if the level of support reaches that of criminal neglect of family will courts intervene in an intact marriage. It falls to a spouse dissatisfied with the level of support within the marriage to bring a divorce action. Thus, at this point, Candy cannot sue Dennis to force him to pay her legal expenses, and Dennis cannot sue Candy to recover the funds spent from the checking account.

However, the common law necessaries doctrine provides a mechanism by which a third party in Elvis's position can recover from one spouse for necessary items supplied to the other spouse. Under that doctrine, the creditor had to show that he supplied to one spouse an item that was necessary and that the other spouse either refused or failed to supply. Necessaries include what is essential for a family's well-being; however, what is considered to meet that test depends on the financial status of the couple. Food, clothing, medicine, medical treatment, transportation, housing, and furniture have all been classified as necessaries. Elvis would argue that Candy's bail and legal defense are necessaries because without them, Candy would remain incarcerated. Her liberty is at stake. See *State v. Clark*, 563 P.2d 1253 (Wash. 1977). The family's well-being, as well as Candy's, required that the spouse who is the primary caretaker for the children and the manager of the house be reunited with the family. The expenditures for the attorney, if reasonable, and for bail are consonant with the family's financial status because Candy has been denied representation by a public defender on the ground that the family's income disqualifies her.

The drug addiction treatment and the reimbursement of the nursing home are likewise expenditures to secure the well-being of the family. Not only Candy's freedom under the plea deal Elvis is working on, but also her health required that she get treatment for her addiction. Both that treatment and the reimbursement are necessary to her freedom.

Elvis is likely to succeed with his action. Dennis should start the divorce process, recognizing that the usual position is that the spousal obligation under the necessaries doctrine continues as long as the marriage does. He will have to wait for the division of the marital property to seek financial redress from Candy, who would probably be entitled to a smaller share because she has dissipated marital assets through her drug habit and criminal activity.

QUESTION #3

I. Jurisdiction to hear Martha v. George

Whether Martha's suit against George to declare their prenuptial agreement a nullity can be heard in federal court at all depends on whether it is the type of case in which the diversity jurisdiction of the federal court is appropriate. First, are the litigants diverse in citizenship? Second, is the amount in controversy sufficient? Moreover, even if the requirements for diversity jurisdiction are met, a court-created exception limits its scope by removing certain domestic relations cases from its purview. This Domestic Relations Exception, first recognized in the mid-nineteenth century, had been treated expansively until the U.S. Supreme Court's decision in *Ankenbrandt v. Richards*, 504 U.S. 689 (1992). In addition, that decision contemplated abstention by the court from a limited class of cases involving domestic relations, even if the exception itself did not apply.

II. The requirements of 28 U.S.C. §1332a

The requirements for federal jurisdiction in diversity cases are diversity of citizenship of the parties, and an amount in controversy that meets a statutory requirement. See 28 U.S.C. §1332 (a). The federal statute requires that the litigants be citizens of different states; this has been interpreted to mean that the litigants, if both are U.S. citizens, are domiciled in different states. Domicile for diversity jurisdiction is evaluated under its federal common law standard, which resembles that of most states: It requires physical residence in the state, and the intent to make the state one's home. Here, Martha is a citizen of Commonalia. For George's citizenship, the court would have to choose between two possibilities, because an individual can have only one domicile. It could be that George is a citizen of Caltex; he has physically resided there for two years. However, the intent requirement for domicile in Caltex is undermined by George's comments to Martha that he would like to go home, and that Leonie had promised to take him home to Commonalia. Moreover, the facts indicate that before his disappearance, George's mental state might have declined. His childlike comments to Martha support that view. He might not have been able to formulate the requisite intent to acquire a new domicile after being removed from his domicile of origin, Commonalia, by Leonie. It is important for Martha to determine whether Leonie has established a guardianship over George, which in most jurisdictions would give her the power to determine where he lived; she might claim that in doing so she established a new domicile for him. The outcome of such a claim would depend on whether establishing a domicile is considered too personal an action for anyone but the party himself to decide.

III. The domestic relations exception and federal abstention

If George is found to be a citizen of Caltex because he is domiciled there, and the amount in controversy is greater than the statutory limit, then Martha might be able to rely on the domestic relations exception for the case to remain in state court. The original nineteenth-century Supreme Court case declining jurisdiction over a domestic relations case, *Barber v. Barber*, 21 How. 582 (1859), said that federal courts have no jurisdiction over suits for divorce and for awards of alimony. Later in that century, expansion began, as the U.S. Supreme Court in *In re Burrus*, 136 U.S. 586 (1890), stated that the "whole subject of the domestic relations of husband and wife, parent and child, belongs to the laws of the States and not to the laws of the United States." Using this phrase, federal trial courts extended the exception to dismiss for lack of federal jurisdiction to cases that might otherwise arise between litigants who were not family members, such as cases in tort and contract, as well as suits for a judgment of divorce, for alimony orders, and for child custody.

The underlying policy justification for the exception was explained when it was retained by the Court in *Ankenbrandt v. Richards*. The justices found that state courts were better suited to domestic relations cases, which "not infrequently involve[] retention of jurisdiction by the court and deployment of social workers to monitor compliance." State courts also have "close association" with state and local government organizations that handle the conflicts arising from intrafamilial litigation, and state tribunals have developed "special proficiency" in dealing with the issues in such cases. *Id.* at 702. In addition, the *Ankenbrandt* court considered that federal court abstention might be appropriate "in a case involving elements of the domestic relationship even when the parties do not seek divorce, alimony, or child custody. This would be so when a case presents 'difficult questions of state law bearing on policy problems of substantial public import whose importance transcends the result in the case then at bar.' . . . Such might well be the case if a federal suit were filed prior to effectuation of a divorce, alimony, or child custody decree, and the suit depended on a determination of the status of the parties." *Id.* at 705. Thus, because family life within each state is legislatively structured by that state in accordance with its norms for the family, federal courts in some situations refrain from intruding into the sphere of domestic relations. The state is a more suitable venue for determining the outcome of cases in which its family policies are implicated.

At the conclusion of *Ankenbrandt* the court found that neither the domestic relations exception nor abstention applied to a tort case for damages for sexual and physical abuse against an ex-husband and his new wife by the man's former wife, acting on behalf of her two daughters. The court's rationale was that the case before it did not seek a divorce, alimony, or child custody decree, but a tort judgment, nor did its issue involve a determination of status of the parties.

Martha's action does not contain a request for divorce, alimony, or child custody, and so is outside the explicit boundaries set by *Ankenbrandt* for the domestic relations exception. It is, rather, a case on the validity of a contract. George's attorney will no doubt point out that this is the sort of "garden variety" case to which the Supreme Court in that case found the exception inapplicable. Although the prenuptial agreement is linked to an alimony determination, because its validity will determine whether an alimony order could be granted if a divorce ever occurred, that connection is indirect.

On the other hand, Martha's attorney should advise her that the *Ankenbrandt* court's recognition of the possibility of federal court abstention in some domestic relations cases offers a rationale on which the federal court might decline to exercise its jurisdiction. The validity of the prenuptial agreement implicates, as the *Ankenbrandt* court required, "difficult questions of state law bearing on policy problems of substantial public import whose importance transcends the result in the case then at bar." This is particularly true when, as in Martha's case, the state has no existing law on prenuptial agreements. Prenuptial agreements differ from "garden variety" contracts; they go to the heart of the state's interest in marriage and the structure of marital families. States' laws on prenuptial agreements reflect the differing norms and values of the states themselves. Thus, they disagree on, among other issues, what the requirements are to avoid procedural and substantive unfairness in contracting; what sorts of financial disclosures are required; what constitutes "unconscionability"; whether invalidating a prenuptial agreement requires that the bargain be unconscionable, or merely that it be unfair or unreasonable; whether the fairness is to be tested at the time of execution or afforded a "second look" to determine its fairness at the time of divorce; and who has the burden of proof in contesting the validity of the contract. Commonalia's choices on these issues inevitably would be determined by its underlying policies regarding marriage and the family. The choices made also have substantial public import, as they could have an impact on parties' decision-making concerning whether to create a marital family, what expectations should be used to structure one's life within it, and whether to end it, beyond the case at bar. This case might well be one that the federal court is justified in declining under abstention doctrine.

Thus, Martha's case could remain in state court if it was found either that (1) George and Martha are both domiciled in Commonalia; (2) the domestic relations exception to diversity jurisdiction applies to Martha's case; or (3) the federal court should abstain from the case because it involves difficult questions of state law bearing on policy problems of substantial public import whose importance transcends the result in the case then at bar. The first and third rationales appear the most likely to succeed.

QUESTION #4

Dell's jurisdictional question must be answered using the Uniform Child Custody Jurisdiction and Enforcement Act (UCCJEA), which has been adopted in some form by all the states. Whether he will succeed with his request for a modification of the custody order to domiciliary parent depends on whether he can make the required initial showing of a change in circumstances that affects the welfare of the child, and if so whether he can show that it is in Frank's best interest for Dell to be domiciliary custodian.

I. The proper jurisdiction for requesting a change of the custody order

The UCCJEA, issued by the National Conference of Commissioners on Uniform State Laws in 1997, the latest and most successful attempt to end parental forum-shopping among states for both initial and modification jurisdiction over child custody decisions, has been adopted in all the states, including Commonalia. This uniform law contains two provisions relevant to Dell's jurisdictional question to end conflicting state decisions concerning a child's custody that had arisen under an earlier uniform act, the Uniform Child Custody Jurisdiction Act (UCCJA). First,

UCCJEA section 201 (a) prioritized one basis for a state court's subject-matter jurisdiction over a child's custody: If the child has a home state, that state has exclusive jurisdiction. *Home state* is defined in section 102 (7) of the statute as the state in which a child lived with a parent or a person acting as a parent for at least six consecutive months immediately before the commencement of a child custody proceeding. At the time of the initial child custody decision concerning Frank, the child had lived for five years with Dell and Edith, and then with Edith alone, in Commonalia. This period included the six months immediately before the child custody litigation; thus Commonalia was the home state with jurisdiction to hand down the initial child custody order.

Second, UCCJEA section 202 established that the court that has made a child custody determination under section 201 has exclusive, continuing jurisdiction over that child's custody until one of two events occurs: (1) the child or the child and one parent have severed their connections to the state and evidence concerning custody issues is no longer available in the state; or (2) a court, whether in-state or not, determines that the child, the child's parents, and any person acting as a parent do not presently reside in the state that had had jurisdiction. Neither of these situations has occurred in this case. Dell, Bitsy (who might have acted as Frank's parent in caring for him during his visits), and Frank still have significant connections to Commonalia. Evidence of such custody-relevant issues as the adults' care for Frank and Frank's relationships with them and others in the state would be available there, along with evidence of Dell's allegations concerning the effect of traveling on Frank himself and on Dell's parenting time. Moreover, Dell, one of Frank's parents, and Bitsy, who might have acted as a parent, reside in the state all year, while Frank resides there for four months each year. Thus, Commonalia, in the absence of an emergency such as abandonment or mistreatment of Frank, is the only state whose courts have subject-matter jurisdiction over determination of the child's custody. Dell need not journey to Mississippi to obtain an attorney and move for modification of the original order.

II. Requirements for a modification of a custody order

Because parents tend to overuse demands for modification of custody orders, the majority of states have an initial requirement that the petitioner for modification show a change, or even a substantial change, in circumstances affecting the child since the original custody order was handed down. If that is satisfied, the court will consider which form of custody is in the child's best interest. Dell can easily show substantial changes in circumstances since the order was handed down; Edith's remarriage and relocation with Frank have removed the child from proximity to his father, making the current custody schedule inconvenient. Frank's new location is three hours from Dell by car, which has had a substantial qualitative impact on Dell and Frank's time together. Dell's remarriage has made it possible for Dell to have Frank living with him for longer periods of time. On the other hand, the result of a best interest test might favor Edith. Edith has been Frank's primary caregiver from his birth until the present. A principal factor in custody decisions is the value of stability and continuity in care for the child. To take Frank away from Edith could be regarded as more disruptive to him than the lengthy drives to and from Jackson.

In addition, Dell has returned to his policy of spending extensive amounts of time at work, rather than with Frank. Moving Frank to Dell's primary custody might leave him in the actual primary custody of Bitsy, who is less familiar to Frank. Dell might do better to work out an arrangement with Edith to share the transportation of Frank, and to cumulate more of his parenting time into larger units so that the child does not have to travel so often.

FAMILY LAW ESSAY EXAM #4

QUESTION #1

Commonalia offers several possible grounds to each spouse in this marriage for divorce, although additional information is required for the usefulness of the fault grounds to be determined. Defenses are available as well, though; Dan's concerns are such that he might best serve his interests by seeking a no-fault rather than a fault-based divorce.

I. Dan's fault grounds against Beth

1. Adultery   It does not appear from these facts that Dan could divorce Beth for adultery. Adultery is usually defined as voluntary sexual intercourse by a married person with a person who is not his or her spouse. Until the latter half of the twentieth century, it was usual for state courts to require proof of reproductive sexual intercourse for the ground to be satisfied; courts were less concerned with the betrayal of the companionate nature of marriage, and more with the potential betrayal of the biological integrity of the family line. Since that time, the focus has shifted to the breach of the duty of faithfulness owed by the spouses to one another. Thus, nonreproductive sexual activities have been held sufficient to fulfill the adultery ground. However, Dan has no basis at present on which to allege that Beth has committed adultery. "Emotional adultery" is a category from pop counseling, not from law. It is unlikely in the extreme that a court would equate adultery, with its physical and psychological risks to the nonadulterous spouse, with a close friendship conducted through correspondence. If Dan cannot find proof that Beth and Charles have ever met one another under circumstances that indicate physical sexual contact, reproductive or otherwise, he will not be able to utilize adultery as a ground for divorcing Beth.

2. Cruelty   In modern divorce litigation, cruelty became an expansive ground on which to get a divorce; the divorce for cruelty can be based on either the physical or the mental mistreatment of the victimized spouse. Mental cruelty includes words or acts that constitute quarreling or derogatory treatment affecting the health, well-being, or peace of mind of the injured party. The defendant's treatment of the spouse cannot be founded on an isolated incident unless that incident constituted a serious threat to the victim's safety. The cruelty alleged has to be seriously harmful to the latter's physical or mental health, so that living together is intolerable or unsupportable. Dan could allege that Beth's hostility to his work, displays of anger because of it, her humiliating him by walking out of the restaurant, and her continued communication with Charles are acts of mental cruelty. Beth's refusal to communicate with Dan unless he agrees to go to marriage counseling also might qualify as cruelty. However, to succeed Dan must demonstrate that her conduct has seriously affected his physical or mental health. Mere nagging, bickering, rudeness, and unkindness have been found insufficient to satisfy the cruelty ground; Beth's repeated demands that he go to marriage counseling with her and her rejection of some of his work would not qualify. In addition, because the facts as known reveal nothing beyond friendship between Beth and Charles, her continued communication with him provides no basis for Dan to claim her treatment of him in refusing to end the correspondence is cruel. If her refusal to communicate with Dan continues, however, it might satisfy the ground if it impairs Dan's health so that living together is intolerable. However, it is possible that Beth could succeed with a defense of recrimination or comparative fault against a cruelty accusation by Dan (see Section II).

   3. Constructive abandonment   Abandonment as a fault ground for divorce requires that one spouse voluntarily live separately and apart from the other without the other's consent and without justification, refusing requests to return made by the injured spouse. Neither Dan nor Beth has moved at this point, although Dan is considering moving. For many years, abandonment has been interpreted as including constructive abandonment; that is, treatment of the innocent spouse in such a manner as to justify his leaving the home because living there is unendurable. The court regards the actions of the spouse who drove the other from the home as, in effect, abandonment. The constructive abandonment must be for the period of time specified for actual abandonment. In these circumstances, the innocent spouse, even though he departed the home, may procure a divorce against the spouse who drove him away. Two facts that Dan has recounted suggest that, if he moves out of the home and allows a year to pass, constructive abandonment is a possible ground on which he could divorce Beth. First, he and Beth have not had sex in some time; denial of sex is considered to constitute constructive abandonment unless the spouse who denies sex to the other has a reason, such as impaired health, that justifies the denial. Gratifying the reasonable sexual needs of one's spouse is considered an obligation of marriage. If Beth continuously denies Dan sex without a justifying reason, and does so for the requisite period, he could bring a divorce on the ground of constructive abandonment. Second, Beth's refusal to speak to him unless he complies with her demand could also be considered constructive abandonment; for spouses to live together without communicating might well be found to be unendurable, and as justifying Dan's departure from the home. However, Dan runs the risk that Beth's treatment of Dan would not be viewed by the court as justifying his departure. There is no indication in the facts that Dan has approached Beth requesting sex, and she has refused. Moreover, if she brings a divorce action for cruelty against him, the court might consider his depictions of her to amount to a fault that would justify her refusal.

II. Beth's fault ground against Dan; possible defenses to fault grounds

   1. Cruelty   Beth could base a petition for divorce against Dan on the fault ground of cruelty such that living together is intolerable. It is clear from Dan's recital of the facts that he has used his writing to mock Beth publicly about private issues that most people would be sensitive about, such as her weight and their marital disagreements. This is not an isolated incident; even in the facts Dan has recited there are multiple instances, and he has implied that more exist. Moreover, in one of his publications, Dan recounted that he sabotaged her effort to return to her career, and influenced her son to do the same, for his and Ron's benefit, possibly undermining her self-confidence and her independence. Dan is aware that he is hurting Beth by his actions; she has told him many times that she is hurt by his depictions of her. However, as the facts indicate, he even uses their disagreements on this issue as material for his column. If Beth can demonstrate that Dan's derogatory treatment affects her health, well-being, and peace of mind, she would have a basis of mental cruelty for divorce.

2. Possible defenses to the fault grounds   Beth would also, in the preceding circumstance, have a defense of recrimination or of comparative fault against Dan's claim that she is cruel. The traditional fault divorce system required that the party requesting the divorce be innocent of a fault that could be the basis for divorce. A successful defense of recrimination would eliminate Dan's ability to use the cruelty ground to divorce Beth because Dan himself was guilty of cruelty. Neither party would have a ground for divorce. If the court uses the defense of comparative fault instead, it would weigh Dan's cruel actions against Beth's and grant the divorce to the less guilty spouse. In such a case, on the facts given, Dan is unlikely to be the party who receives the divorce; Beth's protests concerning her depiction in his work, her leaving him in the restaurant, and her refusal to speak to him unless he agrees to joint counseling are less cruel and humiliating than repeatedly making her a figure of fun in his publications. Dan might also have difficulties of proof, as Beth's alleged cruelty to him, with the exception of her departure from the restaurant, appears to have taken place in their private conversations, whereas Dan has left a paper trail of his humorous depictions of Beth. Dan could attempt the defense of condonation, pointing to the fact that Beth condoned his allegedly cruel actions after he committed them by remaining with him as his wife. She would thus have given up those bases for divorce by forgiving his fault. However, even if that were found, her rejection of him following his most recent use of her in his column indicates that she has not condoned it, and in fact has placed an as-yet-unfulfilled condition — his participation in marriage counseling — on doing so.

III. No-fault divorce on irretrievable breakdown grounds

Considering Dan's concerns about publicity and his doubt over whether he actually wants a divorce, he would be better advised to pursue a no-fault divorce on grounds of irretrievable breakdown than a fault-based divorce. All that he would be required to demonstrate to obtain the divorce would be that he and Beth lived separate and apart continuously for 12 months immediately preceding the action for divorce. This he could do by moving out of their home. He and Beth would not have to make accusations against one another, and develop evidence of each other's fault that, if it became public, might undermine the picture of their family life that Dan has used to become a successful author. During the time period that they were separated, Dan and Beth might be able to work out their differences and reconcile; if they cannot, they can proceed with the divorce. Dan would, of course, be giving up his desire to see the blame for their marriage's breakdown laid entirely at Beth's door. However, he has little chance of obtaining that result under the fault system. He would also face the risk that Beth would decide that she wanted the divorce, even if he did not; either party can ask for the divorce once the no-fault's separation condition has been fulfilled. Because in modern no-fault systems, irretrievable breakdown can be used to secure a divorce if one spouse unilaterally maintains that the breakdown cannot be repaired, protests by the other spouse cannot prevent the divorce. That could also be the result if Beth sought a fault-based divorce, though; if his fault was established, she could obtain the divorce whatever his desires.

QUESTION #2

I. Effect of deliberate inaccuracies on the marriage license

Inaccuracies on the marriage license, even if deliberate, do not in themselves have a nullifying effect on the marriage, any more than an accurately completed license guarantees the validity of the marriage. The marriage license has two functions: It is a means to collect information that will appear on the marriage certificate in the state records, and it is a gatekeeper by which individuals who are not able to marry, such as same-sex couples in most states, and young children in all states, are denied the status. If an inaccurate license enables an individual to marry in violation of state law, whether the marriage is valid is not an effect of the inaccuracy of the license itself, but of state policy concerning the matter about which it is inaccurate. Thus, if someone with a prior undissolved marriage lies on the license application, claiming to be unmarried, and marries on the basis of the license granted, his marriage would be void.

II. Voidable marriage and its ratification

Laura's lie was about her age at the time of the marriage; she claimed to be 18 when she was in fact 17. Age is required by states as a proxy for discernment at the time of the marriage; all states require that parties to a marriage have sufficient intellectual maturity to understand the nature of marriage and give genuine consent to it. Not having attained the particular age required by statute would raise a question of validity if the underage party is so young that the understanding of marriage is impossible. In this case, however, the difference between Laura's actual age at marriage and the age she claimed to be is not great, so it is unlikely that her understanding of marriage was much less than that of an 18-year-old. The marriage is therefore valid.

Even if Laura's understanding of marriage at the time she and Rob wed were questionable, it is immaterial at this time. Lack of the understanding required to consent to the marriage creates a voidable rather than a void marriage. The nullity would have to be found by a court; it is not automatic. Two problems confront Rob, if he wants the marriage to be nullified on the basis of Laura's lie about her age. First, only the party whose understanding is impaired can sue to dissolve the marriage. Laura, not Rob would have had the cause of action. Moreover, voidable marriages may be ratified (also termed "confirmed") by the parties by continuing to live as spouses once the individual who lacked understanding obtains it. In this instance, Rob and Laura have lived together as spouses for 30 years; if their marriage was ever voidable, it has been confirmed.

III. Fraud in the inducement

Rob might attempt to get the marriage annulled because of fraud in the inducement; he would claim that Laura procured his consent to their marriage by misrepresenting her age. Fraud in the inducement requires that there be a misrepresentation as to fact on which the deceived party reasonably relied; there must be a causal relationship between the misrepresentation and the marriage — but for the misrepresentation, he would not have consented to the marriage. The misrepresentation must concern something essential either to the marriage (by the subjective standard of the individual) or to marriage generally (by the objective standards of society). As fraud raises the issue of the consensual freedom of the deceived party, it is regarded as a characteristic of voidable marriages. Under the traditional view of fraud, Rob would be entitled to claim, at most, a relative nullity.

It is hard to see Laura's deception as concerning an essential to the marriage. Using the objective standards, age by itself isn't the basis for a nullity of either sort; it is, as explained earlier, a proxy for discernment. Using the subjective standard, Rob is saying, many years after the fact, that to him it was essential to his marriage 20 years earlier that the person he married not tell lies, especially under oath, be respectful of state law, and not have (even unknowingly) put him in a dangerous position. First, none of these appear particularly related to marriage; these are general virtues. Second, Rob is asking the court to assume that the reactions to this news that he has in middle age are those that he would have had at 22. His whirlwind romance indicates that he was not as cautious then as he appears to have become. He married Laura knowing that her parents disapproved. In addition, he traveled to the next county to avoid confronting Laura's parents before he and Laura were married, which should have aroused his suspicions that they might have been able to stop the marriage from taking place.

If Rob is so affected by his discovery after 30 years of marriage that he no longer wants to be married to Laura, it would be more cost-effective for him to get a divorce, as his nullity action is unlikely to succeed.

QUESTION #3

Two issues must be considered by the court and decided in Bea and Ethel's favor for them to obtain court-ordered visitation with David: the constitutionality of the Commonalia third-party visitation statute, and, assuming it is found constitutional, whether its requirements are met by Bea and Ethel.

I. Constitutionality of statute under *Troxel v. Granville*

1. Liberty interest of parents in the care, custody, and control of their children and resulting presumption   The Fourteenth Amendment of the U.S. Constitution provides that no state shall "deprive any person of . . . liberty . . . without due process of law." This amendment has been characterized by the Supreme Court of the United States as including a substantive component requiring substantive due process, i.e., heightened protection against government interference with certain fundamental rights and liberty interests. One of the earliest liberty interests recognized by the Court was that of parents to control the upbringing and education of their children, to prepare them to meet the obligations they will face. (*Meyer v. Nebraska*, 262 U.S. 390 (1923); *Pierce v. Society of Sisters,* 268 U.S. 510 (1925)). A little more than 20 years later, the Court held that "the custody, care and nurture" of children "reside first in the parents." Since then, numerous decisions have recognized "the fundamental right of parents to make decisions concerning the care, custody, and control of their children." (*Troxel v. Granville*, 530 U.S. 57 (2000)). Additionally, the Court has found that the concept of the family creates a presumption that fit parents' natural affection for their children leads them to act in their children's best interest (*Parham v. J.R.*, 442 U.S. 584 (1979)). Unless this presumption were overcome, under the U.S. Supreme Court's logic, there would not be a reason for the state to interfere in the privacy accorded to the family by requiring fit parents to justify their decisions.

The *Troxel* opinion affirmed a Washington State Supreme Court decision concerning visitation petition by two children's grandparents. The Washington court found unconstitutional as applied the third-party visitation statute under which the trial court had awarded the grandparents more extensive visitation with the children than their single mother, a fit parent, had been willing to allow. Washington's statute permitted any person to petition for a court order of visitation at any time; the only limitation that it placed on the court's decision was that it be based on the judge's estimation of best interest of the child. Most important, the statute did not require the court to weight more heavily the parent's decision as to whether such visitation was in the child's best interest, or to give the parent's decision the presumption of correctness under the best interest standard. In applying the statute, the Washington State trial court indicated that it was starting from the presumption that quality time with grandparents was in the best interest of the child. Thus the statute left the way open for interference with the fundamental liberty interest that the parent had in the care, custody, and control of her children, and in applying the statute, the trial court did not include the statute in its considerations. Thus, the decision below unconstitutionally interfered with the fit parent's fundamental right to make decisions concerning the care, custody, and control of her children.

2. Application to Commonalia's statute   The third-party visitation statute in Commonalia is narrower than Washington State's, but it does not avoid the problem underlying the U.S. Supreme Court's decision in *Troxel*. Commonalia's statute limits the individuals who can request a visitation order to relatives with whom the child has lived in a stable relationship. It also requires the finding that a bond between the child and the third party exists that makes visitation in the best interest of the child. However, the statute does not contain a provision creating a presumption in favor of a fit parent's decision with respect to visitation by the third party. As in Washington State, the trial court could comply with the statute and at the same time unconstitutionally infringe on Jessica's rights by failing to give presumptive weight to her decision to limit Bea and Ethel's visitation and requiring them to overcome the presumption.

However, Commonalia's statute, like Washington State's, does not prohibit the court's applying a presumption that the fit parent's decision is in the child's best interest. The court, by reading the presumption into the statute, could avoid an unconstitutional application, and allow the court to examine the merits of Bea and Ethel's petition.

II. Applicability of the presumption: The "fit parent" requirement

The presumption of correctness given to the parent's decision that a denial of visitation is in the child's best interest is given to decision of a *fit* parent. Bea and Ethel could attempt to deprive Jessica of the presumption altogether by contending that Jessica is an *unfit* parent. The factual allegations would be that Jessica neglected David for four years while she attended college, has inflicted mental and psychological abuse on him by separating him from his long-term caretakers, and has forced him to attend an after school program that causes him emotional distress. They have virtually no chance of success. Because of the parent's protected liberty interest in the care, custody, and control of her child, a finding of parental unfitness requires a compelling justification, such as a risk of some harm. The potential harm must be severe, such as serious physical or serious emotional damage resulting from abuse; sexual abuse; failure to protect the child from such harm or abuse; or neglecting to provide the child with food, housing, appropriate medical care, or education. For a parent to leave her child with known, reliable caretakers while she works and attends college to be better equipped to support the child would not constitute such a harm; nor would requiring the child to attend an after school sports program when his alleged suffering is having to run around. Although severing a child's long-term bond with his care-givers might cause serious psychological harm, that is not what Jessica has done. She has been willing to continue David's relationship with her great-aunts, but under controlled circumstances that she imposed because of their lack of cooperation with her decisions concerning his upbringing. Thus, Bea and Ethel must overcome the presumption that Jessica's decisions were in David's best interest.

III. Application of the statute with the presumption

1. Preliminary requirements of the statute   Before considering the best interest of the child in this case, the court would have to determine if the statute was applicable to Bea and Ethel's petition. The requirements of the statute are that Bea and Ethel be relatives of David; that he previously lived with them in a stable relationship; and that the preexisting relationships that David has with Bea and Ethel have engendered bonds between him and the women. Bea and Ethel meet these requirements. As his mother's great-aunts, they are David's relatives — his great-grand-aunts. David, along with Jessica, lived with the two women for about five years. From the facts given, Bea, Ethel, and David functioned as part of a multigenerational extended family; they not only shared a house, but ate together, and Bea and Ethel participated significantly in David's daily life by taking care of him and giving him individualized attention while his mother attended the university and worked. Thus they fulfill the requirement of having a stable relationship with David. David's bond to Bea and Ethel is demonstrated by his desire to be with them after school; additionally, he appears to regard them as authorities on his own care, as when he used their child care practices to argue against Jessica's. It remains for David's aunts to demonstrate that their visitation is in David's best interest.

2. The best interest of the child standard   Because Jessica is favored under a presumption that her parenting decisions — including the decision to reduce Bea's and Ethel's contact with her son to once a week when she is present — are in David's best interest, the aunts must make an argument that it is in David's best interest to have more frequent and unsupervised visits with them. Determination of the best interest of the child requires a multifactor analysis. This analysis includes factors that are relevant to these facts: the continuity and stability of the child's relationship to those requesting visitation; the wishes of the parents; the child's adjustment to his home, school, and community; and the wishes of the child, if age-appropriate.

Bea and Ethel should have no difficulty establishing the continuity and stability of David's preexisting relationship to them. The same facts that establish the preliminary requirements of their eligibility for visitation would establish that they maintained a continuous relationship with David for five years. It was stable until Jessica reduced their contact with her son. She curtailed the time that they spent with him out of a desire to change the manner in which David was being brought up; thus, she has destabilized the relationship between David and them. His unhappiness with Jessica's new arrangements for his afternoons indicates that David's previously happy adjustment to his home has been shattered. Additionally, David has expressed the desire to return to their care after school and for overnight visits.

The factors that Bea and Ethel rely on, other than the continuity and stability of their relationship with David, do not provide a great deal of support to their request for court-ordered visitation. Part of the reduction of their contact with David occurred because Jessica got her degree from the university and a job that paid well enough for her to afford a home for herself and David. This would likely be seen as a normal change that David should learn to cope with, rather than escape from. The same is true for Jessica's changes in the manner in which David was being brought up by his aunts. The fact that David resists training in areas that his peers at school already have mastered, such as independence, interaction with peers, and toilet training, when no intellectual deficiencies have been found by the school's guidance counselor, indicates that his aunts' care has not encouraged him to mature appropriately as he grows up. As a result, the wishes of the child will have little impact in this case. A 7-year-old is not usually considered to have the maturity and judgment to make reliable decisions as to whose companionship he should have; given David's delayed development in these areas, his preference will likely be discounted.

The factors that favor Jessica under the best interest analysis are the child's adjustment to his home, school, and community and the wishes of the parent. As indicated earlier, according to David's teacher, his adjustment to school was not consistent with that of his peers. The court is likely to regard the teacher's and the guidance counselor's assessments as more reliable than those of David's great-grandaunts because educational professionals are more likely to have expertise and objectivity. Jessica, in requiring more age-appropriate behavior of David, is therefore acting with his best interests both for the present (his ability to make and keep friends in his age group) and for the future, as his responsibilities increase. The changes she has made to his upbringing, such as playdates, encouraging independence and initiative by requiring him to dress himself and otherwise take care of himself, and arranging for him to participate in sports, are consistent with improving his adjustment to his home life (including his personal health), school, and community. In opposing these changes, Bea and Ethel will probably appear to be unwittingly opposing David's best interests. They caused the change in their relationship with David by undermining Jessica's parental authority; they criticized her attempts to get him to take more responsibility to her and to David, including arguing with her about her parenting in front of the child, and getting him to request the contact that she had curtailed. These actions could confuse the child as to what is expected of him.

The factor "the wishes of the parent" strongly favors Jessica. Given the success noted by David's teacher, Jessica's decisions have helped David overcome his earlier lag in social development. This would probably be enough to defeat her great-aunts' petition even without the presumption required under *Troxel*. The presumption reinforces the likelihood that she can defeat her great-aunts' petition: As a fit parent, her decisions on David's upbringing are presumptively in his best interest, and nothing in the facts offers much of a challenge to that.

QUESTION #4

Jurisdictions take radically different approaches to determining whether and how to repay a spouse whose efforts contributed to the success of the other spouse. Very few have adopted Oliver's theory that they should be awarded a percentage interest in their soon-to-be ex-spouse's achievements. Oliver's claim is not that Nelia's voice itself is property, but that her celebrity status is. He is claiming a financial interest in that status on the basis of his contributions to her obtaining it. The ability to make this claim concerning Nelia's career is grounded in the contribution theory of marital property, which in turn is based conceptualizing marriage as an economic partnership. This theory views all the contributions to the enterprise, whether they are direct or indirect, and whatever their nature, as factors in its success. Marital property subject to distribution under this theory frequently takes forms that are intangible rather than tangible, and that are not readily transferable. Courts have equitably distributed between spouses professional licenses, degrees, and practices by making a distributive award of the value of the property, rather than awarding the property itself. The fact that no license or degree exists in this case does not defeat Oliver's claim. The basis on which an award is founded is that a marriage is an economic partnership to which both parties have contributed, through careers and as spouses, parents, and homemakers, and both should share in the income from that investment.

The recognition of what appears to be a personal achievement as marital property is not popular; most jurisdictions have rejected it. First, classifying it as property appears to conflate two separate types of economic determinations following divorce, alimony (also termed spousal support or maintenance) and property division. A major factor in calculating an alimony award is the payor spouse's income and earnings. Those are the same source, future earnings, that is here characterized as property. The result, if Oliver receives an alimony award as well, is that the awards will be duplicative. Second, the valuing of celebrity status as property is highly speculative. Nelia's future earnings as a celebrity can be quantified based on her current status, but that is subject to change. Nelia's voice could decline earlier than expected, as could her popularity. Whereas an alimony award is subject to later modification or termination based on unanticipated changes in circumstances, property awards are not. Third, the calculation of Oliver's contribution to her success both now and in the future is also speculative. Although Oliver taught and trained Nelia, how far Nelia would have gone toward her present eminence without Oliver's help is impossible to determine.

An alternative approach preferred in most states is an award of what is called "reimbursement alimony." This payment reimburses a spouse such as Oliver for his contribution to his wife's development of her voice; that is, after all, the only aspect of her celebrity status that he participated in creating. A calculation of what she owes him could be made based on his usual charges for the services he performed, and for his financial support of her during the early years of her career, adjusted to current values. This reimbursement alimony would be paid in addition to the alimony for his current support; it could be paid in a lump sum or over time. Like a property award, it would not be subject to change, but because it is based on Oliver's actual contributions to her career, it should not be. She has attained her celebrity status partially through his efforts. It is equitable for her to repay those efforts. Although it is unlikely that a court would award Oliver a property interest in her voice, she would be wise to offer him more than reimbursement plus alimony to avoid the risk that the Commonalia court would adopt the minority position.

FAMILY LAW ESSAY EXAM #5

QUESTION #1

The court should invalidate the prenuptial agreement because the agreement is unreasonable, and prior to the execution, Inez was not provided fair and reasonable disclosure of Jerry's property; did not voluntarily and expressly waive any right to disclosure beyond that which Jerry had provided; and neither had nor reasonably could be expected to have adequate knowledge of Jerry's property.

I. The reasonableness of the agreement

The terms of the agreement are such that they appear inadequate to provide for Inez. Inez at present has no income, and has no skills other than exotic dancing. She has not been employed as a dancer for almost ten years, and being ten years older and out of practice, might not readily find employment in that field. Her net worth consists of personal property, which usually is not income-producing wealth; even if it were, its relatively low value of $60,000 would not produce enough for her to live on. Even if she were able to sell the property for full value, it would not support her for very long, so it is unlikely that she could develop career skills sufficient to support her in the long term, considering that she does not even have a high school diploma. Inez would have little financial security after nine years and some months of marriage because she would receive $50,000 in lieu of alimony only if the marriage lasted ten years. As it is, she receives nothing from Jerry on divorce.

Although Jerry is much older than Inez, his financial status is far superior to hers; his net worth is at least over 100 times hers, possibly more. Moreover, much of it is invested in productive property, whereas the only way that Inez can realize any cash value for her property is to liquidate it. Thus, the agreement that provides for Inez to take nothing from Jerry on divorce other than low-value property titled in her name appears disproportionate to the means of the defending spouse, Jerry, and leaves her inadequately provided for.

II. Disclosure requirement

The disproportion between Jerry's means and Inez's does not alone provide a ground for invalidating the agreement. In addition, Inez must prove that the agreement process did not fulfill at least one of the three disclosure requirements for a valid prenuptial agreement under the state statute. In fact, Jerry did not fulfill any of the requirements.

First, Inez was not provided a "fair and reasonable independent disclosure of the property . . . of the other party." The copy of the prenuptial agreement that Jerry provided to Inez contained a partial list of items without further elaborating their value. Although the statute does not specify that values must be included, the purpose of disclosure would be frustrated without it; and "property," usually employed to refer to things, also means the economic rights of a party in those things; that is, their value. Although Inez visited independent counsel, without the full inventory of Jerry's property, the attorney could not provide an independent disclosure to Inez.

Second, Jerry did not procure a written waiver from Inez of any disclosure that she might be entitled to beyond what Jerry had provided; he merely had her sign the incomplete disclosure he had supplied.

Finally, Inez did not have, and could not reasonably be expected to have, an adequate knowledge of Jerry's property. Jerry's secretive attitude toward his financial interests prevented her from obtaining even a general and approximate knowledge of the true value of his assets and income prior to signing the agreement. His avoidance of discussion about his finances suggests that he might have been deliberately practicing concealment of that knowledge from Inez. Inez's knowledge that certain assets existed would not result in knowledge of the value of those assets unless she was unusually financially sophisticated. Inez's observation before the marriage of Jerry's lifestyle is likewise not sufficient to give her knowledge of his income. Inez is unlikely to have possessed the financial sophistication to convert her impressions into actual value.

QUESTION #2

The Hague Convention on the Civil Aspects of International Child Abduction has two principal goals. First, it is intended to obtain the prompt return of children wrongfully removed to or retained in a state that is a party to the Convention. Second, it seeks to ensure that the rights of custody and access under the law of one state that is party to the Convention are respected in the others. It attains these goals by providing a legal process to restore the status quo prior to any wrongful removal or retention, thus requiring those disputing the child's custody to use the appropriate court to effect any change that they seek.

I. Requirements to prove wrongful removal

Maria, because she is petitioning for Rosa's return, must prove that Rosa was a habitual resident of Italy immediately prior to her removal by Quentin. She must prove in addition that Quentin's removal of Rosa was "wrongful," that is, it violated Maria's right of custody under the law of Italy. She must also prove that she was exercising her custodial rights to Rosa at the time that Rosa was removed.

Maria will not have a difficult time proving the facts that meet these requirements. The question of the child's habitual residence is answered by Rosa's continuous residence in Italy with her mother for six years prior to the time that Quentin seized her. She had been attending school there, and has friends and extended family there. She has not lived in the United States since she was two years old. The removal breached Maria's custodial rights under the law of Italy; Maria had registered the Commonalia custody order granting her primary physical custody and joint legal custody of Rosa. It thus became effective as Italian law. Maria was also exercising her custodial rights to Rosa when Quentin removed her. She was Rosa's physical caretaker on an everyday basis. Therefore, Quentin wrongfully removed Rosa.

II. Quentin's defenses

Quentin could offer the newly issued court order from the Commonalia district court as evidence that he had sole custody of Rosa at the time that he took her. This court, under the Uniform Child Custody and Jurisdiction Act (UCCJEA), has exclusive continuing jurisdiction over Rosa's custody. The Commonalia court made the initial custody determination consistent with the UCCJEA rule that the home state of the child at the time of the custody determination is the forum with exclusive jurisdiction over her custody. Rosa had lived with her parents in Commonalia for at least the six consecutive months required for home state identification. Because a parent—Quentin—still resides in Commonalia, its status as the home state has not been lost; it continues to have exclusive jurisdiction over her custody in every U.S. state. Unfortunately for his case, Quentin did not register this order in Italy, which would have made it effective there as Italian law. Therefore, under Italian law at the time he kidnapped his daughter, Maria was joint custodian and had primary physical custody over their child, and the conclusion is again that his removal of Rosa was unlawful.

Although the Hague Convention provides affirmative defenses, the facts do not indicate that any of them apply to Quentin's case. The five affirmative defenses are (1) the grave risk of harm to the child if she were returned; (2) fundamental principles of human rights and fundamental freedoms of the requested State—the U.S.—do not permit her return; (3) the child is now settled in her new environment; (4) the person from whom the child was removed was not exercising custody rights at the time of removal; or (5) the child, who is mature enough for her wishes to be taken into account, objects to being returned. Thus, under the Hague Convention, Rosa should be returned to Maria in Italy.

III. Equitable doctrines and the Hague Convention

U.S. federal courts are divided as to whether their equitable power to deny relief to a petitioner can be invoked in cases of child abduction under the Hague Convention. If they do, the equitable principle "unclean hands" might be applied in this case. This doctrine states that he who asks for equitable relief must come with clean hands, that is, the petition of one whose behavior has been inequitable in the matter in which he seeks relief will not be heard, however improper the alleged behavior of the defendant. Thus, Quentin could point to Maria's behavior in interfering with his visitation as evidence that she herself behaved inequitably in the matter of Rosa's custody. Therefore, her petition for Rosa's return should be dismissed.

One jurisdiction has refused to apply the doctrine of unclean hands, declaring that it is inconsistent with the Hague Convention on the Civil Aspects of International Child Abduction. First, the focus of the Convention is on protecting the well-being of the child, not on punishing the conduct of the parties, except to the extent that that impacts the child's well-being. That goal is best served by restoring the status quo that existed before a wrongful removal. This outcome leaves the judgment of what is best for the child with the courts empowered to make substantive custody determinations. Second, the doctrine could be used to foster the parental behavior that was found so damaging to children's well-being, a cycle of abduction and reabduction by their parents. A court that rejected the application of the equitable principle in such cases could not find in Quentin's favor.

Other courts have applied an equitable principle to proceedings brought under the Hague Convention: the fugitive disentitlement doctrine. Under this doctrine, one who has abused the American criminal process by defying or fleeing from judicially imposed obligations is not entitled to petition a U.S. court for a remedy to an injury he has received. Fugitive disentitlement does not apply to the facts of Quentin and Maria's case. However, considering that U.S. courts have invoked one equitable principle to supplement the Convention's written rules, a court could decide that other equitable principles, such as the unclean hands doctrine, apply to it as well. A court that did so, given Maria's interference with Quentin's visitation under the first order, might find that her case could be dismissed for unclean hands.

QUESTION #3

I. The presumptions concerning existence of a valid marriage

To receive Hank's estate under Commonalia's intestacy law, Wilma must establish that she was validly married to Hank at the time of his death. First, she must prove that she and Hank validly married at all; the marriage certificate from their ceremonial marriage and, if available, supporting evidence, such as witness testimony, would demonstrate this. Because the states of the U.S. have a policy of favoring marriage, two presumptions have been developed to ease the burden on the party alleging that it exists. The first presumption is that a marriage validly entered into continues until the death of one of the parties. The facts indicate that Hank and Wilma validly married; they had none of the impediments to marriage, were competent, and included all required ceremonial elements. Wilma at first appears on this analysis to be entitled to the presumption, but in fact she is caught in the crossfire of conflicting presumptions concerning the existence of a marriage. The second presumption, also arising out of the policy of favoring marriage, is that the last marriage in a series of marriages by one person is valid. Wilma married Sam after she married Hank; therefore, the Texas marriage is the last marriage in the series of her marriages. Because this presumption is given priority over the first one, Wilma is not presumed to have been married to Hank at the time of his death; she is presumed to be married to Sam, and must overcome that presumption by proof that her marriage to Hank was never dissolved, but continued to his death. If so, her marriage to Sam would have been invalid, and she would be Hank's surviving spouse.

II. Proof that a marriage continued until the death of one of the parties

How one proves that a marriage continued until the death of one party without the benefit of the presumption is the issue. Once again, Wilma must prove that a valid marriage between her and Hank took place. Then she must prove that her marriage to Hank continued until his death. The methods for proving that a marriage continued until the death of one of the parties differ slightly in different states. The more difficult method is a search of the records of divorce and annulment in every U.S. jurisdiction, regardless of whether the parties lived there or not. That is the minority position. The majority position requires a search of the divorce and annulment records in every jurisdiction in which she or Hank had been domiciled, showing that neither of them divorced the other, or obtained a declaration of nullity. If she finds no documentation that Hank procured either type of dissolution in the jurisdictions where she is required to search, she has proof that her marriage to Hank lasted until his death.

III. Wilma's potential obligations to Sam for alimony and marital property division

Whether one who entered an invalid marriage can obtain marital benefits such as alimony and a division of marital property varies with the jurisdiction. If Caltex has either the doctrine of common law marriage or of putative marriage, Wilma might be obligated to Sam for these benefits of marriage.

1. Common law marriage   A few states in the United States still permit the confection of valid common law marriages within their borders; additional states are willing to recognize the validity of a common law marriage entered into in one of the states that permits its confection. If Commonalia is one of these, Sam could have claims against Wilma for equitable distribution of marital property and for alimony.

A valid common law marriage has four requirements: a mutual agreement between the parties to enter the relationship of legal marriage at the present time; cohabitation as husband and wife following that agreement; holding themselves out to the community as married, thus gaining a reputation of being married; and having the capacity to be married, that is, no disqualifying impediments or defects of consent. Wilma and Sam went through a state marriage in Caltex; all states include a mutual agreement to enter legal at the present time as part of their ceremonies. Following the ceremony, Wilma and Sam lived together as husband and wife, according to the facts. They held themselves out to the community that they lived in as married and had that reputation, again according to the facts. Wilma could claim that her failure to divorce Hank indicates that she did not consent to marry Sam; she was avoiding marriage rather than entering it. However, Wilma's public expression of consent to that status would be hard for her to deny credibly. What Wilma and Sam lacked, however, was freedom from disqualifying impediments. Wilma had a prior existing marriage to Hank at the time that she married Sam, as her own search of state records will show.

In most jurisdictions that allow common law marriages to be validly confected, this impediment would be a bar until the dissolution of the earlier marriage through death or divorce. At that point, a new agreement between the parties to enter legal marriage would validate their common law marriage. Thus, after the dissolution of Wilma's marriage to Hank through his death, if Wilma and Sam again agreed to be husband and wife at present, they would have a valid common law marriage. In addition, a few jurisdictions do not require this new agreement after the impediment to the common law marriage has ended. A valid common law marriage comes into being automatically on the dissolution of the earlier marriage. If either of these possibilities exists in Wilma and Sam's jurisdiction, Wilma could be Sam's legal spouse if she is found to have entered an agreement subsequent to Hank's death, or in the second type of jurisdiction, even if she did not. Because common law marriage is in fact legal marriage in the jurisdictions that recognize it, a divorce is required to terminate it, and the financial incidents that might flow from divorce, such as alimony and a division of marital property, could flow to Sam. Wilma's inheritance from Hank would most likely not be considered part of the marital property; many jurisdictions exempt property inherited by one of the parties to a marriage from equitable distribution on divorce. However, Wilma's new wealth would provide a source for an alimony award to Sam.

2. The putative marriage (also known as "putative spouse") doctrine   Even if Sam does not qualify as Wilma's common law spouse, Wilma might have financial obligations toward him. A minority of jurisdictions in the United States adhere to the putative marriage doctrine, also termed the putative spouse doctrine. This doctrine is an equitable remedy for one who unknowingly contracted an invalid marriage. Under it, one who is not validly married can recover on its annulment or other dissolution some or all of the benefits ordinarily awarded to a spouse. The requirements for one seeking to have putative spouse status are that the party who claims that status entered in good faith into an apparently valid marriage that, because of some defect unknown to him, is in fact invalid. The extent of the spousal benefits granted varies in different jurisdictions, but alimony and a share in the marital property are commonly among them.

If Caltex has adopted this doctrine, Sam could qualify for the benefits ordinarily awarded a former spouse if he could establish that he was entitled to recognition as a "putative spouse." He entered into an apparently valid marriage through the state ceremony for marriage. With respect to Sam's good faith, according to the facts, Wilma did not tell him of her earlier marriage to Hank. The facts also do not indicate any suspicious behavior on Wilma's part, such as visiting Hank in Commonalia, after the marriage; there appears to be no reason that Sam should have known that his "wife" was a bigamist. The facts also indicate that Sam learned for the first time of Wilma's prior marriage after Hank's death. Thus, Sam appears to be entitled to the status of a putative spouse, and might be able to claim alimony and a share of marital property as if he and Wilma had been validly married.

QUESTION #4

There are two arguments in favor of Thea taking a child's share of Paul's estate. First, under the paternity statute, Leda, acting for Thea, should immediately appeal the dismissal of Thea's paternity action. The trial court's interpretation of "reasonable period," using it to foreclose a suit brought three months after Paul's death and a month after his child's birth, is inconsistent with the purpose of the statute. Second, that interpretation of the statute would make it an unconstitutional discrimination against an out-of-wedlock child.

I. A judgment of paternity within a "reasonable time" of the father's death

Substantively, Leda's paternity action presents no difficulty on the facts given. Actions to establish the paternity of a nonmarital child may set the standard of proof at the preponderance of the evidence (*Rivera v. Minnich*, 483 U.S. 574 (1987));

posthumous paternity actions often require a higher level, the clear and convincing standard. The facts establish that Leda and Paul were faithful to one another, and the DNA test results will therefore establish that Paul was Thea's father. The obstacle is the court's interpretation of "reasonable period" to exclude a suit brought within four months of Paul's death. That decision is inconsistent with the statute's purpose in imposing a time limitation on posthumous adjudications of paternity. The statute furthers the state's interest in the just and orderly administration of estates of its domiciliaries. It provides a time period for legally unrecognized children of the decedent to establish their relationship to him, and thus accomplishes the probable intent of the deceased that all his children be treated equally, the assumption underlying the intestacy statute. It also prevents stale claims from being brought when proof of the relationship might no longer be available and the estate has been distributed among the recognized heirs. The time period in Commonalia is flexible, which permits the court to determine whether in a given case any delay was reasonable or not.

In this case, the delay was short; Leda filed suit a month after Thea's birth, which is about three months after Paul's death. Her suit does not create the problems of a stale claim; Leda has the evidence required to prove paternity, and Paul's estate has not yet been distributed. To dismiss it frustrates the statute's purpose in fostering justice in estate distribution without serving the other state policy underlying it. Thus, the appellate court would be likely to reverse the trial court's dismissal.

II. Constitutional protection of nonmarital children's inheritance rights

The appellate court has an additional reason for finding that the trial court's interpretation of "reasonable period" is untenable. It is not only inconsistent with the state's own policies concerning intestacy, it is also inconsistent with protections provided to nonmarital children under the Fourteenth Amendment to the U.S. Constitution. Nonmarital children had for centuries been subjected to discriminatory treatment by state statutes either barring them from rights accorded to marital children, or affording them lesser rights — for example, allowing them to take as heirs in intestacy only if no marital children existed. The U.S. Supreme Court in the late twentieth century invalidated many of these statutes as discriminatory. Although it did not declare nonmarital children to constitute a suspect classification, it applied heightened scrutiny to the statutes that treated these children differently because they touch on fundamental personal rights. States have thus been required to demonstrate a substantial relationship between their discrimination against nonmarital children and an important state interest.

States have an important interest in the just and orderly administration of estates, which this statute is intended to serve. However, the statute would not fulfill the court's requirement of having a substantial relationship to that interest if the court upheld the trial court's interpretation of "within reasonable period" of the father's death as less than four months. The reasons are the same as those for viewing this interpretation as inconsistent with the state's own purposes in enacting the statute. The problems of stale claims of inheritance would not commonly arise in such a short period of time. The disposition of an estate usually takes longer than four months, and so most are unlikely to be disrupted by claims that are made slightly more than three months after the death of the father. The availability of DNA testing has reduced concerns about unjust distributions caused by the passage of time producing fraudulent claims, which motivated the Supreme Court to permit time limits in the 1970s. Moreover, even at that time, the difficulty of proving paternity could not be used to create an "impenetrable barrier" that would "shield otherwise invidious discrimination." See *Gomez v. Perez,* 409 U.S. 535 (1973). If the state's statute were interpreted to exclude Thea's case, that is what she would face. The first two methods of establishing her relationship for purposes of inheritance are foreclosed to her by her father's inaction before his death; the third would limit the time allowed for action by Leda, Thea's representative, in a manner not required by state policy. In fact, such a short period would be in violation of the state's interest in the just distribution of estates because it might exclude those with just claims. Thus, the appellate court should rule in Leda's favor.

Family Law
Multiple Choice
101 QUESTIONS

ANSWER SHEET

Print or copy this answer sheet to all multiple choice questions.

1.	A B C D	28.	A B C D	55.	A B C D	82.	A B C D
2.	A B C D	29.	A B C D	56.	A B C D	83.	A B C D
3.	A B C D	30.	A B C D	57.	A B C D	84.	A B C D
4.	A B C D	31.	A B C D	58.	A B C D	85.	A B C D
5.	A B C D	32.	A B C D	59.	A B C D	86.	A B C D
6.	A B C D	33.	A B C D	60.	A B C D	87.	A B C D
7.	A B C D	34.	A B C D	61.	A B C D	88.	A B C D
8.	A B C D	35.	A B C D	62.	A B C D	89.	A B C D
9.	A B C D	36.	A B C D	63.	A B C D	90.	A B C D
10.	A B C D	37.	A B C D	64.	A B C D	91.	A B C D
11.	A B C D	38.	A B C D	65.	A B C D	92.	A B C D
12.	A B C D	39.	A B C D	66.	A B C D	93.	A B C D
13.	A B C D	40.	A B C D	67.	A B C D	94.	A B C D
14.	A B C D	41.	A B C D	68.	A B C D	95.	A B C D
15.	A B C D	42.	A B C D	69.	A B C D	96.	A B C D
16.	A B C D	43.	A B C D	70.	A B C D	97.	A B C D
17.	A B C D	44.	A B C D	71.	A B C D	98.	A B C D
18.	A B C D	45.	A B C D	72.	A B C D	99.	A B C D
19.	A B C D	46.	A B C D	73.	A B C D	100.	A B C D
20.	A B C D	47.	A B C D	74.	A B C D	101.	A B C D
21.	A B C D	48.	A B C D	75.	A B C D		
22.	A B C D	49.	A B C D	76.	A B C D		
23.	A B C D	50.	A B C D	77.	A B C D		
24.	A B C D	51.	A B C D	78.	A B C D		
25.	A B C D	52.	A B C D	79.	A B C D		
26.	A B C D	53.	A B C D	80.	A B C D		
27.	A B C D	54.	A B C D	81.	A B C D		

FAMILY LAW QUESTIONS

1. Assume that the legislature in a U.S. state became alarmed because the number of impoverished households containing minor children was increasing. These households were usually headed by a divorced mother. In an effort to reduce the divorce rate, and with it, child poverty, the legislature passed a statute requiring completion of a nonreligious premarital counseling session before a marriage license could be issued. Attending the counseling, which lasts for a weekend, costs $500. The state provides no funds toward this cost. Alex and Bethany are unemployed and indigent; Bethany is pregnant with Alex's child. They are engaged, but cannot reasonably expect to have $500 to pay for the counseling and obtain a license. With an American Civil Liberties Union attorney representing them, they sue the state for depriving them of their fundamental right to marry. How is the court likely to rule?

   A) The court will strike down the requirement as unconstitutional because the U.S. Supreme Court has recognized the right to marry as a constitutionally protected fundamental right of privacy, so the state cannot impose any financial burden on access to it.

   B) The court will not strike down the requirement as unconstitutional because it is rationally related to the important state interest of reducing child poverty.

   C) The court will strike down the statutory requirement as unconstitutional if it finds that although the state has a compelling interest in reducing child poverty, the statute completely deprives the couple of their fundamental right to marry by means that are both underinclusive and overinclusive.

   D) The court will not strike down the statutory requirement as unconstitutional if it finds facts supporting the conclusion that most child poverty in the state results from the parents' divorce.

2. Which of the following statements concerning state prohibitions on marriage between close relatives in the U.S. is **not** true?

   A) A marriage between relatives who are too closely related under the law of the state where the marriage is contracted is voidable rather than void.

   B) The states are divided on the issue of whether first cousins can validly marry one another.

   C) All states permit marriage between relations who are second cousins or more distantly related.

   D) No state permits marriage of an individual to his or her lineal ancestor (parents, grandparents, etc.) or to his or her lineal descendant (children, grandchildren, etc.).

3. Andy is a developmentally disabled 50-year-old man with an IQ of 65 who works as a cook in a fast-food restaurant. He lives at a group home for the developmentally disabled. Bella is a 49-year-old woman, also developmentally disabled, who lives at the same group home. She is employed as a cleaner at a hospital; her IQ is 55. Both have state-appointed guardians who handle their financial affairs. The two of them have fallen in love and want to marry. Which of the following statements reflects the position of most states on their ability to marry?

A) They cannot marry because the fact that guardians have been appointed to handle their financial affairs indicates that they lack the mental capacity to give consent to the contract of marriage.

B) They cannot marry because they might still be capable of producing children, who would then become wards of the state.

C) They can marry if both of them have sufficient capacity to understand the nature of the marriage contract and the duties and responsibilities incident to it.

D) They can marry only if their guardians supply the consent for them.

4. Queenie and Finn are high school students who want to marry. Finn is 18 years old. Queenie has just turned 17 years old, and their state requires that minors can only marry with the permission of one of their parents. Queenie's parents adamantly refused to give their consent. Queenie and Finn obtained a marriage license by lying on the application form, claiming she is 18. They married in a state ceremony before a justice of the peace. They moved into Finn's bedroom at his mother's home. After a couple of months, they tired of married life and split up, and Queenie returned to her parents' home. Shortly thereafter, Finn files a suit in family court for divorce from Queenie. Queenie replies by denying the validity of the marriage because she was underage, and asks for an annulment. Which of the following states a possible outcome?

A) The court will observe that the couple does not require a divorce or annulment because a marriage of a minor without parental permission is void, but will grant an annulment in response to Queenie's request.

B) The court will rule in favor of Queenie, because the marriage of a minor without parental permission is voidable, and the two did not ratify the marriage owing to the brevity of their relationship.

C) The court will rule in favor of Finn if it finds that Queenie, although a minor, had sufficient understanding of marriage to give valid consent to it, and thus they are validly married.

D) Any of the above, depending on the jurisdiction.

5. Which of the following traditional requirements for finding a marriage voidable on the ground of fraud was made more expansive in the late twentieth century?

A) The fraud must be material to the consent of the person alleging fraud to the marriage; that is, his or her consent would not have been given without it.

B) Only the victim of the fraud can petition for annulment of it.

C) The fraud must affect the essentials of marriage, that is, marital issues related to cohabitation, sexual relations, or procreation.

D) The fraud must relate to the facts at the time the marriage was confected, not to future developments.

6. Debbie has married Floyd, whom she had met at a political campaign event for a candidate that she passionately supported. Floyd represented himself as a strong supporter of her candidate and his progressive platform, and he volunteered to work with her group on the ultimately unsuccessful campaign. After they married, Debbie discovered documents in Floyd's desk indicating that Floyd was an operative for the Tarahu, a right-wing "militia" organization in their state that seeks to overthrow the current U.S. government. He had participated in the campaign to gather information on the politician and sabotage his chances. The Tarahu's goal is to return the United States to its "true role" as a white supremacist state. Debbie is horrified by what she's discovered about Floyd's beliefs and actions. When she confronted him, he admitted to them, and refused to give up his beliefs or the group, but said she could continue to see her friends of other races because they were "a good cover." Debbie is seeking an annulment of their marriage for fraud. She says that she would never have married someone with Floyd's political beliefs. What is the likely outcome of her case?

A) The court would grant Debbie an annulment under the modern subjective test of "essential to the marriage"; although his political views are unrelated to cohabitation, sexual relations, or procreation, the facts support her allegation that she regarded political compatibility as essential to her marriage.

B) The court would deny Debbie an annulment because a difference in political viewpoints does not go to the essentials of a marriage because it is unrelated to sexual relationships, cohabitation, or procreation.

C) The court would deny Debbie an annulment because to grant one would make the voidability of a marriage depend on the popularity of a particular political group or set of beliefs.

D) The court would grant Debbie an annulment because if Floyd engages in violence in the future, Debbie's life might be in danger.

7. Joseph, a citizen of a foreign country, has come to the United States as a university student whose student visa is about to expire. He wants to remain here, but he does not have permanent resident status. He has met Nancy, a straight-A nursing student and U.S. citizen, at the university. Nancy is in need of money to finish her degree because budget cuts imposed on education

during a financial crisis eliminated her scholarship, and her family has no money to assist her. Joseph pays Nancy to go through a marriage ceremony with him, agreeing that they will not have sexual relations or live together, and will divorce after two years. The marriage ceremony meets the state's requirements of validity. They have none of the state's impediments to marriage. However, they do not share housing, living expenses, or a sexual relationship. Two years later, the Immigration and Naturalization Service (INS) arrests Joseph for remaining in the United States after the expiration of his visa, and is attempting to deport him. His defense is that he is validly married under state law to a U.S. citizen. What is the most likely result?

A) Joseph will be deported because the validity of the marriage under state law does not mandate that the INS give it effect for immigration purposes.

B) Joseph will be given permanent resident status and allowed to remain in the United States because he is validly married to Nancy under state law, which is the law that governs domestic relations in the United States.

C) Joseph will be deported because in every state, the husband and wife must cohabit in a matrimonial domicile for the marriage to be valid.

D) Both A and C.

8. Elizabeth and Fiona were lesbian partners who married in 2008 in Connecticut, one of the few states that permit such couples to marry. For employment-related reasons, they moved to Montana in that same year. In 2004, Montana's citizens had added an amendment to their state constitution that read, "Only a marriage between one man and one woman shall be valid or recognized as a marriage in this state." Elizabeth and Fiona's marriage has now broken down. Elizabeth files for a divorce in Montana, requesting alimony and distribution of the property acquired since the marriage. Fiona responds that because Montana does not consider them to be married, a divorce action is not available to Elizabeth. What is the most likely ruling from the Montana court?

A) The Montana court will dismiss Elizabeth's divorce action because the federal Defense of Marriage Act prohibits states from recognizing same-sex marriages.

B) The Montana court will dismiss Elizabeth's divorce action because it is premised on recognition of validity of her marriage to Fiona; Montana's constitutional amendment indicates a strong public policy contrary to recognizing same-sex marriages contracted in another state as valid.

C) The Montana court will allow Elizabeth's divorce action to proceed because each state is required by the Full Faith and Credit clause of the U.S. Constitution to recognize marriages validly contracted in another state.

D) The Montana court will dismiss Elizabeth's divorce action because Elizabeth and Fiona's marriage in Connecticut took place after Montana had passed its constitutional amendment.

9. Roberta is a postoperative male-to-female transsexual woman. She and Herbert, who has been male since birth, wish to marry. In most U.S. jurisdictions that have confronted the issue, will they be permitted to marry or not, and for what reason?

A) They would not be permitted to marry in most states that have considered the issue because in the majority of these, the courts have held that the sex of the transsexual partner was not affected by the sex reassignment treatment and surgery.

B) They would be permitted to marry by most states that have considered the issue because Roberta is now female, and therefore there is no impediment to her marriage to a male, Herbert.

C) They would be permitted to marry in most states that have considered the issue because if the state still recognized Roberta as male, male-to-female transsexuals would be permitted to contract valid marriage with partners who are women from birth, thus legalizing same-sex marriage.

D) Both B and C.

10. Michael and Norma became engaged when he was 73 and she was 64. Both had been married before and widowed. Because Michael had periodically experienced erectile dysfunction and was afraid of the side effects of medication, they agreed prior to marrying that their marriage would not include sexual intercourse. However, a few months into the marriage, Norma began asking for sexual intercourse and when Michael said no, she repeatedly suggested Viagra. Michael wants to sue to enforce the prenuptial agreement that he and Norma made. If he does, how is the court likely to rule?

A) The prenuptial agreement is unenforceable because the court would be intervening in an intact family to impose an arrangement concerning their marital responsibilities.

B) The prenuptial agreement is enforceable, but has not been breached because Norma has not been successful in obtaining sex from Michael.

C) The prenuptial agreement is unenforceable because it attempts to modify a noneconomic marital obligation.

D) Both A and C.

11. Lacy and Tod have been cohabiting for four years in a jurisdiction that does not allow common law marriage. Neither has an existing marriage, they are unrelated to one another, and they are of opposite sexes. Lacy very much wants to marry Tod. Tod, who is an elder of the True Way Church, has told his pastor and Lacy that he wants to "get right with God" in his relationship with Lacy. He and Lacy went through the True Way Church's legally recognized marriage ceremony with their pastor, who is a qualified marriage celebrant in the state, officiating. They fulfilled all the mandatory requirements for marriage in their state. The ceremony included the pronunciation of the vows taking one another as husband and wife. Twenty-five of their friends from the church were witnesses to the event. However, prior to going through the ceremony, Lacy had at Tod's request signed a document stating that they did not subjectively intend to marry one another through this ceremony. Tod had deposited the agreement in the safe in his home office. Three months later, Tod had a heart attack and died. His will left nothing to Lacy, who has filed suit in Tod's succession for the elective share of the surviving spouse. Angela, Tod's executrix, opposes Lacy's request. She contends that Tod and Lacy were never married, and offers the signed agreement as evidence. How should the court rule?

A) The marriage is void because one or both of the parties did not have the subjective intent to marry, despite creating the appearance of a valid marriage.

B) The marriage is void because Tod and Lacy entered an enforceable prenuptial agreement that it would not be valid before going through the ceremony.

C) The marriage is void but the putative spouse doctrine would apply to give Lacy the elective share of the surviving spouse.

D) The marriage is valid because it is contrary to public policy for parties who met all the ceremonial and substantive requirements for marriage to contract privately to avoid the effects of marriage.

12. Which of the following is **not** a requirement for common law marriage in the states that recognize such marriages?

A) An agreement to contract marriage (i.e., be husband and wife) at the time that the agreement is made.

B) Competency to marry, that is, lack of an impediment that would void the marriage contract.

C) Holding oneself out as married within the community, as evidenced by being reputed to be married.

D) Cohabitation as husband and wife for at least seven years.

13. Using the titles "Mr. and Mrs. Dodgson," Lewis and Alice Dodgson cohabited for 14 years in a state that permits confection of valid common law marriage. Everyone in the community in which they lived treated them as a married couple, and they held their bank account and rented property as husband and wife. They had agreed to be husband and wife when they moved in together, but rejected the public ceremony of marriage as created by a corrupt consumerist culture. They were not related to one another, neither had been married before they began cohabiting, and they are not of the same sex. They have no children. Alice discovered that Lewis had been purchasing lottery tickets, resulting in a bitter argument. Because of Alice's intolerance of his "harmless

fun," Lewis left her. He moved to a different town in the same state to start over. Neither party ever obtained a divorce. A year after he left Alice, Lewis married Grace, who insisted on a formal marriage in her church. Seventeen years later, Lewis and Grace are still together; Lewis is still childless. That year, Lewis purchased the sole winning ticket for a $68 million lottery jackpot. After collecting his prize, Lewis was killed in a one-car accident in his new sports car. He left no will. The state in which Lewis, Alice, and Grace live makes the surviving spouse of a childless decedent the decedent's sole heir in intestacy. Who would inherit Lewis's fortune under the law of most jurisdictions?

A) Alice would inherit Lewis's fortune to the exclusion of Grace because, as she and Lewis never divorced, her common law marriage to him was not dissolved at the time of his "marriage" to Grace, and his marriage to Grace was absolutely null ab initio.

B) Grace would inherit Lewis's fortune because Lewis's common law marriage to Alice, being unrecorded, did not require a formal divorce to terminate it. Their separation for over a year terminated it, and Grace's subsequent marriage to Lewis was valid.

C) If the state in which the three were domiciled recognizes the putative marriage doctrine, Alice and Grace would share the estate if Grace was in good faith on entering and during her putative marriage to Lewis.

D) Either A or C.

14. When Ann and Bob were college students at Iowa State in 1994, Ann became pregnant with Bob's child. They privately confected a common law marriage; Iowa permitted such marriages then, and still does. They lived as husband and wife in Iowa until 2008, when they moved to Virginia because Bob's company transferred him. Bob has been killed by a negligent driver in Virginia. Ann has sued for wrongful death. Virginia does not permit common law marriages to be confected within its borders, and does not permit recovery for wrongful death by a nonrelative who is not a legal spouse of the deceased. Which of the following answers states the rule that is ordinarily applied to determine whether Ann could recover for Bob's wrongful death as his spouse?

A) Because the Full Faith and Credit Clause of the U.S. Constitution mandates that each state recognize the public records of the others, the Virginia court must recognize Ann and Bob's valid Iowa common law marriage as valid in Virginia as well.

B) Under the conflict of laws principle on comity for marriages validly contracted in another state that could not be validly contracted in Virginia, a marriage valid where contracted need not be recognized as valid if it violates the strong public policy of another state in which recognition is sought; therefore, Ann and Bob's valid Iowa common law marriage will only be recognized as valid in Virginia if Virginia has no strong public policy against such marriages.

C) Under the conflict of laws principle on recognition, a marriage valid where contracted will be everywhere recognized as valid; therefore the Virginia court must recognize Ann and Bob's valid Iowa common law marriage as valid in Virginia as well.

D) Under the conflict of laws principle on recognition, a marriage valid where contracted need not be recognized as valid in another state if the parties to the marriage are no longer domiciled in the state where the marriage was contracted; therefore, the Virginia court need not recognize Ann and Bob's valid Iowa common law marriage as valid in Virginia as well.

15. Alexandra and Bradley were married in the Roman Catholic Church in 1987; they divorced in 2000. Three years later, they agreed to remarry. They obtained a marriage license; one evening Bradley stopped at the rectory of their parish church to ask the parish priest to perform the ceremony for them. The priest replied that because the Church does not recognize civil divorce, it does not require a second ceremony. The priest then signed and dated the portion of the license headed "Marriage Certificate," and sent it to the county Records Office. Alexandra and Bradley moved in together. In 2008, Bradley filed for a no-fault divorce. Alexandra filed for an annulment. In their jurisdiction, which does not permit common law marriages, which of the following is true?

A) Bradley's request for a divorce will be granted because they were remarried by the priest's action in completing the marriage certificate after the couple had agreed to marry again.

B) Bradley's request for a divorce will be granted because the couple's intent to remarry and their good faith belief in the priest's statement that they were still married were sufficient to marry them.

C) Alexandra's request for an annulment will be granted because her second purported marriage is void; in a state that does not permit common law marriages, a formal ceremony of solemnization is required for valid marriage.

D) Alexandra's request for an annulment will be denied because the marriage certificate signed by a qualified celebrant, the parish priest, and on file in the county records office creates a conclusive presumption of marriage.

16. Darla and James lived in Calvin, a small town located ten miles from Comanche, a much larger town where the residents of Calvin went for shopping, entertainment, and professional services. However, Comanche was located across the border in a different state from that in which Calvin was located. When Darla and James decided to get married, they drove to Comanche, which had a county clerk's office, and procured a marriage license. On St. Valentine's Day, 2000, they were married in a traditional religious ceremony conducted by the pastor, Reverend Hite, at their church in Calvin. Reverend Hite was authorized to perform marriages in both of these neighboring states. Hite filled out the information required for a marriage certificate on the license for the couple, scratching out the name of the state that issued the license and filling in the name of Darla and James's state of domicile. He returned the completed certificate after the ceremony to the clerk of the county court in Comanche. The clerk filed the marriage certificate in the public records of his state. Darla and James lived together for eight years, and had two children.

In 2008, James, who wanted to divorce Darla, found out from his attorney in Comanche that he had to file for a divorce from Darla in the nearest county seat in the state of their domicile. He also learned that the legislatures in both states had outlawed common law marriages. James hired a lawyer in the state where he and Darla lived and filed for a divorce. Darla in her answer petitioned for a declaration that the marriage was void because of the couple's failure to obtain a state marriage license. Although the state statutes did not list lack of a license as a cause of a void marriage, as they did for bigamous and incestuous marriages, state law requires that the parties to the marriage obtain such a license and present it to the officiant, and makes failure to do so a misdemeanor. She also contended that the pastor who officiated at their wedding had no authority to perform a marriage ceremony in their state of domicile without a valid state marriage license, again a requirement of state law; the officiant's failure to do so is also a misdemeanor. She pointed out that although she and James had obtained a marriage license from the neighboring state, they had not met that state's statutory requirement for creating a valid marriage: a marriage ceremony within that state's borders. The district court agreed with Darla. It found that no divorce could be granted because the attempted marriage was void. James has appealed that decision. How should the appellate court rule?

A) The appellate court should reverse because the requirement of a marriage license is directory rather than mandatory; its absence creates a penalty on the couple and the officiant, but does not void the marriage.

B) The appellate court should reverse the trial court's decision because James and Darla were in good faith when they ceremonially married, and therefore are putative spouses.

C) The appellate court should affirm the trial court's decision because recognizing an unlicensed marriage as valid would authorize common law marriage, contrary to the state legislature's express policy.

D) The appellate court should affirm the trial court's decision because otherwise the state would be unable to verify whether recipients of benefits tied to marriage merited those benefits.

17. Troy, an officer in the U.S. Army from a wealthy family, met Cressie, a singer, while he was on leave a week before his unit was to deploy to Afghanistan. The two spent the entire week together, and at the end of it, Troy proposed and Cressie accepted. Troy purchased a diamond ring for $35,000 and presented it to Cressie as her engagement ring. They planned to marry when

Troy's present tour was over in 18 months. While Troy was in Afghanistan, Cressie e-mailed him every day concerning wedding plans. She booked a wedding venue, giving a nonrefundable deposit, and also booked flights for her three best friends to fly in to attend. Nine months into his tour in Afghanistan, Troy realized that Cressie did not know where Afghanistan was, or why the U.S. Army was there. His attempts to communicate with her on any subject other than her wedding, her clothes for her wedding, her shoes (whether for the wedding or not), and her friends' thoughts on these subjects were failures. Troy wrote to Cressie telling her that he had had second thoughts and was calling off the wedding; he asked that she send the ring to his mother. Cressie refused to part with the ring. What would the most likely result be if Cressie sued Troy for breach of promise to marry, asking for $150,000 in damages for lost expenses and social expectations, and Troy counterclaimed for return of the ring?

A) If Cressie could prove that her fault did not cause the breach, she would receive an award for whatever damages she could prove were caused by the breach, and would be able to keep the ring because Troy was at fault in breaking the engagement without a serious cause.

B) Cressie's suit for breach of promise to marry would likely be dismissed because most jurisdictions have eliminated that cause of action because of the changes in sexual mores and in the status and power of women.

C) Cressie would have to return the ring because it was a conditional gift, and the condition (her marriage to Troy) was not fulfilled.

D) Both B and C.

18. Troy's mother, Hester, delighted that her son was getting married, had sent Cressie a $10,000 gift certificate toward her wedding dress at a fashionable designer's shop. She also invited Cressie to lunch. Hester enjoyed Cressie's company so much that she took Cressie to a jewelry store and bought her a ruby-studded gold brooch shaped like a shoe. She pinned it to Cressie's jacket, and said, "The money's for the wedding, but this is just because you're you." When Hester discovered that Troy had called off the wedding, she asked for the gift certificate and the brooch back. Cressie refused to return them. What should be the result if Hester sues for their return?

A) Cressie must return the gift certificate and the brooch because they were conditional gifts, given by Hester in contemplation of a marriage that did not take place.

B) Cressie must return the gift certificate, but need not return the brooch because Hester's statement indicates it was not given to her in contemplation of marriage, but just out of fondness for her.

C) Cressie need not return either the gift certificate or the brooch because Cressie did not cause the cancellation of the marriage.

D) Cressie need not return the gift certificate because it did not specify that it was given in contemplation of her marriage to Troy, but she must return the brooch because, had she not been engaged to Troy, she would not have met his mother.

19. Alan Anderson, a political journalist for a newsmagazine, married Beth in San Francisco, California in 2003. While on assignment in Texas in 2007, he met and married Catherine. Catherine had no idea that Alan was already married to Beth. The travel required for Alan's work enabled him to maintain two separate households, one in Texas and one in California. However, in 2010, Catherine saw a picture on the Internet of Alan and Beth at the 2010 Political Journalism Awards banquet. The photo was captioned, "Alan Anderson of Newstime magazine and his wife, Beth." Catherine's investigation confirmed Alan's prior undissolved marriage. Both California and Texas recognize the putative marriage doctrine. Under that doctrine, which of the following statements is **not** true?

A) Catherine requires an annulment or a divorce to terminate her putative marriage to Alan.

B) Catherine's marriage to Alan is void because of the impediment of his prior existing marriage.

C) If Catherine had a good-faith belief that her marriage to Alan was valid, then she is entitled under the putative spouse doctrine to spousal benefits such as alimony and a share of what would have been marital property.

D) Good faith for the purpose of the putative spouse requires that the party invoking the doctrine neither knew nor should have known of the invalidity of his or her marriage.

20. Debra Parker has an established reputation as a scientific researcher at her state's flagship university. She recently married Sam Wilty, who is a colleague in her department. She submitted the record of their marriage to the University's personnel office so that she and Sam could receive a cost break that the university's group health insurance offers to spouses. When Debra received her first paycheck after her marriage, her name appeared on it as "Debra Wilty." She discovered from the personnel office that on all her records, her name had been changed. The administrator in charge of personnel records insisted that a married woman's legal name is her husband's last name, and that hers must be changed to comply with her legal status. Which of the following is true?

A) At common law, to continue to have the legal name "Debra Parker" after her marriage, Debra must go through the state's legal process to change her surname from "Wilty" to "Parker."

B) A married woman who wishes to change her legal surname to her husband's last name can now only do so by legal process.

C) Married women's use of their husbands' last names was not practiced at common law, but became the law in some U.S. jurisdictions through statutes or court decisions.

D) Unless Debra's jurisdiction has legislated otherwise, or its courts have determined otherwise, her legal surname remains "Parker" after marriage; the common practice of taking the husband's surname was a matter of custom rather than a legal requirement at common law.

21. What presumption and burden of persuasion exist concerning the validity of successive marriages entered into by the same person?

A) When a person has contracted successive marriages, the latest in the series is presumed to be valid.

B) When a person has contracted successive marriages, the earliest in the series is presumed to be valid.

C) When a person has contracted successive marriages, the burden of persuasion shifts from the later marriage to the earlier one if the first spouse presents evidence that the earlier marriage remains undissolved.

D) A and C.

22. April and Brandt married in 1993. At that time, Brandt was in his third year of medical school; April put him through school by working as a file clerk. Once Brandt finished medical school, internship, and his residency, he joined a successful surgery practice. April looked forward to a very comfortable standard of living without having to scrimp and save on Brandt's $500,000-per-year salary. However, aside from buying a house, Brandt was unwilling to change his poor-student lifestyle. He saved every penny that he could. He kept large amounts of cash in several banks; his investments were extremely conservative. Fifteen years later, April and the two children that she and Brandt had had were living in a house furnished from thrift stores. Their groceries came from a discount superstore. Neither April nor Brandt had credit cards. Brandt did the shopping for the family and paid by cash or check. He was unwilling to replace their old appliances, so April had learned to repair the washer and dryer. When the furnace of their house ceased working during a bitter winter and April couldn't repair it herself, Brandt refused to pay for its repair. April and the children have recurring colds and occasional flu. April has consulted a lawyer about suing Brandt for support payments to enable her to run the house in accordance with Brandt's income. However, she does not want to leave Brandt; she believes that would devastate their children and Brandt, whom she still loves, as well. Which of the following principles would be relevant in April's suit?

A) The level of the obligation of support within marriage is calculated on the basis of the spouses' incomes, and a court can order a spouse to make up any deficiency.

B) In the absence of a separation or divorce, a court ordinarily will not intervene in an intact family to resolve a dispute as to the standard of living to be maintained.

C) If one spouse has endangered the family by failing to supply the necessities of life despite his or her ability to do so, the other can obtain a support order even without separation or divorce.

D) Both B and C.

23. Using the facts in question 22, assume that instead of suing Brandt, April convinces a repairman to attempt to fix the heater, and when he could not, to replace it, promising that her husband would send the repairman a check when Brandt returned from work. When Brandt comes home, he refuses to pay, saying that he had not authorized the man to make the replacement. The repairman sues Brandt for payment. Under what circumstances can the repairman win his suit?

A) If the jurisdiction in which April and Brandt live has not discarded the doctrine of necessaries.

B) If the heater is found to be a necessary, considering Brandt's ability to pay and standing in the community.

C) If Brandt is found to have refused to furnish this necessary to April.

D) All of the above.

24. Wally is suing Pastor Flynn, the minister of the church that Wally and his wife Brenda used to attend, in tort for the alienation of Brenda's affections. Wally has requested compensatory and punitive damages. Wally and Brenda had been married for six years when Wally, an Army officer, was deployed to Afghanistan. Before the deployment, Brenda and Wally appeared to be a loving young married couple. They went out socially with other married couples. They testified that they had sexual relations several times a week. While Wally was first deployed, Brenda talked to him nearly every day and the two exchanged regular e-mails. Brenda suffered from feelings of guilt because she and Wally had a serious disagreement before his departure for Afghanistan: Brenda wanted to get pregnant by Wally before he left because she wanted to have his child, and she feared that he might not return. Wally refused because he was afraid that he might leave Brenda to raise a child alone. Brenda told Pastor Flynn about her feelings of guilt, and he invited her to counseling sessions. During these, Flynn persuaded Brenda that Wally was being selfish, and probably didn't want her to have a child. Flynn began an affair with Brenda; while it was going on, Brenda's calls and e-mails to Wally became less frequent and more distant in tone. Brenda ended her relationship with Flynn, despite his arguments that it was therapy for her anxieties, after six months. Although she and Wally have not gotten a divorce, Wally testified that there was no way to regain the trust they once had. Brenda testified to her

self-hate and fear that Wally could never believe in her enough to start a family. They have spent thousands of dollars on individual and couples counseling. How is a court in most jurisdictions likely to rule?

A) The court would find in favor of Pastor Flynn because his behavior is not a proximate cause of Brenda's affair; her consent is.

B) The court would dismiss Wally's case for failure to state a cause of action on which relief could be granted.

C) The court would find in favor of Pastor Flynn because Wally and Brenda's disagreement, and Brenda's seeking Flynn's counseling, prove that their marriage was damaged prior to her affair with Flynn.

D) The court would find in favor of Flynn because he did not owe Wally a duty to refrain from seducing his wife.

25. A few states have passed a covenant marriage statute offering a type of marriage that can be voluntarily chosen by the couple. Which of the following is **not** true of covenant marriage statutes?

A) The purpose of covenant marriage statutes is to allow couples greater flexibility in structuring their marriages to decrease the likelihood of marital conflict.

B) Covenant marriage statutes require couples to have counseling before the marriage and before initiating a divorce.

C) Covenant marriage statutes either make obtaining a no-fault divorce more difficult or eliminate the possibility altogether.

D) Covenant marriage statutes were introduced as an attempt to reduce divorce rates.

26. In the case of *Boddie v. Connecticut,* 401 U.S. 371 (1971), the U.S. Supreme Court decided that due process prohibits a state from denying access to its courts to indigent individuals who are seeking a divorce. What is the reason for the court's finding?

A) Because marriage is fundamental to our society, and state courts are the only legal instruments for dissolving it, a state cannot deny access to those seeking this adjustment of a fundamental relationship for their genuine inability to pay.

B) The Supreme Court recognized the right to divorce as a fundamental privacy right implicit in the Fourteenth Amendment's protection of liberty.

C) The Supreme Court recognized that access for all persons to the courts is a right guaranteed under the Due Process Clause of the Fourteenth Amendment, so it cannot be placed by the states beyond anyone's reach.

D) Both A and C.

27. Under the modern interpretation of cruelty as a fault ground for divorce, which of the following situations would be most likely to support a finding of cruel treatment against a spouse who is the defendant in a fault-based divorce action?

  A) Plaintiff husband Alec, a very tidy man, complained that during their ten-year marriage, the defendant wife Barbara was a messy housekeeper with a disorganized kitchen; she had poor time management skills that made her unreliable, and sometimes sent their children to school in mismatched clothing because she hadn't sorted the clean laundry; and she would bicker with him when he criticized her instead of trying to improve.

  B) During their 20-year marriage, the defendant husband Don hit the plaintiff wife Candace in the face once, knocking her down, in the course of an argument about whether he was rude to her mother, but she was not seriously injured and he was not physically violent before then or afterward.

  C) The defendant wife Eliza, who was an NCAA volleyball player, married her physically inactive math teacher, plaintiff Frank, who is 20 years older than she is, right after graduating from college six years ago. During any disagreement about rearing their two children (ages 2 and 4) she slaps him, punches him in the torso, kicks his shins, or twists his arm until he agrees with her. Frank does not respond in kind.

  D) Helen and Gene were married ten years and had three children; according to plaintiff Gene, the defendant wife Helen would "review" his sexual performance after they had sex, and give a rating based on movie ratings. She frequently rated his performance a "bomb," and never gave him more than one star. Helen admits to the actions, but says that she was "teasing." Gene says her behavior was unjustified because he did nothing to deserve such a low rating.

28. In July 1905, before no-fault divorce had been adopted by any U.S. jurisdiction, heiress Ginger Waltzer Bruce discovered that her husband, Harry Bruce, an impecunious geology professor, had married her only to get access to her millions. She wanted to divorce him, but had no evidence that he had committed any fault that would provide a basis for a divorce action against him. So she made an agreement with Harry: She went to a hotel accompanied by another man; the two dined and danced publicly with great shows of affection. At 1 a.m., they checked into a hotel room, registering under the names of Mr. and Mrs. Smith. Ginger and the man spent the evening playing checkers. The next morning, they ordered breakfast from room service. As they were eating, Ginger's husband Harry burst into the room, accompanied by the family attorney and a photographer, who photographed Ginger in a pink negligee sitting on the lap of the other man, feeding him grapefruit sections. The other man wore his pajamas. If Harry brought a divorce action on grounds of adultery, what would have been the most likely result?

A) Harry would have obtained a divorce judgment on the ground of adultery provided the court did not make a finding of collusion by Harry and Ginger.

B) Harry would not have obtained a divorce judgment on the ground of adultery because the photographs did not show sexual intercourse taking place.

C) Harry would not have obtained a divorce judgment on the ground of adultery because he had no eyewitnesses to sexual intercourse between Ginger and the other man.

D) Ginger could bring an action to divorce Harry on the basis of her adultery with the other man.

29. Use the same facts as in question 28, except that no agreement existed between Harry and Ginger. Instead, Ginger said to Harry when he confronted her in the hotel room, "I suppose that you'll divorce me now." Harry answered, "Not at all. I forgive you," and took no action to dissolve his marriage to Ginger. Ginger returned to the house she shared with Harry, and initially they resumed living as a married couple, including sexual relations. However, after a few months, Ginger refused to have sexual relations with Harry, despite his frequent requests. In 1907, Harry moved from the matrimonial domicile. In 1910, Ginger sued Harry for divorce on the ground of abandonment (also known as desertion) for more than three years, the period required by their state's statute. Harry countersued for a divorce from Ginger on the same ground. What would have been the most likely result?

A) Harry cannot obtain a divorce for abandonment because Ginger continued to live in the matrimonial domicile with him until he moved out.

B) Harry can obtain a divorce for abandonment because persistent refusal of one spouse to have sexual relations without a cause related to the health (physical or mental) of that spouse is considered behavior that forces the other spouse to leave the matrimonial abode, and thus constructive abandonment (also known as constructive desertion).

C) Harry can obtain a divorce on the grounds of adultery, using the photos of and witnesses to Ginger's night at the hotel with the other man in 1905.

D) The court will refuse on the basis family privacy concerns to consider the extent of the sexual relationship between husband and wife as a fault ground for divorce.

30. Use the facts of question 28, but not those of question 29, and these additional facts: Assume that shortly after the discovery of Ginger and the other man in the hotel, Harry brought an action for divorce against Ginger on grounds of adultery. He introduced the evidence of witnesses to Ginger and the other man's actions. Ginger testified on the stand to her adultery with the other man. The court, however, refused to grant the divorce to Harry. Harry appealed the judgment. Which of the following would be the most likely result?

A) The appellate court would reverse the trial court's decision and remand because of its manifest error; by 1905 social standards, the overwhelming evidence would have supported a finding in Harry's favor.

B) The appellate court would affirm the trial court's decision because the social consequences of being divorced for adultery were much more severe for a woman than for a man in 1905.

C) The appellate court would reverse the trial court's decision because Ginger had confessed to adultery on the stand, contrary to her own interest.

D) The appellate court would uphold the trial court's decision if it was based on a sua sponte determination that the evidence for adultery had been fabricated to obtain a divorce by means of a fraud on the court; deference would be given to the trial court in its findings of fact, as it could evaluate the credibility of the witnesses.

31. Use the facts of question 28 above, but not those of questions 29 and 30 above, and these additional facts: Assume that Ginger said to Harry when he confronted her in the hotel room, "I suppose that you'll divorce me now." Harry answered, "Not at all. I forgive you," and took no action to dissolve his marriage to Ginger. Instead of returning to live with Harry, Ginger moved out of the matrimonial domicile into a house of her own in the same year, 1905. In 1908, the legislature of the state where Harry and Ginger both were domiciled passed a statute creating a cause of action for divorce for a spouse who has been living separate and apart from the other spouse for seven or more years. In 1912, seven years and one day after she moved from the house she shared with Harry, Ginger filed an action for divorce on grounds of living separate and apart. Harry contested the divorce, arguing that allowing Ginger to use the separate and apart ground would be an unconstitutional impairment of their contract of marriage by a state's statute. At the time of his and Ginger's marriage, that contract could only be terminated on the fault grounds in the state's divorce statute, and he had not committed any of the faults. What is the likely result of Ginger's action?

A) Ginger's action would be dismissed, and the court would rule, on the basis of the U.S. Constitution, that the new ground for divorce was only available to couples who married after the "separate and apart" statute's effective date in 1908.

B) Ginger's action would be dismissed because she and Harry had not lived separate and apart for seven years after the passage of the statute creating that ground for divorce.

C) Ginger would obtain a judgment of divorce on the basis of living separate and apart from Harry for seven years.

D) Harry would not be able to obtain an alimony award in these circumstances because Ginger received a divorce judgment against him.

32. In the late nineteenth century, Rochester met Bertha, a cousin of a college friend, while he was vacationing in Barbados. After a whirlwind courtship, he brought her home to his mansion in Rhode Island. Bertha's behavior was erratic; occasionally she would yell at Rochester and physically assault him. As time passed, the behavior manifested itself more often; after two years of marriage, it was clear that she was severely mentally ill with what today would be called paranoid schizophrenia. Rochester set up an apartment for her in the mansion where she could live luxuriously, but in isolation because of her dangerous actions. He visited her every evening. She has punched Rochester, attempted to strangle him, and finally set his house on fire with him in it, injuring him severely. If Rochester filed for divorce, and the state's divorce provisions were typical of the era, what result would be most likely?

A) Rochester could not secure a divorce from Bertha because insanity constituted a defense to fault.

B) Rochester could secure a divorce from Bertha on the ground of cruelty.

C) Rochester could secure a divorce from Bertha on the ground of constructive abandonment.

D) Rochester could secure an annulment of the marriage for error as to the person.

33. Andrew and Barbara married in 1997. They agreed in writing prior to marrying to have an "open marriage" in which sexual activities with other partners by either spouse would be acceptable within the marriage. One afternoon, Andrew came home early to discover Barbara having sexual intercourse with their next-door neighbor, Carl. In a common law fault-based system, which of the latter is most likely to be true?

A) Andrew could divorce Barbara for adultery.

B) Andrew could not divorce Barbara for adultery because to do so would breach their prenuptial contract to accept sexual activities of the spouse with other partners.

C) Andrew could divorce Barbara for adultery because their prenuptial agreement is a nullity.

D) Andrew could not divorce Barbara for adultery if she presented the common law defense of connivance.

34. Alice sues her husband Bob for divorce on the ground of adultery under a fault-based system that maintains the common law defenses to a divorce action. Bob defends the action by alleging that Alice had committed habitual drunkenness, a fault ground under the state statute. He counterclaims for divorce on that basis. Alice defends by pointing to Bob's adultery. If each spouse is proven to have committed a fault, which of the following is **least** likely to be the result?

    A) The court could deny a divorce to Alice on the basis of the defense of recrimination.

    B) The court could grant the divorce to Alice because although she committed the fault of habitual drunkenness, Bob's fault of adultery has comparative greater weight and thus his defense of recrimination would fail.

    C) The court could grant the divorce to Bob because Alice's fault of habitual drunkenness has comparatively greater weight and thus her defense of recrimination would fail.

    D) The court could dismiss both parties' divorce actions because they have come to court with "unclean hands."

35. Which of the following is **not** a characteristic of the grounds for divorce under modern no-fault divorce statutes in the United States?

    A) The ground for the divorce is not the fault of either party, but the court's determination that the marriage has irretrievably broken down (sometimes characterized as "irreconcilable differences" between the spouses).

    B) The grounds permit the court to grant a divorce if it determines that there is no reasonable prospect of reconciliation of the spouses.

    C) The traditional defenses to a divorce action are inapplicable to no-fault grounds because they attempt either to excuse the conduct of the spouse accused of a fault, or to ameliorate his or her guilt because of the other spouse's actions.

    D) The divorce cannot be granted if one of the parties makes a credible argument that reconciliation is possible.

36. For a state to grant a divorce that must be recognized under the Full Faith and Credit clause of the U.S. Constitution, which of the following is required?

    A) Both spouses must be domiciled in the state that grants the divorce.

    B) At least one of the spouses must be domiciled in the state that grants the divorce.

    C) The state that grants the divorce must be the state of the spouse's most recent matrimonial domicile.

D) The state that grants the divorce must be the state with the greatest relationship to the couple and the marriage.

37. Phillip, owner of an import–export company, is married to Ellen in North Carolina. He has been having an affair with Mary, who is now pregnant with his child. Phillip wants to divorce Ellen to marry Mary so that the child is born within the parents' marriage. However, the type of divorce he would qualify for under North Carolina law would require at least a year to complete. Having heard that Nevada permits a person to obtain domicile there in six weeks, and has a six-week no-fault divorce process, Phillip travels there and rents a hotel room for seven weeks. He brings with him only the clothing and other items that he would need for that period. He continues to work at his import–export business, using the hotel's business center, his room's telephone, and its Internet access with his own laptop computer. He makes no changes in his mailing address, voter registration, or driver's license. He does not move his bank account from North Carolina, but uses an ATM in the hotel lobby for cash. Once six weeks have passed, he files for a Nevada no-fault divorce and sends the divorce summons and petition to Ellen back in North Carolina. She does not answer or appear. As soon as the divorce is granted, Phillip returns to North Carolina and moves in with Mary, who is planning their wedding. Ellen files for a North Carolina divorce from Phillip on the fault ground of adultery. Which of the following would justify a ruling by the North Carolina court that Phillip's Nevada divorce is void, and thus not entitled to full faith and credit?

A) The Nevada divorce was granted ex parte.

B) Phillip's actions in Nevada are insufficient to establish domicile because they do not evince the intent required for domicile: to remain a resident of Nevada indefinitely or permanently.

C) Because Phillip's matrimonial domicile was North Carolina, that state has exclusive jurisdiction over his and Ellen's divorce.

D) Phillip's Nevada divorce is void because divorcing Ellen without her participation is a denial of due process rights under the U.S. Constitution.

38. Derrica Isla is a Caribbean nation that requires only a one-day separation of the parties to a marriage for a no-fault divorce, whether it is unilateral or bilateral. It also requires only 24 hours of residence in Derrica by either spouse for its courts to have jurisdiction over a divorce, whether ex parte or not. Victor wishes to divorce his current wife, Diane, to marry Nikki. He flies to Derrica. After Victor has been present on the island for 24 hours, he appears in court through local counsel and receives a divorce judgment. Will Victor's divorce be recognized by U.S. states as valid, so that he and Nikki can validly marry?

A) The divorce will be recognized in the United States because the Full Faith and Credit clause of the U.S. Constitution mandates recognition of foreign divorces that are valid in the country that issued them.

B) The divorce will be recognized by U.S. states under the principle of comity (deference to the judgments of a foreign country based on mutual respect) because it comports generally with U.S. standards of due process and substantive fairness.

C) The divorce will not be recognized by most U.S. states because the one-day residency requirement for subject matter jurisdiction over divorce by the courts of Derrica Isla is insufficient to fulfill the domicile requirement needed to satisfy due process demands under U.S. standards.

D) The divorce will not be recognized by most U.S. states because only the federal government has the power under the U.S. Constitution to recognize a divorce judgment from another sovereign nation's court.

39. As soon as Victor returned to the United States from Derrica Isla, he told Nikki that he had divorced Diane and was free to marry. Victor and Nikki married immediately. After eight months of marriage, Victor became dissatisfied and sued for an annulment on the basis that his marriage was bigamous: At the time he married Nikki, he was still married to Diane. In most U.S. jurisdictions, would Victor be granted an annulment?

A) Victor would not be granted an annulment because he has come to court with unclean hands, having benefited from the divorce he claims is invalid.

B) Victor would not be granted an annulment because he is estopped from doing so by obtaining a divorce decree invalid on the basis of jurisdiction and causing Nikki to rely on it.

C) Victor would be granted an annulment because his divorce was void for lack of subject matter jurisdiction; he therefore committed bigamy, which makes his marriage void ab initio.

D) Both A and B.

40. Which of the following statements articulates the doctrine of divisible divorce in migratory divorce actions?

A) In an ex parte divorce action against an absent spouse, the court can divide the marital property and determine spousal support.

B) Under the Fourteenth Amendment's Due Process Clause, the issues of marital property division and the award of spousal support must be divided from an ex parte divorce for adjudication because these economic incidents are property rights that require personal jurisdiction, based on minimum contacts with the state, over both parties to a divorce.

C) A divorce cannot be awarded against an absent spouse if issues of property division and spousal support remain unresolved.

D) Divorce jurisdiction is divided into that for no-fault divorces, which can take place ex parte, and for fault-based divorces, which require the presence of both parties.

41. Which of the following is **not** true of court awards of alimony (also known as maintenance and spousal support) on dissolution of the marriage?

A) An ex-spouse whose fault was the basis for the divorce cannot be awarded alimony because to do so would reward that party's destruction of the marriage.

B) An ex-spouse whose fault was the basis for the divorce can be awarded alimony regardless of his or her fault in all but a very few states because most states have adopted the theory that many elements are at work in the breakdown of a marriage.

C) An ex-spouse whose fault was the basis for the divorce can be awarded alimony if he or she can demonstrate that the other spouse was equally at fault.

D) An ex-spouse whose fault was the basis for the divorce cannot be awarded alimony in most states because most states have abolished alimony as based on gender discrimination.

42. Brenda, a former cashier in a supermarket, and Larry, the manager of a big-box store, had dropped out of high school to marry 15 years ago. Larry has brought a no-fault divorce action against Brenda. He wants a divorce because Brenda has developed an incurable neurological disease that partially paralyzed her face. As a result of paralysis of her lips, her speech is slurred and often difficult to understand. She drools continually, and has to wipe her mouth and chin with a handkerchief every few minutes. She had to quit her job because of this impairment. Larry does not want to live with her anymore. The two do not own enough property for Brenda to support herself for more than six months on her share, so she has requested permanent periodic alimony. Larry opposes any alimony for Brenda, arguing that she can support herself. He points out Brenda is only 33 years old, and, although not highly skilled, could get a job someplace like the Quik-Stop gas station and food store a block from their former apartment, which is always advertising for clerks. She has her share of the marital property to live on until then. He also points out that doctors develop cures for formerly incurable diseases every year; hers might be next, and she'd be able to get an even better job. How is the court most likely to rule?

A) The court is most likely to rule that Brenda must liquidate her share of the marital estate and exhaust it before she can receive an award of alimony.

B) The court is most likely to rule that Brenda is entitled to permanent periodic alimony because the effects of her disease make it extremely unlikely that a business will hire her for any position for which she has the skills; if her health situation changes, Larry can move for a modification of the original order.

C) The court is most likely to rule that Brenda is entitled to rehabilitative alimony for 12 months; if shortly before the end of that time, Brenda has still not found a job that pays well enough for her to live on its wages, she can move for a modification of the original order.

D) Either A or B.

43. George, a successful dental surgeon in his early 40s, had been making $250,000 a year fixing the smiles of the rich and famous. He and his former wife Allison, to whom he was married for 18 years, divorced two years ago, when George began talking about living up to their religion by reducing their standard of living. Because their state sets alimony in accordance with the standard of living prior to the divorce, George has been paying court-ordered alimony of $3,000 per month to her to supplement what she earns as a primary school reading specialist, which is $22,000 a year. He has sold his practice to volunteer with Dentists Without Borders, a nonprofit organization that sends dentists to impoverished areas of the world. George has performed cleft palate surgery on dozens of children with great success. However, his income from his investments is now around $40,000 a year. He has moved for a reduction in his alimony payments to Allison, alleging as a change in circumstances the reduction in his income. Which of the following is **unlikely** to play a part in the court's decision of the case?

A) The court will evaluate whether George's career change was made in good faith; lack of good faith might, depending on the jurisdiction, prevent the court from granting any reduction.

B) If the court finds that the benefits to George of participating in Dentists Without Borders do not outweigh the burdens to Allison of a reduction in the alimony she receives, it will deny him a reduction in alimony regardless of the answer to the question of his good faith.

C) The court will refuse to consider benefits and burdens that are not financial in nature in determining whether a reduction is warranted.

D) If the court determines that a reduction in alimony is warranted, it can recalculate George's alimony obligation on the basis of his current level of income.

44. Anna and Bob obtained a no-fault divorce after seven years of marriage because Bob revealed to Anna that he is gay. The court has ordered Anna to pay alimony to Bob. The courts of their state have long held that the obligation

to pay court-ordered alimony ceases on the death of either the payor or the recipient, and on the remarriage of the recipient. Anna has discovered that Bob is now cohabiting with Carl. The jurisdiction does not permit or recognize same-sex marriage. She has asked her attorney whether a court would terminate her alimony payments to Bob under these circumstances. The issue is de novo in the jurisdiction. What would her attorney respond?

A) A court would terminate Anna's alimony payments because she should not be forced to support the lifestyle that destroyed her marriage.

B) Anna's alimony payments will be terminated because Bob and Carl are in a de facto marital relationship; therefore the underlying rationale for termination on remarriage applies to Bob and Carl's cohabitation as well.

C) Anna's alimony payments will not be terminated because as Bob and Carl are not married, they have not taken on the mutual support obligation that would replace Anna's obligation to Bob.

D) Either B or C.

45. Which of the following is **not** a difference that distinguishes the community property system of marital property from that used in noncommunity property states?

A) Under a community property regime, each spouse has, from the moment it is acquired, an undivided half-interest in property acquired during the marriage that is classified as community, whereas ownership follows title during the marriage in other states.

B) Under a community property regime, the community is terminated by divorce, whereas in other states, the marital estate only comes into existence on divorce.

C) Under a community property regime, no property acquired during the marriage is exempted from the community that is subject to division on divorce; under the system of noncommunity property states, property acquired during marriage by gift or inheritance is considered to be separate property.

D) Under a community property regime, the property is subject to division if the termination of community occurs through death as well as through divorce; under the system in noncommunity property states, the property acquired during the marriage is divided between the spouses at divorce, but if the dissolution of the marriage occurs through death of a spouse, title governs ownership.

46. Zelda and Yves were married in a state that utilizes an equitable distribution system for property division on divorce. Zelda had purchased a house for $70,000 20 years prior to their marriage, and had already paid off the mortgage loan she had taken out before the marriage took place. The couple made that

house their home during the five years of their marriage. At the time of their divorce, it was worth $150,000 owing to market forces. Three years after they married, Yves's father died, leaving him $150,000 worth of oil company stock, as well as interest-paying bonds. Yves and Zelda used $10,000 of the interest to buy antiques to furnish the house. The rising price of gasoline has caused the value of the stock to rise to $200,000. Which of the following would be true in most equitable distribution jurisdictions?

A) Because Zelda and Yves used the house that Zelda had purchased prior to marriage as their matrimonial domicile, it is no longer separate property, and will be included in the distribution of the marital property.

B) Although Yves received the stocks and bonds from his father's estate during the marriage, they are separate property that is excluded from the equitable distribution of marital property because they were acquired by inheritance from a third party.

C) The antiques purchased with the $10,000 earned by the bonds belong to Yves because the funds used to purchase them can be traced directly to Yves's separate property.

D) Both B and C.

47. Assume that, during the marriage, Zelda and Yves were both wage earners. Zelda earned $60,000 per year as an accounts manager, and Yves earned $90,000 per year as an accountant. They acquired the following in the course of the marriage: (1) A joint bank account containing $12,000; (2) certificates of deposit titled in Zelda's name worth $60,000; (3) a Peugeot automobile titled in Yves's name currently valued at $24,000; (4) a Chevrolet Malibu titled in Zelda's name currently valued at $15,000; (5) personal property stored in their home, currently valued at $45,000. What principle is most likely to provide the starting point for the trial court in dividing the property?

A) The trial court will begin with the presumption that all property that is classified as marital is to be divided equally between the parties.

B) The trial court will begin with the presumption that property titled in the name of one party is to be awarded to that party, and that property titled in both names is to be divided equally between the parties.

C) The trial court will begin with the presumption that the property is to be divided in accordance with the relative monetary contribution of each party to the support of the marital household; thus, Yves should receive one and one-half times the property that Zelda receives.

D) The trial court will begin with the presumption that the economically weaker party is to receive a larger share of the marital property.

48. Which of the following is **not** considered marital property subject to division in most U.S. jurisdictions?

A) Professional degrees or licenses earned during the marriage.

B) The enhancement of one spouse's earning capacity during the marriage that is derived from his rights of personality, and to which the other spouse contributed.

C) Intellectual property rights acquired from work performed during the marriage.

D) Enterprise goodwill; that is, the goodwill of a business that does not depend on any particular owner.

49. Paula and Tom have been married for 20 years; Paula has been a traditional homemaker and caregiver to their children, while Tom pursued his career at a major oil company. Tom and Paula are getting a divorce. Along with their other assets, Tom has a vested pension at the oil company. He cannot access it until he retires. He is at least 15 years from retirement. Paula asks for a division of the vested pension benefits and distribution of a share to her. What would the court determine concerning whether and how the vested pension benefits would be divided?

A) Vested pension benefits will be distributed to Paula in proportion to the number of years worked at the business during their marriage in relation to total years worked.

B) The pension benefits should not be treated as marital assets because it is not known whether or not Tom will receive them.

C) The pension benefits should be equally divided between the two spouses.

D) Because Paula has not been paid for her duties of homemaker and child caregiver, she should receive a larger share of the pension benefits.

50. Sandra and Ted were married in Arkansas in 1986. Sandra was a highly successful country-western singer. In 2009, Sandra moved to Las Vegas, Nevada, and divorced Ted. Ted, who has continued to live in Arkansas, has filed suit in federal court in Nevada for alimony in the amount of $10,000 per month; he maintains that Sandra's monthly income is over $80,000. The federal district court dismissed the suit for lack of jurisdiction. Ted has appealed; how should the federal appeals court rule?

A) The federal Court of Appeals should reverse the district court's decision and remand for a trial on the merits because the requirements for diversity jurisdiction — diversity of citizenship of the parties and an amount in controversy in excess of $100,000 — have been met.

B) The federal Court of Appeals should affirm the district court's decision because a claim by an ex-spouse for an award of alimony falls under the judicially created "domestic relations exception" to federal diversity jurisdiction.

C) The federal Court of Appeals should reverse the district court's decision because the judicially created "domestic relations exception" to federal diversity jurisdictions applies only to actions directly related to the marital status (e.g., divorce, nullity of marriage) and child custody orders.

D) The federal Court of Appeals should affirm the district court's decision because domestic relations cases have been expressly excluded from federal jurisdiction by statute since the Judiciary Act of 1789.

51. Mindy, a young widow, met and married Nathan in Plano, Texas in 1999. She and her son from her earlier marriage, Josh, moved into Nathan's home in Plano. Josh was 2 years old when the marriage took place. From the beginning, the marriage was stormy. Mindy and Josh left Nathan in 2008, when after a six-hour argument in which the couple screamed at one another and threw crockery and furniture, their neighbors called the police, who at Mindy's request escorted Mindy and Josh to a hotel. Mindy has divorced Nathan and moved to Oklahoma. As Josh's custodian, she is suing Nathan on Josh's behalf in tort for the intentional infliction of mental and emotional harm during the violent argument. Josh has suffered from post-traumatic stress disorder since the episode. She brought the suit in federal court in Texas, asking for $1 million in damages. The trial court dismissed the case for lack of jurisdiction, citing the domestic relations exception. Mindy has appealed. How should the federal Court of Appeals rule?

A) The federal Court of Appeals should reverse the federal district court and remand the case because it is not within the narrow limits of the exception; it is a tort case that could arise between any two parties.

B) The federal Court of Appeals should affirm the federal district court because the tort arose out of the marriage of Mindy and Nathan and her custody of Josh; Josh's welfare is a matter of state expertise and state jurisdiction.

C) The federal Court of Appeals should reverse the trial court and remand the case because although Mindy was married to Nathan, Josh is unrelated to him; the domestic relations exception applies only between husband and wife and blood relatives.

D) None of the above.

52. In 1890, Mary, an upper-middle-class unmarried woman living in a common law jurisdiction, became pregnant by Derek, who was also unmarried but refused to marry her. She gave birth to a son she named Andrew. Which of the following rights were available to Andrew?

A) Andrew would be an heir in intestacy on Mary's death.

B) Andrew would be an heir in intestacy on Derek's death.

C) If Mary predeceased her parents, Andrew could represent Mary (i.e., inherit through her) as an heir in their intestate successions.

D) None of the above.

53. "Lord Mansfield's Rule" is one among a number of rules of evidence that the English courts used in actions to identify the legal father of a child born to a married mother prior to the discovery and use of DNA. These rules favored finding the husband to be the father and therefore the child to be "legitimate." Which of the following states "Lord Mansfield's Rule," which was used in both English and U.S. courts in paternity adjudications?

A) The husband of the mother was presumed to be the father of a child born to his wife during the existence of their marriage or within 280 days of its dissolution by his death.

B) The presumption of the husband's paternity could only be defeated by proof of his inability to reproduce or of his lack of access to his wife during the time period when the child was conceived.

C) Both the husband and the wife were prohibited from testifying that the husband did not have access to the wife during the time period when the child was conceived.

D) If the husband succeeded in disavowing the child born within the marriage, the common law treated him as illegitimate.

54. Teresa and Seth have been cohabiting without marrying for five years. After their first year together, Teresa gave birth to a child, Ursula. Seth signed as Ursula's father on her birth certificate, and he and Teresa have consistently acted, in private and public, as though he were the child's father. This year, Gerald showed up at their home; he is Teresa's husband, whom she had married eight years earlier. She left him a year after they married and has not seen him since. Unknown to Seth, Teresa and Gerald were never divorced. When he was unsuccessful in persuading Teresa to return to him, Gerald filed suit for joint custody with Teresa of Ursula. He argued that he is presumptively Ursula's legal father under the common law principle that the husband of the mother is presumed to be the father of a child born during the existence of the marriage. The trial court ruled that under the common law presumption, Gerald is irrebuttably presumed to be Ursula's father, and refused to admit Teresa and Seth's DNA evidence of Seth's biological paternity. The court ordered joint custody of Ursula in Teresa and Gerald. Teresa and Seth have appealed. How is the appellate court most likely to rule?

A) The majority of the states now have legislation or case law permitting rebuttal of the marital presumption, such as the Uniform Parentage Act (UPA), so the appellate court is most likely to reverse and remand for a trial on the evidence submitted by Seth that he is the father of Ursula.

B) The appellate court is most likely to reverse and dismiss Gerald's claim because, by residing with Ursula for the first two years of the child's life and holding himself out as her father, Seth has established a parent–child relationship with her, and is now presumed to be her father under the UPA sec. 204.

C) The appellate court is most likely to affirm the trial court's decision because in most states, the time limit on a contest paternity under the marital presumption is two years; it is too late for Seth to challenge Gerald's paternity of Ursula.

D) The appellate court is most likely to affirm the trial court's decision because, when two men both have presumptions of paternity of a child in their favor, the policy of favoring marital families requires that the marital presumption prevail.

55. Harry and Wanda, a married couple, wanted to have children but had been unable to conceive a child during their five years of marriage because of Harry's low sperm count. They sought help at a fertility specialist's clinic. With Harry's written consent, using an anonymous sperm donor's semen, Wanda was impregnated by means of in vitro fertilization. During Wanda's first trimester, tensions developed between the couple and they separated. Harry filed for a no-fault divorce from Wanda, and because Wanda consented to the divorce, obtained it three months prior to the child's birth. Once the child is born, Wanda sues Harry for child support. Harry maintains that because he and Wanda divorced before the child was born, he is not the child's father. Assume that the jurisdiction's assisted conception statute contains the types of provisions most prevalent in U.S. jurisdictions. How should the court rule?

A) Wanda's request for child support should be denied because she consented to ending the marriage to Harry before the child was born.

B) Wanda's request for child support should be denied because Harry's suit for divorce impliedly revoked his consent to be the father of her child.

C) Wanda's request for child support should be granted because most states' assisted reproduction statutes provide that the husband who consents to his wife's artificial insemination with donated sperm is the father of the child, and Harry was Wanda's husband at the time of his consent.

D) Wanda's request for child support should be denied because she chose to carry the child to term despite the divorce from Harry.

56. Registered same-sex domestic partners Mia and Olive wanted to have a child; Mia was to be the birth mother. Under the supervision of an obstetrician specializing in reproductive technology, Mia was artificially inseminated. Rather than using an anonymous sperm donor, Mia and Olive got the consent of Olive's closest male relative, her cousin Jason, to use sperm that he donated, waiving, as the state assisted reproduction statute required of sperm donors, his

parental rights. Mia conceived using Jason's sperm and gave birth to a son, Tom. Jason saw the child once, at his christening. When Tom was 3 years old, Jason decided that he wanted to have a paternal relationship with the child. Mia and Olive refused. Jason has sued for joint custody with Mia and, in the alternative, visitation. Mia and Olive have asked to be recognized as Tom's only parents. The trial court granted Jason's request for joint custody. Mia and Olive have appealed. If the jurisdiction's assisted reproduction statute contains the types of provisions most prevalent in U.S. jurisdictions, how should the appellate court rule?

A) The appellate court should affirm the trial court's award of joint custody to Mia and Jason because it is in Tom's best interest to have a father.

B) The appellate court should reverse the trial court's ruling and dismiss the case because assisted reproduction statutes typically provide that a non-spousal donor of semen has neither parental rights nor parental obligations, such as child support, with regard to a child conceived by the donee.

C) The appellate court should affirm the trial court's judgment because the typical state assisted reproduction statute's provision that a nonspousal donor of semen has neither parental rights nor parental obligations violates Jason's fundamental right to the care, custody, and control of his child, and is therefore unconstitutional.

D) The appellate court should reverse the trial court's findings and dismiss the case because an unmarried biological father has no parental rights to custody or visitation with his biological child, who is legally the child of no one.

57. Assume the same facts in question 56. When Tom was 7 years old, Olive and Mia separated; Tom remained with Mia. Mia originally allowed Olive to keep Tom at her apartment overnight and to visit him at Mia's house. Owing to disputes with Olive about Tom's care, Mia ended the contact between Tom and Olive. Olive has sued to be recognized as Tom's parent, and thus as having standing to request custody, visitation, or both. She argues that the state's assisted reproduction statute establishes the husband of the mother as the legal parent of her child born by artificial insemination, and that as the registered domestic partner of Mia at the time of Tom's conception and birth, and his joint caretaker for seven years, she was entitled to the same recognition. Which of the following positions has a state court taken on recognizing parental rights and responsibilities in two parents of the same sex?

A) An assisted reproduction statute that recognizes a man as legal father of a child to whom he has no biological relationship because he consented to his wife's artificial insemination that produced the child, but does not recognize a mother's consenting registered same-sex partner as a legal parent in the same circumstances, violates state constitutional protections against discrimination based on sexual orientation; the status of parent must be extended to both.

B) In accordance with the Uniform Parentage Act, a child may have two parents of the same sex if the nonbiological parent consented to the artificial insemination of the birth mother and informally acknowledged the children as her own.

C) The former same-sex partner who developed a relationship with her partner's child has no standing to request parental rights such as custody and visitation after separation from the natural parent unless an act of the legislature extends such rights to former partners in that situation.

D) All of the above.

58. Annette wanted to have a child, but knew that it was medically impossible for her to carry a child to term. She contracted with Barbara, who agreed to serve as a "gestational surrogate"; that is, to carry an embryo formed from Annette's egg to term, and surrender the child to Annette when it was born. Annette's egg was fertilized in vitro by sperm from her husband, Rolf; then the embryo was transplanted into Barbara's womb. All went well until Barbara gave birth to the child. She has refused to surrender the child to Annette and Rolf. They have sued to enforce the gestational surrogacy agreement, and to have Annette named as the child's mother on his birth certificate. How is the court most likely to rule?

A) The court will enforce the gestational surrogacy agreement if it meets the requirement of a valid contract without further analysis.

B) The court will find Barbara to be the mother of the child by analogy to children born through egg donation; in those situations, the woman who gives birth to a child using the egg of another woman is considered to be the natural mother of the child.

C) The court will find Annette to be the mother of the child because, although either she or Barbara could be recognized as mother of the child, the surrogacy agreement shows that Annette intended to procreate and raise a child; this intention entitles her to be recognized as the child's mother.

D) The court will recognize Annette as the mother of the child because the child has her genetic makeup rather than Barbara's.

59. Which of the following is **unlikely** to be a factor used by a court in making an initial child custody decision between the parents on the basis of the best interests of the child?

A) The emotional ties of love and affection between each party and the child.

B) The willingness of each party to encourage and facilitate a close and continuing relationship with the other party.

C) The responsibility for care and rearing previously exercised by each party between each party and the child.

D) The financial resources available to each party to provide for the child's material needs.

60. Every state permits the parents of children of divorce to seek modification of a court's judgment determining child custody, even though any subsequent judgment would be based on litigation of the same issue (child custody) by the same parties. Given the principle of res judicata, what is the explanation given in almost every state for allowing a party to an earlier child custody case to bring a modification action?

A) It is a violation of res judicata for them to do so, but that principle is trumped by the state's parens patriae duty to protect children living within its borders.

B) Because it would be a violation of res judicata for the same parties to relitigate the same issue on the same facts seeking a different ruling, child custody modification cases can only be heard if a party alleges that the facts leading to the original judgment have changed since it was handed down.

C) Because it would be a violation of res judicata for the same parties to relitigate the same issue on the same facts seeking a different ruling, parties to the original child custody litigation are considered to waive that principle by implication in bringing the original action by which the court determined placement of the child.

D) None of the above.

61. Alberto, a Hispanic-American, and Beatrice, an American of English descent, were married in 2002. They are now getting a no-fault divorce. Each has asked for sole custody of their son, Carlos, who is 6 years old. The judge found that sole custody in Alberto was in the child's best interest, while granting visitation to Beatrice. In his reasons, the judge stated that in Alberto's custody Carlos would experience greater stability. He would continue to be in the care of Alberto's parents after school, as he was at present, to which Beatrice has objected. The judge stated Carlos would continue to attend his present bilingual school, which also provided a great educational advantage for the future; Beatrice objects to his attending the bilingual school. The judge added that Carlos would be more comfortable living in his father's Hispanic community because he "looks and sounds Hispanic." Beatrice has appealed. Should the judge's custody order be affirmed?

A) The judge's order should be affirmed because although he considered race as a factor, it was not his sole or decisive consideration in determining child custody.

B) The judge's order should be reversed because in making it, he considered racial resemblances (appearance and language) between the child and his father; any use of race as a factor in awarding custody violates equal protection.

C) The judge's order should be affirmed because placing Carlos in his mother's sole custody could confuse him as to his gender identity.

D) The judge's order should not be affirmed because for a child of tender years, there is a strong preference for maternal custody.

62. Assume that the trial court's determination in question 61 was upheld on appeal, and Alberto has sole custody of Carlos. Beatrice, not having custody, has been awarded "reasonable visitation" with Carlos. It is overnight visitation, scheduled every other weekend, alternating holidays, and four weeks during the summer; in addition, she has Carlos one evening during the week from 4 p.m. until 8 p.m. For the purposes of this question only, assume that on several occasions, Carlos has complained to his father that Beatrice didn't do anything but sleep during his visit, not getting dinner until he woke her and reminded her to do so. Alberto had noticed that Beatrice was losing weight, and asked her about her health; she told him that her doctor had diagnosed her with major depression, and none of the medications he prescribed for her have worked. Beatrice also told Alberto in front of Carlos that life doesn't seem worth living without Carlos with her. A few days later, Beatrice attempted suicide by taking an overdose of her prescription medication. Although she is recovering, Alberto is concerned that her continued visitation with Carlos might result in harm to his son. What should Alberto do?

A) Alberto should ask the court to restrict Beatrice's time with Carlos to supervised visitation, so that it only occurs when either he, one of Beatrice's family members or friends, or a professional child welfare worker is present.

B) Alberto should ask the court to terminate Beatrice's visitation with Carlos because it could seriously endanger Carlos's physical, mental, or emotional health for him to be exposed to her depression and suicidal thoughts.

C) Alberto should ask the court to terminate Beatrice's parental rights on the basis that she is an unfit mother to eliminate Beatrice's constitutional right to contact with Carlos.

D) Alberto should ask the court to suspend Beatrice's visitation until she demonstrates that she is no longer mentally ill.

63. Assume that the trial court's decision in question 61 was upheld on appeal, and Alberto has sole custody of Carlos, but that the events in question 62 did not occur. Two months after Alberto received the favorable judgment from the Court of Appeals, Beatrice petitions the trial court for a modification of the

original order; she requests sole custody of Carlos. She complains that Alberto was over a half-hour late delivering Carlos to her for two of her visitations. On another visit, Carlos arrived with a bruise and a cut on his cheek; he'd fallen at school the day before, and Alberto hadn't taken him to a doctor. Carlos has said on each visit that he misses her. She claims that the present custody is dangerous to Carlos's physical and emotional health and safety, and that Alberto is attempting to interfere with her visitation by delivering Carlos late. Alberto opposes modification. If the underlying facts prove true, how is the court likely to rule?

A) The court will likely rule in favor of Beatrice because Alberto's neglect of Carlos's injury and of his duty to provide Beatrice with scheduled visitation, along with Carlos's desire to be with his mother, indicate that Alberto's sole custody is not in the best interest of the child.

B) The court will likely rule in favor of Alberto because the facts that Beatrice recounts do not prove the existence of a substantial change in circumstances that make the present custody order no longer in the child's best interest.

C) The court will likely rule in favor of Alberto because the facts that Beatrice recounts do not prove the existence of a substantial change in circumstances, and that the benefits of transferring custody to Beatrice would outweigh the negative effect of it on providing a stable environment for Carlos.

D) Either B or C.

64. Assume that Alberto has had sole custody of Carlos for a year. Alberto has a sexual relationship with a woman named Sandi; they began it six months ago. Two months ago, she moved into Alberto and Carlos's home. Beatrice has learned from conversations with Carlos that Sandi shares Alberto's bedroom, and that the couple regularly engages in romantic gestures such as hugging, kissing, and sitting with their arms around each other in front of Carlos. Beatrice considers the romantic behavior by an unmarried couple in front of a 6-year-old, when combined with the shared bedroom, to be inappropriate. She has petitioned for a change of custody to sole custody in herself, with liberal visitation by Alberto, including overnight stays provided Sandi doesn't stay overnight at the same time. Alberto opposes her petition and wants to maintain the current custody arrangement. How might the court rule?

A) Custody will be modified to sole custody in Beatrice with the conditions she has requested because Alberto's nonmarital sexual relationship, including shows of affection, is a substantial change in circumstances that meets either standard for modification of a custody order. These facts indicate that he is unfit to provide guidance in moral and social norms to a child.

B) The court will deny Beatrice's request despite the substantial change in circumstances because the facts don't indicate any negative effects of Sandi's presence on Carlos.

C) Either A or B.

D) None of the above.

65. Assume that, instead of the situation described in question 64, Beatrice learns from Carlos's teacher that Alberto is in a relationship with a man named Felix. Although Felix has not moved into Alberto's home, Carlos told the teacher that Felix is a frequent visitor, usually eating dinner with Alberto and Carlos. He often spends the night. Carlos also had told her that his dad and Felix say that Felix sleeps on the couch, but when Carlos gets up in the night, Felix isn't on the couch. Carlos also said that he has seen Felix coming out of Alberto's bedroom in the morning. Beatrice asked Alberto to end Felix's visits but Alberto has refused. Beatrice now has petitioned for a modification to sole custody in herself, with liberal visitation for Alberto, including overnight stays, provided Felix doesn't stay overnight at the same time. Alberto opposes her petition and wants to maintain the current custody arrangement. How might the court rule?

A) Custody will be modified to sole custody in Beatrice with the conditions she has requested because Alberto's nonmarital sexual relationship meets the threshold for modification, a substantial change in circumstances, and either standard for granting a modification; these facts indicate his failure to provide guidance in moral and social norms to his child.

B) The court will deny Beatrice's request despite the substantial change in circumstances because the facts don't indicate any negative effects on Carlos of Felix's presence.

C) Custody will be modified to sole custody in Beatrice with the conditions she has requested imposed on Alberto's visitation because his nonmarital sexual relationship meets the threshold for a court to consider modification of a custody order, and Carlos's question and observations to his teacher indicate either standard for modification will be met. His father's relationship is confusing him and causing him to be curious about matters inappropriate for a 6-year-old, and Alberto has placed his own desires over his son's development by refusing to exclude Felix from the home.

D) Any of the above.

66. Amy and Brad obtained a divorce; they sought, and received, joint legal custody of their 5-year-old daughter, Tammy, with Amy given residential (also known as primary physical or domiciliary) custody. The two lived in the same town, 20 minutes from one another. Brad has visitation with Tammy one entire week and one additional weekend a month, and for six weeks in the summer. Custody of Tammy was harmonious for two years. Amy has now remarried. Her new husband, Charlie, a building contractor, lost his business owing to the recession; after a long search he has found a job in another state, 500 miles from Amy's and Brad's current hometown. Amy wants to join him there with Tammy. She has filed a request with the proper court to modify the existing custody decree so that she and Tammy can relocate to live with Charlie. Brad opposes the request. What must Amy establish in most jurisdictions to succeed in her request?

A) Amy must establish that the relocation is for a legitimate purpose and is reasonable to achieve that purpose, and if Brad seeks to demonstrate that the relocation is not in the best interests of the child, must counter his demonstration.

B) Amy must establish that she has a good-faith reason for the move and that it will not interfere with the best interests of the child or prevent reasonable visitation by the child's father.

C) Amy must establish, on the basis of the court's full and detailed inquiry into the relevant facts and circumstances, that modification permitting her to move with Tammy is most likely to serve the best interests of the child.

D) The rules of the different states governing permission for interstate relocation of a custodial parent vary greatly, but usually include establishing the elements of a good-faith (or legitimate or reasonable) purpose, and serving the best interests of the child.

67. Della and Edward married when they were students at the University of California, Los Angeles, 13 years ago. Three years later they moved to New York. While in New York, they had two children: Frederick a year after moving there and Gail two years later. When Gail was 5, they decided to divorce. Without any further discussion with Edward, Della moved back to California with the children. There she filed an action for divorce and a custody action, requesting sole custody of Frederick and Gail. Edward filed a divorce action and a custody action requesting sole custody of the children in New York two weeks later. Which court has jurisdiction over the action for custody of Frederick and Gail?

A) California has jurisdiction over the child custody action because Della's suit was the first one filed; Edward's New York action will be dismissed on grounds of lis pendens because he lost the "race to the courthouse."

B) Under the Uniform Child Custody Jurisdiction Enforcement Act (hereafter UCCJEA), because the children lived in California with a parent on the date that the proceeding was commenced, California is their home state and thus has jurisdiction over the initial custody determination.

C) Under the UCCJEA, because the children lived in New York with a parent for at least six consecutive months prior to the date when the proceeding was commenced, it was the home state of the children; because a parent still lives in New York, and the children lived there within six months before the commencement of the proceeding, New York still has jurisdiction over the initial custody determination.

D) Under the UCCJEA, because one parent lives with the children in a state other than the children's home state, the home state court will determine which state has the most "significant connections" with the children and the custody action, and recognize that state's jurisdiction.

68. Using the facts given in question 67, assume that New York is found to have jurisdiction over the initial determination of Frederick's and Gail's custody in accordance with the UCCJEA. The New York court awarded joint custody to the parents, with Della having physical custody in California during the school year, and Edward having the children in New York during the three-month summer vacation. The parents alternate physical custody on major holidays. Della takes Frederick and Gail back to California after the custody award was handed down. When their school year ended nine months later, Della did not send the children to Edward at his home in New York; instead, she filed a motion in a California court for modification of the original order from joint custody to her sole custody. Edward requests that the New York court find Della to be in contempt; the New York court does so. Does the California court have jurisdiction to modify the New York child custody order under the UCCJEA?

A) No, because once New York made an initial custody determination consistent with the UCCJEA, that state retains exclusive continuing jurisdiction over the matter, unless neither the child nor either one of the parties to the action still lives in New York, and there is no longer substantial evidence available there concerning the child.

B) Yes, because Frederick and Gail have lived with their parent Della in California for at least six consecutive months prior to the commencement of the modification proceeds, so California is now their home state.

C) No, because once New York made an initial custody determination consistent with the UCCJEA, it retains exclusive continuing jurisdiction over the matter regardless of the location of the evidence concerning the children and the domicile elsewhere of the parties to the original action.

D) Yes, because substantial evidence concerning Della's custody of the children will be located in California.

69. Using the facts in questions 67 and 68, assume that while Della has the children with her in California, Della and Edward's neighbor in New York, Henry, files a request in California family court for a determination of the paternity of Frederick and Gail. Although he has never developed a personal relationship with the children or claimed them as his own before, he asserts that he, not Edward, fathered the children during a five-year affair with Della. Edward opposes the request, and moves for its dismissal. Which of the following is most likely to be the case?

A) Henry's suit would be dismissed because the "marital presumption" — that the husband of the mother is the father of any child born during the marriage or within 280 to 300 days of its termination by death or dissolution — is irrebuttable.

B) Henry's request would be granted because a biological parent has a due process right under the U.S. Constitution to establish a relationship with his child.

C) Henry's request would not be granted because he had not acknowledged the children and had never held them out as his own.

D) Henry's request would not be granted because, although a majority of states allow rebuttal of the marital presumption, those states usually require that the suit be brought by the presumed father, the mother, or the putative father within two years of the child's birth.

70. Using the facts of questions 67 through 69, assume that Edward is **not** the biological father of Frederick and Gail. Which of the following is not a requirement for a court to find him to be the equitable parent of Della's children under the Equitable Parent Doctrine in states (like California) that recognize it?

A) Della cooperated in the development of a father–child relationship between Edward and her children.

B) Della has no objection to continuation of the father–child relationship between Edward and her children.

C) Edward desires to have the rights afforded to a parent.

D) Edward is willing to take on the responsibilities of a parent, including child support.

71. Marla and Frank, an unmarried couple, had a child, Derek, 11 years ago. Marla ended their relationship a year later because Frank had become involved with a violent criminal gang, and his parental rights were terminated. In need of additional income to support Derek, Marla, who had a full-time clerical position, enlisted in the National Guard. Marla's cousin Sybil and her husband Paul provided care for Derek when Marla had National Guard duty. Marla's unit has been called up for two tours of duty in the Middle East in the past seven years; during them, Sybil and Paul had taken Derek to live with them. During the past seven years, owing to Marla's military deployments, Derek has lived with Sybil and Paul for a longer period of time than he has lived with his mother. When Marla returned from her most recent deployment, Sybil and Paul offered to adopt Derek. Marla refused. Sybil and Paul then filed suit requesting custody of Derek, arguing that it would be in Derek's best interest. At trial they demonstrated their care for him during his prolonged stays at their home, and the stable home life he has had with them. Marla opposed, testifying that she placed Derek with Sybil and Paul on the understanding that the placements were temporary, and only because she could not refuse to perform her National Guard duties. She stated that she now qualified for better-paid civilian employment on the basis of her National Guard record. Derek, now 11, refused to state a preference when asked in camera by the judge. How should the court rule?

A) The court should award custody of Derek to Sybil and Paul because Derek's best interests are served by remaining in the stability provided by their home environment.

B) The court should award custody of Derek to Sybil and Paul because Derek's best interests are served by being placed in a two-parent home with a male parent who can serve as Derek's role model as he matures.

C) The court should investigate whether Marla or Sybil and Paul constitute Derek's "psychological parent(s)," and place Derek with whoever fulfills that role.

D) The court should award custody of Derek to Marla because the natural parent who is not found to be unfit is presumed to be the proper custodian of her minor child in the absence of an exceptional circumstance under which the child would suffer detriment (or in some states, substantial harm) from the parent's continuing care. Marla's absences owing to military service do not constitute such a circumstance.

72. Ernest and Betty married 18 years ago. They had two children, Liz, born 15 years ago, and Kitty, born 13 years ago. Ernest and Betty divorced four years after Kitty's birth. After an initial attempt at joint custody, Ernest received sole custody of the children a year after the divorce because of Betty's continual interference with his parenting time. Two years after getting custody, Ernest married Edith. Edith adopted the traditional homemaker and mother role in the family, developing an excellent relationship with Ernest's two daughters. This year, Ernest was killed in an automobile accident. Betty now has sole custody of Liz and Kitty, whose emotional distress at their father's death has increased since moving to Betty's house. Betty will not allow her daughters any contact with Edith. Edith has filed a petition with the family court requesting visitation with Liz and Kitty once a week, between the hours of 4 p.m. and 8 p.m. Betty opposes the request. There is no statute in their state providing for nonparent visitation. How might the court rule?

A) The family court could dismiss Edith's request for lack of standing because there is no common law right for a stepparent or other nonparent to have continuing contact with a stepchild over the objections of a parent, and the state has not acted to modify the common law.

B) The family court could find that Edith has standing because she stands in loco parentis to Liz and Kitty, and grant visitation over Betty's objections provided it presumed, on the basis of a parent's fundamental constitutional right to rear her children, that the fit parent's decision was in the children's best interest, and that Edith had overcome that presumption.

C) The family court could grant visitation over Betty's objections on the grounds that continuing the relationship with Edith is in the best interests of the children who are clearly suffering emotional trauma from losing their father and their relationship with their stepmother.

D) Either A or B.

73. Which of the following statements is **not** a characteristic of the Hague Convention on the Civil Aspects of International Child Abduction (hereafter Hague Convention), implemented in the United States through the International Child Abduction Remedies Act (ICARA)?

A) The primary use of the Hague Convention is to obtain a new custody determination in the nation-party to which the child has been abducted.

B) The Hague Convention provides that a child will be returned to the custodian recognized under the law of the child's habitual residence if the child was wrongfully removed to or retained in a nation-party unless the child was removed for more than a year and is settled in his or her new environment.

C) The Hague Convention permits the court to take the child's objection to return into consideration if he or she is of sufficient age and maturity for his or her views to be taken into account.

D) The Hague Convention provides exceptions that allows a court to refuse to return the child to the lawful custodian if the opposing party establishes that there is either a grave risk that the child would be exposed to harm or otherwise placed in an intolerable situation, or that the return of the child would violate fundamental principles of human rights and fundamental freedoms.

74. Which of the following is **not** an element required to prove that a child was wrongfully removed or retained under the Hague Convention?

A) That the child was living in his or her state of habitual residence immediately prior to such removal or retention.

B) That the removal or retention took place by threat or use of force.

C) That the removal or retention breached the petitioner's custody rights under the law of the child's habitual residence.

D) That the petitioner was exercising his or her custody rights at the time of removal or retention.

75. Brian, an American, and Annick, a French citizen, met and married while he was a graduate student in France and she was studying art at the same university. Brian became a research scientist with a biochemical company, and Annick was a photographer. Brian kept his American citizenship, but the couple remained in France. Three years later, they had a daughter, Chloe. The couple and their child lived in France except for occasional visits to Brian's parents in the United States. When Chloe was 2 years old, her parents obtained a divorce in France. Annick was awarded custody of Chloe and Brian received liberal visitation. When Chloe was 4, Brian obtained permission from Annick to take the child to New York with him to visit his parents. He and Chloe flew from France to New York on round-trip tickets, with their return scheduled six weeks later. However, a week before the scheduled return, Brian called Annick and asked to be allowed to keep Chloe for an additional two weeks for his parents' 40th wedding anniversary. Annick agreed, but arranged to fly to New York two weeks later to retrieve Chloe and take her back to France. Meanwhile, Brian, who had decided to relocate to New York, petitioned a New York court for custody of Chloe. He obtained a court order naming him temporary custodian. Upon arrival, Annick was served with it and with an order not to leave the jurisdiction with Chloe until the issue of custody was determined. How should the trial court rule?

A) The trial court should rule in favor of Brian because Annick had given him permission to take Chloe to the United States and to stay the additional two weeks, so he had not wrongfully removed Chloe from France.

B) The trial court should rule in favor of Brian because France is no longer Chloe's state of habitual residence, as she has been living in New York for two months.

C) The trial court should rule in favor of Brian because otherwise, his right as an American citizen to live in the United States would be violated.

D) The trial court should rule in favor of Annick because France is the state of Chloe's habitual residence, and Chloe is being wrongfully retained in the United States.

76. Assume the same facts as question 75, except that Brian did not take Chloe to visit his family in New York and has not relocated to the United States. When Chloe was 4, Annick remarried; her new husband, Daniel, is a U.S. citizen who resides in Oregon. Annick plans to move there with Chloe. She has told Brian about these plans; he objects to them, as it will limit his visitation with his daughter. Assume that French law requires the consent of a divorced parent who has visitation with a noncustodial child to the custodial parent's removal of the child from the country; it also requires the custodial parent's consent should the noncustodial parent remove the child. This right is termed a divorced parent's ne exeat right. Without obtaining Brian's consent, Annick moves with Chloe to Oregon. Brian brings suit in the U.S. District Court there to obtain Chloe's return to France under the Hague Convention, saying that Annick wrongfully removed Chloe in "breach of rights of custody attributed to a person . . . under the law of the State in which the child was [theretofore]

habitually resident," protected by Art. 3(a) of the Convention. Annick responds that Brian has no "rights of custody under the French law," only of visitation; therefore the Convention does not apply. How should the court rule?

A) The court should rule that the ne exeat right was not a "right of custody" under the Convention, but only a right to participate in decision-making; therefore, the Convention's return remedy was not authorized.

B) The court should rule that Chloe should be returned to France because the ne exeat right is a right of custody, the right to make a joint determination of the country in which the child will reside.

C) The court should rule that Chloe should be returned to France because to interpret the Convention as not providing a return remedy for removal of a child in violation of a ne exeat right contradicts the Convention's purpose of deterring parents from seeking a friendlier forum for deciding custody disputes.

D) Both B and C.

77. Rachel and Sam were married in California 11 years ago. Their son Ben was born there two years later. The parties' marital relationship gradually deteriorated and they agreed to a divorce, which they obtained when Ben was 4 years old. In the divorce, they stipulated to a child custody plan that gave Rachel sole custody of Ben and gave Sam liberal visitation. Rachel decided to move to Israel, where her parents lived; she and Sam both had dual U.S.–Israeli citizenship. In Israel, Rachel registered the custody order from the California court and secured approval of it from a Rabbinical court in Haifa. Sam had no objection to the move, as he frequently visited Israel in connection with his employment, and saw Ben on those occasions, as well as during visitation in the United States. However, owing to a downturn in the economies of both the United States and Israel, Sam lost his job and could no longer travel to Israel. Rachel sent Ben to visit Sam in California in accordance with the child custody plan when Ben was 8 years old. Ben was supposed to stay for one month; Rachel had purchased a round-trip ticket for him. However, at the end of the month, Sam did not let Ben return to Israel, but retained him in California, where Ben completed the third grade. During this period, Sam moved twice for financial reasons, most recently this past spring, when he had to change school districts. Ben has few friends in his new school, and doesn't participate regularly in extracurricular activities; he spends most of his time after school playing video games and watching television. Rachel initially attempted to resolve the issue of Ben's return without litigation. However, this summer, she sued in federal district court in California for Ben's return to Israel, basing her claim on the Hague Convention. Sam has defended, saying that the child is well-settled in his new location in California. How should the court rule?

A) The court should allow Ben to remain with Sam because Rachel delayed a year before she filed suit for Ben's return to Israel.

B) The court should return Ben to Rachel because Sam retained him in violation of her custody rights; this action requires the court to return the child to the state of habitual residence automatically.

C) The court should return Ben to Rachel if it finds that the child is not "well-settled" in his new environment because Rachel waited for over a year prior to filing her petition.

D) The court should allow Ben to remain with Sam because Rachel, who had stayed behind in Israel, was not exercising her rights of custody at the time when Ben, who had been in the United States for a month, was retained.

78. Fred and Ethel had been married for three years and had one child, Doris, when they divorced in Oregon. At the time of the divorce, the state trial court awarded joint custody to the two parents. Two years later, Ethel wanted to move to Maryland, where her employer's head office was located; she had been offered a promotion to an important senior position. She requested a modification of the joint custody order to sole custody in herself so that she and Doris could move. Fred opposed, and asked for sole custody in himself. Because of docket delays, the Oregon court could not complete its deliberations prior to the date on which Ethel was to report to work in Maryland. The court granted Ethel's request for modification from joint custody to sole custody in Ethel and allowed her to relocate with Doris, but it made the new order temporary to give itself time to make a more studied determination. On arriving in Maryland, Ethel registered the Oregon order of sole custody and obtained a Maryland court order enforcing the Oregon order. The Oregon court, having received additional information about the care provided to Doris by Ethel and by Fred, entered an order granting permanent sole custody to Fred. Fred filed suit in federal district court under the Parental Kidnapping Prevention Act (PKPA), alleging that Maryland's order enforcing sole custody in Ethel, rather than in Fred, violated the act's provision for recognition of out-of-state custody decrees. He requested that the federal court declare the Maryland order invalid and enjoin Maryland from enforcing it. He also requested that the federal court declare the Oregon order to be valid and order Maryland to enforce it. Ethel has opposed, requesting continued enforcement of the Maryland order. How should the federal court rule?

A) The federal court should dismiss Fred's suit because the PKPA does not create an implied private cause of action in federal court to determine which of two conflicting custody orders is valid.

B) The federal court should find in favor of Fred because the PKPA is intended to make custody determinations subject to the Full Faith and Credit clause of the U.S. Constitution.

C) The federal court should find in favor of Ethel because once she registered the only existing order from Oregon and Maryland issued an order enforcing it, the purpose of the PKPA had been fulfilled.

D) The federal court should find in favor of Fred by inferring a federal cause of action because any other decision would render the PKPA nugatory.

79. Buddy and Cindy, who married ten years ago, lived in North Dakota with the four children of their marriage. Six years later, Cindy filed a divorce action against Buddy in North Dakota. Both Cindy and Buddy requested sole custody of the children pendente lite, and permanent sole custody once the divorce was granted as well. Cindy and the children moved to New Hampshire after the divorce but before the court had made a custody determination. Records of North Dakota's department of child welfare revealed that both parents had a history of domestic violence, and that Cindy had physically abused the children. One month after Cindy and the children left, the North Dakota divorce court entered an order granting Buddy immediate custody of his and Cindy's children.

One month after the order was granted, the New Hampshire Department of Health and Human Services (DHHS) initiated a child protection action and was granted custody of Cindy and Buddy's children. The ground for transferring custody to the state was that Cindy had abused the children after arriving in New Hampshire, and that custody in Buddy would put the children at risk of harm because he had never protected the children from their mother's abuse while the family lived together in North Dakota. Two months later, Buddy registered the North Dakota custody order with the New Hampshire court. The DHHS then petitioned to extinguish the parental rights of both parents, accusing them of unfitness. Buddy moved to dismiss the DHHS petition. He argued that the Parental Kidnapping Prevention Act (PKPA), 28 U.S.C. sec. 1738A, deprived the New Hampshire court of the necessary subject matter jurisdiction to place the children in state custody because North Dakota had already issued a custody order prior to New Hampshire's exercise of jurisdiction. Exclusive, continuing jurisdiction over the matter was therefore in the North Dakota court, and the New Hampshire court was attempting to modify, contrary to the express provisions of the PKPA, the orders of the state with subject matter jurisdiction. How should the New Hampshire court rule on Buddy's motion?

A) The New Hampshire court should dismiss the DHHS's case; the termination order would be a custody determination attempting to modify North Dakota's earlier order, and North Dakota has exclusive, continuing jurisdiction over custody of these children under the PKPA.

B) The New Hampshire court should dismiss Buddy's case because the PKPA applies only to child custody disputes between private parties, not to child protection cases in which the state is a party.

C) The New Hampshire court should dismiss Buddy's case because the PKPA applies only to interstate abductions of children, not to unilateral removal by a parent who at the time of the removal was exercising her custodial rights.

D) Either A or B.

80. The Indian Child Welfare Act (hereafter ICWA), 25 U.S.C. §§1901-63, substitutes tribal for state court jurisdiction in certain child custody proceedings. Which of the following statements concerning the Act is **not** true?

A) The ICWA provides for the possibility of tribal jurisdiction in proceedings arising out of divorce of the parents, foster care placements, terminations of parental rights, preadoptive placements, and adoptive placements that determine the custody of children who qualify as Native American under the Act.

B) Under the ICWA, adopted children of Native American parents do not qualify as Native American children whose custody is subject to tribal jurisdiction unless they are also eligible for membership in the tribe, and are biological children of members of the tribe.

C) The ICWA grants to the tribal court exclusive jurisdiction over any child custody proceeding involving a Native American child domiciled within the tribe's reservation, except in a few instances where jurisdiction is vested by another statute in the state.

D) The ICWA requires transfer to tribal court of a case involving a foster placement or a termination of parental rights proceeding involving a tribal child who is not domiciled on the reservation, unless the tribal court declines, either parent objects, or the state court finds good cause not to transfer the case.

81. Andy and Berta are two minor Native American children, registered members (like their parents) of the Puyallup tribe, which is recognized by the federal government. The parents and the children did not live on the reservation. The state removed Andy and Berta from their parents' home as deprived children. The state contacted the tribe, which agreed not to request transfer of the case so that the state could seek to reunite the family. If the family reunification efforts failed and the state sought to terminate the parents' rights, the state and the tribe agreed that the children would be placed with Puyallup foster parents. After unsuccessfully attempting for two years to reunite the family, the state terminated the biological parents' rights without notifying the tribe. The state placed the children with non-Native American foster parents. The foster parents then sought to adopt the children in state court. On discovering this, the tribe requested transfer of the case to its tribal court, located in a different state hundreds of miles away. The foster parents objected, and the state court held a hearing on their objection without notifying the tribe. It then denied the tribe's transfer request, finding "good cause" under the ICWA to do so because almost two years had passed since the children began

living with the foster parents. The tribe has appealed this decision in state appellate court. How should the appellate court rule?

A) The appellate court should affirm because transfer at this point would delay the children's adoption by the adults with whom they have been living in a stable relationship for almost two years.

B) The appellate court should affirm because the most relevant evidence as to the children's relationship with their foster parents is located in the state that has been exercising jurisdiction over the deprived child proceeding and the attempted rehabilitation.

C) The appellate court should reverse because the tribal court has exclusive jurisdiction over tribal families under the ICWA.

D) The appellate court should reverse; requiring the tribes to request transfer before the state had exhausted its reunification efforts would undermine efforts of tribes and state welfare agencies to work together to reunite Native American families, and the further delay in this case was not caused by the tribe.

82. The facts are the same as in question 81. Assume that the appellate court has upheld the trial court's decision to deny transfer to tribal court, but not its reasoning. The appellate court found instead that tribal jurisdiction over custody cases concerning Native American families who are not domiciled on the tribal reservation is restricted to two types of proceedings listed in section 1911(b) of the ICWA: termination of parental rights and foster care placement. In this case, both these steps have already occurred; adoptive placement is the question before the court. Because the Puyallup tribe did not make its request at the time of the earlier proceedings, transfer to its tribal court is not only not required, but not allowed. The tribe has appealed this decision to the state Supreme Court. How should it rule?

A) The Supreme Court should reverse because the requirement (with very limited exceptions) that state courts transfer termination and foster placement proceedings to tribal courts that request it does not preclude the transfer of other types of proceedings, such as preadoptive placements and adoptions, to tribal court.

B) The Supreme Court should reverse because the ICWA, as a matter of policy, identifies tribal courts as the preferred forum for issues concerning the relationship between Native American tribes and tribal children; therefore, the statute should be read expansively in granting that jurisdiction.

C) Both A and B.

D) The Supreme Court should affirm the appellate court's decision because transferring the case to the tribal court, which has no subject matter jurisdiction over it under the unambiguous language of the ICWA, would result in a null judgment.

83. In 1984, the federal government, in an effort to make court-ordered child support more reasonable and consistent in the states, conditioned the states' receipt of federal welfare funding on each state's adoption of statutory child support guidelines that the state could devise. However, the federal government had to approve a state's guidelines to receive welfare funding. By 1989, all the states had adopted such guidelines. Which of the following statements correctly describes an effect of the guidelines on judicial awards of child support?

A) A state's child support guidelines are advisory, not mandatory.

B) The amount of child support calculated by means of the guidelines is irrebuttably presumed to be the proper award.

C) A court can deviate from the state's guidelines in making a child support award, but it must supply written or oral on-the-record reasons justifying doing so.

D) The guidelines are unfair to the payee parent because they do not provide a means for courts to deal with special circumstances, such as special educational needs of the child or extraordinarily high income of the payor parent.

84. Which of the following is the method of calculating child support used by the majority of U.S. states?

A) The flat percentage of income model, under which the child support obligation is a percentage of the payor parent's income; the percentage increases with the number of children to be supported.

B) The income shares method, under which the court (1) adds together the monthly incomes of the two parents to determine their combined income; (2) locates on a chart the basic support obligation to be paid by two parents at that income level with the number of children they must support; (3) adds any extraordinary expenses for the children to the basic support obligation to obtain the total support obligation; (4) calculates what percentage of the combined income is attributable to each parent; and (5) multiplies the total support obligation by the percentage of combined income attributable to the payor parent to arrive at his or her child support obligation.

C) The Melson formula, which (1) allocates to each parent the amount of his or her income needed to provide for his or her basic needs; (2) treats any amount beyond that as excess income, available to meet the child's (or children's) basic support needs; (3) satisfies the amount needed for basic support of the child from both parents' excess income in proportion to each parent's income; (4) draws on any excess income of each parent beyond what is required to meet the child's basic support needs for an additional "standard of living payment" to enable the child to share in the parent's standard of living.

D) None of the above.

85. Which of the following is **not** a true statement concerning the modification of a child support order?

A) The usual ground for a modification of a child support order is substantial change in the circumstances of the payor (obligor) parent, the payee parent, or the child.

B) The child support awarded under the order can be modified by the court in either an upward or a downward direction, depending on the nature of the change that is demonstrated.

C) An increase in the payor parent's income since the original order is insufficient to constitute a change in circumstances justifying increase in the child's award unless an increase in the child's need during that period is also demonstrated.

D) A decrease in the payee parent's income since the original award can be the basis for a modification increasing the amount that the payor parent must contribute, even if the award itself remains the same.

86. Natasha and Oscar divorced after five years of marriage and two children, Melissa and Paul. Oscar received domiciliary custody of Melissa and Paul; Natasha has been paying Oscar child support in the amount of $700 per month. Natasha then had an affair with Quentin, and had his child, Robert. Shortly after Robert's birth, Quentin died of complications from diabetes. Natasha has now filed a motion to modify the child support order for Melissa and Paul by reducing the amount of their award to $400 per month. Her basis for the request is her support obligation to Robert. How would the court rule?

A) The court would deny the request for a downward modification of the award for Melissa and Paul. Natasha voluntarily changed her circumstances after that award by choosing to take on the cost of an additional child; she should not be allowed, by her voluntary choice, to reduce Melissa and Paul's standard of living, or impose greater financial burdens on Oscar.

B) The court would grant a downward modification of the award for Melissa and Paul by deducting the amount required for Natasha to support Robert from Natasha's available income because a later-born child should not be financially disadvantaged by birth order.

C) The court would deviate from the state's child support guidelines because the additional child provides a sufficient basis for doing so. The court would modify the existing order so that the children are treated as equally entitled to share in Natasha's standard of living. On the basis of the sources of income available to each child, it would determine an award amount for the children of the first family that allows Natasha's additional child to be supported at an equitable level.

D) Any of the above awards, depending on whether the jurisdiction had adopted the rule of "first family first," or of "second family first," or of additional children as a justification for equitable deviation from the state guidelines.

87. During their seven-year marriage, Alan and Dorothy, both schoolteachers, had two children. On their divorce, Alan received custody of the children and a $300 per month child support award. Dorothy remarried; her new husband Robert is a corporate executive with an income of $3 million per year. Alan has moved for a modification of child support. He is seeking an increase in child support based on Dorothy's second husband's earnings. How is the court most likely to rule?

A) The court will deny Alan's motion because Dorothy's marriage to Robert does not impose a child support obligation on her new husband.

B) The court will recalculate the child support amount by including in Dorothy's income one-half of Robert's income, and modify the award upward.

C) The court will recalculate the child support by imputing Robert's contribution to Dorothy's living expenses to her as income, and modify the award upward.

D) The court will deny Alan's request in any noncommunity property state because Dorothy has no legal claim on Robert's earnings.

88. Bella divorced Christopher, a highly successful sports lawyer; Bella was awarded sole custody of their three children because Christopher was so involved in his work that he had little time for them. Incensed that he was unable to obtain child custody and must instead pay a substantial amount of child support every month to the woman who divorced him, Christopher quit his job to join an order of devout men in his religion who study its sacred texts, attend worship rituals, and meditate all day rather than earning wages. They are supported by donations made to the group rather than to its individual members. The principal donor to Christopher's group is a trust fund that Christopher created shortly before joining the order. The trust property is Christopher's wealth. Christopher has now asked for a downward modification of his child support order because he has no regular income of his own. Bella opposes Christopher's request. How is a court likely to rule?

A) Because Christopher's loss of income has resulted from his free exercise of his religion in creating the trust fund to foster one of its practices, and in joining the group himself, the court must modify the child support order to avoid violating the First Amendment of the U.S. Constitution.

B) Because it appears that Christopher did not change his career in good faith, but only out of spite to defeat his ex-wife's child support award, the court would deny Christopher's request for modification.

C) Because Christopher voluntarily changed his career, the court would deny his request for a modification of child support to avoid penalizing the children for their father's professional decision.

D) Either of B and C, or both of them.

89. Assume that Christopher in question 88 lost his attempt to modify his child support obligation. He now has left the religious order he had joined and returned to his highly successful sports law practice. However, he had ceased paying his child support obligation when he joined the order, and has continued to refuse to pay. Bella obtained a determination from the state's family court that Christopher has willfully failed to pay his child support obligation in a timely manner, and is ignoring an order that he pay his arrears plus interest, and resume monthly payments. Christopher continues to refuse to pay. Bella has now submitted a complaint against Christopher to the state bar association. What enforcement mechanism, available in several states, is Bella seeking to bring to bear on Christopher?

A) Christopher could be dismissed from his law firm because of the complaint.

B) In a number of states, Christopher's license to practice could be suspended by the state bar association on the basis of the court determination; it would continue to be suspended until he complies with the court order.

C) Christopher would be ineligible to run for public office because of the complaint.

D) Both A and C.

90. The state in which Christopher and Bella live provides that a noncompliant child support obligor can be held in either criminal or civil contempt by the family court. Which of the following statement(s) do(es) **not** state genuine difference(s) between the two types of contempt?

A) The purpose of civil contempt is to obtain compliance; the purpose of criminal contempt is to punish the obligor.

B) An obligor charged with criminal contempt is entitled to more extensive federal constitutional protections, such as the presumption of innocence and the right to counsel, than one charged with civil contempt.

C) An obligor can go to prison if found in criminal contempt, whereas an obligor found to be in civil contempt will not.

D) Both A and B.

91. Which of the following is **not** a mechanism through which Bella can attempt to enforce Christopher's child support obligation against him in the case in question 88?

A) Bella can seek a garnishment or wage assignment through which the amount of Christopher's child support payment will be withheld from his paychecks and turned over to her directly.

B) If Christopher owes more than $5,000 in arrearages and seeks to travel abroad, Bella can have the state welfare agency notify the federal Department of Health and Human Services to deny his passport application or restrict or revoke his current passport.

C) If Christopher wins a lottery, his winnings can be seized and used to satisfy his child support obligations.

D) If Christopher attempts to declare bankruptcy, Bella can have the bankruptcy court dismiss his case.

92. Mr. and Ms. Kay married in Reno, Nevada, where they had met while attending a convention. They then moved to Cyriac, New York, Mr. Kay's hometown, with Ms. Kay relocating from her home state of North Carolina. After two years, they had a daughter, Dot; three years after Dot's birth they had a son, Sylvester. After nine years, they divorced in New York. The New York trial court awarded Ms. Kay custody of the children, and child support in the amount of $600 per month. Mr. Kay then moved to California, and has never returned to New York. After two years, he stopped sending Ms. Kay the court-ordered child support payments. Ms. Kay wants to enforce the support order against Mr. Kay in California. Which of the following is **not** a true statement of the law concerning interstate enforcement of child support orders?

A) Under the Uniform Interstate Family Support Act (UIFSA), Ms. Kay can travel to California, register the New York child support order in California and obtain enforcement of it by the California courts, which cannot modify it.

B) Ms. Kay cannot obtain enforcement in California because the California court would be enforcing an order of a court in New York, which lacks personal jurisdiction over Mr. Kay.

C) Under the UIFSA, Ms. Kay can have the New York child support enforcement agency (called a "Title IV-D agency") forward the order to the California Title IV-D agency for registration and enforcement by the California courts.

D) Ms. Kay can rely on a federal statute, 28 U.S.C. sec. 1738B, that grants to the state first issuing a valid child support order the continuing, exclusive jurisdiction over that order as long as the children or Ms. Kay continue to live in New York; using it, she can register the New York order for Sylvester and Dot's support with the California Title IV-D agency, and obtain enforcement according to New York law without modification by a California court.

93. In the United States, which of the following is the most common reason for a child support order to be terminated?

A) The minor child whose support was ordered has died.

B) The minor child whose support was ordered has attained the age of majority, or if after that point he is still a full-time student in high school, graduates after reaching majority; or attains the age set by the state (usually 19 or 20) for terminating the support of a child still in secondary school.

C) The child whose support was ordered has graduated from college.

D) The minor child whose support was ordered has been emancipated by membership in the military and assignment to active duty.

94. Ted and Ursula, who were married for 12 years and have been divorced for five years, have a daughter, Della. On her parents' divorce, Della's father received sole custody because her mother had no interest in raising her. Ursula has visitation and pays child support. A year ago, Della, who was then 14 years old, eloped with a 24-year-old musician, Jerry. When Ted located the pair two weeks later, they had already married. Della returned with her father to his home to live. Jerry was arrested and ultimately convicted of statutory rape; he is imprisoned in the state penitentiary. Six months later, a court found Della and Jerry's marriage to be voidable and annulled it. The ground for the annulment was that Della, because of her youth, had lacked the mental capacity to give consent to the marriage to Jerry. Ursula, who now has remarried and has two children by her second spouse, has just learned of Della's elopement and its consequences. Ursula has filed suit in state court to be reimbursed for the child support that she has paid since Della's elopement, arguing that Della was emancipated at the time of her marriage and was from that time no longer entitled to child support. Ursula has asked the court to terminate her child support order, and has stopped making support payments to Ted. Ted maintains that the judgment of nullity of the marriage means that Della was not emancipated. How is the court likely to rule?

A) Because, in all states, marriage emancipates a minor who becomes a spouse, the validity of Della's marriage at the time it took place resulted in Della's emancipation, which cannot be reversed; therefore Ursula should receive reimbursement of the child support paid and an order terminating her support obligation.

B) Because Della's marriage was voidable rather than void, its nullification means that the cause of Della's emancipation has ceased to exist, and Della is once again an unemancipated minor, entitled to support from her family; Ursula should only receive reimbursement of the child support paid during the six-month period before the marriage was declared void.

C) Although a minor's marriage can trigger emancipation, the court must examine whether the marriage created a relationship inconsistent with the minor's subjection to parental control and care to determine whether emancipation was effected; in this case, no such relationship was created, as evidenced by Della's continued residence in the parental home with parental support and the declaration of nullity of the marriage.

D) Either B or C.

95. Queenie, an unmarried 16-year-old junior in high school, became pregnant by her classmate Noah, who is 18 years old. She knows that she and Noah have no future together; he has already been arrested on several occasions for assault and battery and destruction of property. She has decided to put the baby up for adoption. Her parents agree that she should do so. When she told Noah of her plan, he opposed it; he was planning on raising the child with her, and says that if he can't, he'll raise the baby without her. He filed a declaration of his paternity of her child in the state's putative father registry. He offered Queenie money to help with her expenses, but she refused to take it. Queenie has met with an attorney who specializes in arranging private adoptions that take place immediately after the state-mandated waiting period of five days after birth. She informed him of Noah's objections, and asked whether Noah could prevent the adoption. What would the attorney respond?

    A) Noah will not be able to prevent the adoption because at the time the adoption takes place he will have no established relationship with the child.

    B) Noah will be able to prevent the adoption immediately after birth if he acts quickly to establish a relationship with the child because he has a fundamental parental right to the care, custody, and nurture of the child.

    C) Noah will be able to prevent the adoption because, as the biological father, he has a fundamental right to the care, custody, and nurture of his child.

    D) Noah will not be able to prevent the adoption because he would not be a fit father for the child.

96. The facts are the same as in question 95, but Queenie has decided that there is less risk to the child if she has an abortion rather than placing the child for adoption with strangers or, even worse, having him raised by Noah. She told Noah her decision, and he objects to it for the same reason that he objected to the adoption. Can Noah prevent Queenie from obtaining an abortion?

    A) Noah can prevent Queenie from having an abortion because he registered as the unborn child's father in the putative father registry and has attempted to support Queenie; thus, he has obtained the right to establish a relationship with his child, which will be denied him if she has an abortion.

    B) Noah can prevent Queenie from having an abortion if a court finds, in balancing the interests of both parents, that his interests in protecting life and parenthood outweigh Queenie's interest, which is based on speculative fears about the child's upbringing.

C) Noah cannot prevent Queenie from having an abortion because the U.S. Supreme Court has found the pregnant woman rather than the unborn child's father to have the right under the U.S. Constitution to make a decision whether to carry that child to term.

D) Noah cannot prevent Queenie from having an abortion because he is not married to her.

97. The facts are the same as in question 96, with the following additions: Now Noah has informed Queenie's parents, whom he knows to be opposed to abortion on religious grounds, of Queenie's decision to get an abortion. The parents agree with Noah that Queenie should carry the unborn child to term, although they still want her to place the child for adoption as originally planned. Queenie's parents have told her that because she is a minor, under a state statute that has been found to be constitutional, she must obtain the permission of at least one of her parents to have the abortion, and that they have applied for an injunction to block her from having one. Will Queenie's parents succeed in preventing her from having an abortion?

A) No, because a pregnant woman's right to decide to have an abortion is founded on her liberty interest in her bodily integrity, and is therefore absolute.

B) Not necessarily, because if the state statute is constitutional, it must provide the option for Queenie to secure a court determination that Queenie is mature enough to decide for herself whether to have an abortion despite her parents' objections; if it does not, the court will strike it as unconstitutional.

C) Yes, because the parents' fundamental right to the care, custody, and control of their minor child without state interference means that they, rather than Queenie, have the ultimate decision-making power over her reproductive status.

D) Yes, because Queenie's parents' right to control their minor child and their interest in protecting life, balanced against Queenie's interest in not carrying the unborn child to term and giving birth, will be found to be the weightier interest by the court.

98. Use the same facts as in question 97, except for this change for the purposes of this question only: Assume that Queenie's father ordered her to leave the family home after learning that she is pregnant. Queenie's mother, upset by her husband's reaction, moved out of the family home as well. She rented a two-bedroom apartment into which she and Queenie have moved. Queenie's mother is supporting Queenie as well as herself from her own funds, but knows that these will not last through Queenie's pregnancy. She has also found out from Queenie that Noah has no income and is unlikely to have one any time soon. Queenie has been unable to obtain a part-time job, and her mother refuses to allow her to quit school to take a full-time job. Instead, Queenie's mother asked Queenie's father for support for their daughter, but he refused. Queenie's mother brings an action for support on behalf of Queenie. How will the court rule?

A) By becoming pregnant, Queenie has been emancipated; thus, her father is no longer required to support her, despite the fact that she is still a minor.

B) Because she is residing apart from her family's domicile, Queenie is emancipated, and thus her father is no longer required to support her, despite the fact that she is still a minor.

C) Because Queenie is an unmarried minor whose only support and only residence are with a parent, she is not emancipated, and thus is entitled to support from her father.

D) Because Queenie has not been able to get a part-time job, she is not emancipated, and thus is entitled to support from her father.

99. Tammy is 16 years old. She left her parents' home during an argument with them, after her parents mistakenly accused her of having an affair with one of her teachers. After two days at a friend's house, Tammy dropped out of school and moved to a larger city than her hometown. She obtained a full-time job at a factory by lying about her age. She has rented an efficiency apartment and has been self-supporting for over a year. Tammy's parents began searching for her when they discovered she was no longer staying with any of her friends. Tammy's employer has discovered that she is a minor, and has said she must have her parents' consent to work in the factory. Tammy told him that she is emancipated, so consent is not required. Which of the following states Tammy's status under the law?

A) Tammy is emancipated despite being a minor because she has established her independence of her parents by living in a different residence, beyond their sphere of influence and without their support.

B) Tammy is not emancipated despite her independence because her parents have not consented to or acquiesced in her emancipation.

C) Tammy is emancipated because her parents' action in letting her leave their home constituted consent to her emancipation.

D) Tammy is not emancipated because emancipation for a reason other than marriage or attaining the age of 18 requires a court order.

100. Dennis and Dooley, ages 8 and 10, are brothers who are known throughout their neighborhood as "hell-raisers" for the amount of damage they have caused while roughhousing. One afternoon, when their parents were indoors, the boys decided to imitate martial arts moves that they had seen in a movie, using broom handles that they had sawed off their parents' brooms as fighting sticks. Because their own yard was small, they went into their next-door

neighbor George's much larger yard. As they were practicing, they crashed through George's sliding glass patio doors. Fortunately, neither of the boys was badly injured. However, George has demanded that the boys' parents, Henry and Alice, replace the broken doors. Henry and Alice have consulted an attorney to learn whether they are liable for the broken doors. The jurisdiction has not passed any statutes imposing greater liability on parents than that which exists at common law. Which of the following statements of their liability is most likely?

A) Because it was reasonably foreseeable that Dennis and Dooley, given the fact that they have already caused damage to property in their neighborhood, would damage George's patio doors, it was Henry's and Alice's duty to prevent such damage, and they are therefore financially responsible for replacing the glass doors.

B) Henry and Alice are strictly liable for the destruction of the glass doors by their children because a parent has a duty to control his or her minor child to prevent the child from causing damage to others, regardless of whether it is intentional or unintentional, foreseeable or unforeseeable damage.

C) Because Dennis and Dooley are too young to have been able to foresee the damage to George's patio doors, their parents Henry and Alice are not responsible for the damage.

D) Because it was Dennis and Dooley who damaged George's patio doors, they, rather than Henry and Alice, are responsible for the damage.

101. René and Estelle were married and had two children, Edgar and Gerta. When Edgar was 3 and Gerta was 5, René deserted Estelle for Olivia. Estelle has divorced René for adultery and abandonment, and has received sole custody of the children. René has visitation but has never exercised it. After a year, Estelle returned to court requesting that the children's last name, De Gas, be changed to her own last name, Musson, to which she had returned after the divorce. She points out that this would make the children's names consistent with her own, and thus identify them as a family for both practical and emotional purposes. She also has demonstrated that René has never even tried to exercise his visitation with the children since he deserted the family; Edgar is now 5 and Gerta is 7. Estelle introduced evidence that René plans to move back to his native country, France. René points out that the children have borne his last name for years, and to change it now would be confusing for them and for those who maintain records, such as the hospital and their school. He also maintains that although he has not actually decided to return to France permanently, if he did so, it would be helpful for the children to have the same last names as he did on their passports. Finally, he maintains that as the children's biological parent who is paying child support, he is entitled to have the children identified with him by their names. On what legal basis is a court most likely to decide whether to change the children's surname?

A) The court will presume that continuity in the children's surname is in the children's best interest, and so the present last name will be maintained unless the presumption is overcome by Estelle.

B) The court will presume that the choice of the custodial parent is in the children's best interest unless the presumption is overcome by René.

C) The court will consider the best interest of the children without regard to any presumption, but will consider continuity as a factor in its decision.

D) Either A or C.

101 ANSWERS & ANALYSIS

FAMILY LAW ANSWERS & ANALYSIS

1. Issue: Protection of the Right to Marry as a Liberty Interest

The correct answer is **C**. The statute is underinclusive because it does not address other causes of child poverty than divorce — Alex and Bethany's child will be poor whether or not they divorce — and overinclusive because it prevents the couple from marrying on the basis of their economic situation, whether they are likely to divorce or not. Thus it is not "closely tailored" to effectuate the state's interest. The U.S. Supreme Court required that this standard be met in *Zablocki v. Redhail*, 434 U.S. 374 (1978), which recognized the right to marry as a liberty interest protected by strict scrutiny. A is wrong because reasonable regulations that do not substantially burden the right, including financial ones such as a marriage license fee, can be imposed by the state. B and D are wrong because they employ a rational-basis test that is not appropriate for a fundamental right.

2. Issue: The Characteristics and Effect of State Prohibitions on Close Relatives Marrying

The correct answer is **A**. A marriage between relatives considered too close under the law of the state where the marriage took place is void, not voidable, so answer A is **not** true. B is true; the states are approximately evenly divided on the issue. C and D are also true; no state prohibits marriage between parties who are second cousins or more distantly related, and all states prohibit marriages between lineal ancestors and descendants.

3. Issue: The Mental Capacity Required for Consent to Marriage

The correct answer is **C**. The mental capacity required for consent to marry is the ability to understand the nature of the marriage contract and marital responsibilities, interpreted in a minimalist fashion; see *Edmunds v. Edwards*, 287 N.W.2d 420 (1980). A is incorrect because it equates the consent required for commercial contracts (e.g., making purchases, investing one's wages) with the consent required to enter the marriage contract. Although marriage is a contract, it differs in its nature from other contracts, and thus in the mental capacity required to consent to it. See 82 ALR 2d 1040, 1046 (1962). B is incorrect because capacity to marry is not evaluated on the basis of the suitability of the parties as parents. D is incorrect because the guardians in this instance have been appointed to handle the parties' financial affairs, not to make personal decisions for them.

4. Issue: The Validity of a Marriage in Which at Least One Party Is Below the Statutory Minimum Age Required by the State

The correct answer is **D**. The three answers all present possible decisions by a court because treatment of marriage below the statutory age of consent without parental permission varies from state to state. A would be correct in a state that regards such marriages as void. The marriage that is absolutely null is contrary to public policy, and cannot be ratified; it does not require a declaration of nullity to prevent it from having effect, although courts grant annulments in such cases on request of one of the parties. B would be correct in a jurisdiction that regards such marriages as voidable; such marriages have effect until an annulment is granted, and may be ratified if the parties live as husband and wife after the minor attains the age of consent, or is found to have sufficient understanding to consent, depending on the jurisdiction. C is also possible in a jurisdiction that does not treat the age of consent as a bright line rule for voidability, but evaluates the understanding of the underage party to determine whether she was able to give consent; it is lack of that understanding that makes the marriage voidable. Hence, any of the answers could be the ruling of a court, depending on how the jurisdiction treats underage marriages.

5. **Issue: The Traditional Requirements for Annulment of a Marriage on the Ground of Fraud and Their Modern Modification**

The correct answer is **C**. A, B, and D are incorrect; they refer to traditional elements of the fraud ground for annulment that have not been expanded. Thus, annulment for fraud still must be sought by its victim, and requires that the deception be material, causally related to the victim's consent, and of a serious nature. It also must affect the essentials of marriage, as in C. That term has been redefined in an expansive fashion during the years since the end of World War II. The essentials of marriage are no longer confined to matters concerning cohabitation, sexual relations, and procreation. Courts have recognized that a subjective test of what is essential to a particular couple's marriage is appropriate in an era of companionate marriage.

6. **Issue: The Modern View of the Essentials of (the) Marriage**

The correct answer is **A**. The traditional view of "essentials of the marriage" as restricted to its sexual and procreative functions has been replaced by the view that essentials of marriage can include significant issues that would have dissuaded the complaining party from the marriage had the fraud not occurred. See *Kober v. Kober*, 211 N.E. 2d 817, 819 (N.Y. 1965) (woman's marriage to a man who had concealed his Nazi affiliations and rabid anti-Semitism from her was voidable). Only a court that veers from the modern, subjective view of essentials of the marriage would take the approach in B, which is incorrect; it states the judicial position of the late nineteenth and early twentieth centuries. C is incorrect because it also departs from the modern trend because it rejects the test of "essential to the marriage" as being a subjective one; the modern test would only look to whether compatibility with Debbie's political views was significant and essential to Debbie, not whether it was a norm required by most people. See *Wolfe v. Wolfe*, 378 N.E.2d 1181 (Ill. 1978) (Roman Catholic husband entitled to nullification of his marriage for fraud where wife informed him that her previous husband had died — even forging a death certificate — when in fact they had divorced and he was still alive). D is also incorrect, as the pertinent facts in an annulment for fraud are those that exist at the time the marriage is confected, not future developments.

7. Issue: The Effect of a Marriage Valid Under State Law but Entered into as Part of a Scheme to Obtain Permanent Residence for a Foreign National

The correct answer is **A**. Under the U.S. Supreme Court's decision in *Lutwak v. United States*, 344 U.S. 604 (1952), state recognition of the validity of a marriage entered into as part of a scheme to evade U.S. immigration and naturalization law is immaterial to the application of that law. B is wrong because it states the contrary principle. C is wrong because no state imposes a requirement of cohabitation in a matrimonial domicile on ceremonial (as opposed to common-law) marriages for them to be valid. D is wrong because although A is true, C is not.

8. Issue: State Recognition of Same-Sex Marriages Validly Confected Out-of-State

The correct answer is **B**. Recognition of the validity of an out-of-state marriage that is contrary to state law is based in comity and evaluated by conflict of laws principles. The basic principle that a marriage valid in the state where contracted is valid in other states as well has an exception if the marriage violates a strong public policy of the state asked to give recognition. Montana's constitutional amendment indicates such a policy. A is incorrect because the Defense of Marriage Act does not prohibit states from recognizing same-sex marriages; it says that they are not required to do so under the Full Faith and Credit clause of the U.S. Constitution. C is wrong because marriage has historically not been considered to be governed by the Full Faith and Credit clause. D is wrong because the time of the passage of the Montana amendment is irrelevant on these facts.

9. Issue: The Recognition of Marriage of a Postoperative Transsexual to Someone of the Transsexual Partner's Former Sex

The correct answer is **A**. Although only a small number of states' courts have spoken on this issue, only one of those has ruled in favor of permitting such a marriage. B is erroneous because the courts deciding against the transsexual's marriage have done so on the ground that the sex of the transsexual partner remains unchanged even after surgery. Thus, the impediment of same sex to a valid marriage with Herbert still exists. C is wrong because the courts that have so decided have not confronted the fact that on their logic, same-sex marriages could result. D is wrong because both B and C are wrong.

10. Issue: Enforceability of a Prenuptial Contract That Attempts to Modify the Noneconomic Rights and Duties of Marriage

The correct answer is **D**. Although almost every jurisdiction has recognized the enforceability of contracts to vary at least some of the *economic* rights and duties of marriage, enforcement of a contract to abrogate a noneconomic right or duty that the state attributes to marriage is contrary to public policy. Those rights and duties of state marriage exist regardless of whether the spouses intended to take advantage of them. See Restatement of the Law of Contracts, sec. 587. Thus C is a true statement. In addition, courts will not intervene in an intact marriage to resolve a dispute about the nature and extent of the parties' sexual relationship. Thus A is a true statement as well. Therefore D, which includes both of these reasons, is the correct answer. B is incorrect because it states that the prenuptial agreement is enforceable.

11. Issue: Whether a Marriage That Would Be Otherwise Valid Will Be Found Not to Be So Because One or Both of the Parties Did Not Have the Subjective Intent to Marry

The best answer is **D**. Parties who fulfill the substantive and ceremonial requirements for marriage cannot contract privately to avoid the effect of that status. Otherwise, it would be impossible for any third party, including the state, to determine by objective means whether any given couple was truly married if they claimed its benefits. A is incorrect because to base determination of the validity of a marriage on subjective intent would open the way to fraud. B is wrong because the parties could not enforceably contract to change the effects of the state's legal regime of marriage. C is wrong because the putative spouse doctrine applies to a spouse or spouses who attempt to marry, but fail to do so because of a good faith mistake; here, the couple is attempting not to marry despite having all the exterior signs of a valid marriage. See *Crosson v. Crosson*, 668 So. 2d 868 (Ala. Civ. App. 1995), *Bishop v. Bishop*, 308 N.Y.S.2d 998 (1970), *Lester v. Lester*, 87 N.Y.S.2d 517 (Dom. Rel. 1949), and *Schibi v. Schibi*, 69 A.2d 831 (Conn. 1949).

12. Issue: The Requirements for Common Law Marriage in States That Permit It to Be Entered Into

The correct answer is **D**; cohabitation as man and wife for seven years is **not** a requirement of common law marriage. Although cohabitation as husband and wife is required for common law marriage, no particular number of years is required. In contrast, the other three answers all state genuine requirements for common law marriage: agreement to marry presently, lack of impediments, and holding out as married within the community.

13. Issue: Requirement for Dissolution of Common Law Marriage and Effect of Putative Marriage on Inheritance

The correct answer is **D**. A is accurate because Lewis's common law marriage to Alice is a valid marriage, despite its informality, and is dissolved in the same ways that ceremonial, formal marriages are: death and divorce. B is incorrect because lack of recordation of a marriage certificate for common law marriages makes enforcement difficult, but doesn't lessen the requirement of a divorce for remarriage. Thus, Lewis's failure to procure a formal divorce prior to remarriage made that attempted marriage void. However, C is accurate if the state recognizes the putative marriage doctrine. Under it a good faith putative spouse receives marital benefits despite the absolute nullity of her marriage; Grace would share in the inheritance with Alice if the state and Grace meet those conditions. Therefore, D, which recognizes that either A or C might be the case, is the correct answer.

14. Issue: Application of the Conflict of Laws Principle on Recognition of Marriages to Common Law Marriage

The correct answer is **B**. Recognition of the validity of an out-of-state marriage that is contrary to state law is based in comity and evaluated by conflict of laws principles. These in general call for recognition in other states of the validity of a marriage that was valid where contracted; however, it includes a "strong public policy" exception. See Sec. 283 of the Restatement (Second) of Conflict of Laws. A is incorrect despite a couple of Louisiana cases that invoke it; validity of a marriage contracted in another state is determined by conflict of laws rather than Full Faith and Credit principles. C is incorrect because the conflict of laws principle on recognition of marriage contains an escape mechanism for states in which a strong public policy is violated by the marriage at issue. D is incorrect because the conflicts principle for recognizing out-of-state marriages contains no exception for a change of domicile.

15. Issue: Ceremonial Requirement for Marriage Where Common Law Marriages Are Not Allowed

The correct answer is **C**; Alexandra and Bradley needed to comply with the requirement of a ceremony to remarry after their valid civil divorce. A is wrong because no marriage ceremony took place; only one party was present, and the celebrant merely signed the certificate instead of presiding over the required consent by each party to take the other as spouse. B is wrong because a good faith religious belief in their continued marriage does not create a civil marriage. D is wrong because the presumption of marriage created by a marriage certificate on file in the public records is not irrebuttable, and would be rebutted by the lack of a ceremony.

16. Issue: Whether a Marriage License from the State Where the Marriage Ceremony Is Performed Is a Mandatory or Directory Requirement for a Valid Marriage

The correct answer is **A**. The state's laws, described in Darla's arguments, specify marriages that are void, and do not include unlicensed ones. The penalty prescribed for failure of the parties to obtain, and the officiant to require, a state license for marriage is not that the marriage is void, but that the parties have committed misdemeanors. Because the legislature has not expressly indicated that an attempted marriage without a license is a nullity, the requirement is not mandatory for a valid marriage; it is directory only. See *Carabetta v. Carabetta*, 438 A.2d 109, 110 (Conn. 1980); *Rivera v. Rivera*, 2010 N.M. App. Lexis 96. B is incorrect because putative spouse status is a consequence of a void marriage; therefore, reversal of the trial court's decision would not be warranted. C is incorrect because common law marriage is one lacking a marriage ceremony, not merely a marriage license. D is incorrect because although public records are the usual method of determining whether a couple qualifies as married, the marriage can be proven in other ways, such as by witness testimony.

17. Issue: Actions in Relation to Breach of Contract to Marry

The correct answer is **D**. Although answer A states the former requirements for the breach of contract action and for determining ownership of the ring given in contemplation of a marriage that did not take place, the "heart-balm action" for breach of promise has been eliminated in the majority of jurisdictions, either by "anti-heart-balm statutes" or by judicial decision. A also stated the traditional view that the ring, despite the fact that it was a conditional gift, was only returnable if the donee broke the engagement or if it was called off by mutual consent. However, the present view of courts that have considered the issue is that no matter who ends the engagement, the donee must return the ring, and applies the rule for conditional gifts. B states accurately the modern position on breach of promise actions: They are considered irrelevant given the changes in sexual mores and the position of women, so most jurisdictions would dismiss the case. C accurately states the modern position on the ownership of the engagement ring once the engagement has been called off. Thus D is the proper choice.

18. Issue: Return of Gifts Given by Third Parties in Contemplation of the Donee's Marriage

The correct answer is **B**. A is correct with regard to the gift certificate, because the wedding for which Hester thought Cressie would buy the wedding dress was the marriage to Troy. However, Hester's words in giving the brooch indicate that Hester gave it because she liked Cressie herself very much, regardless of her status as Troy's fiancée. That is the position of answer B. C states the wrong result for the gift certificate and the wrong principle for Cressie's retaining the brooch. D states the wrong result and the wrong principle for both gifts.

19. Issue: The Requirements and Effects of the Putative Marriage Doctrine

The correct answer is **A**. A putative marriage is not a valid marriage, but a remedy for a good-faith party in a marriage that is an absolute nullity, void *ab initio*. Therefore, no divorce is required; and because the marriage is void rather than voidable, no annulment is required, although the good-faith party may file for one as a step in obtaining some or all of the effects of marriage. Answers B, C, and D are all true components of the doctrine.

20. Issue: The Legal Effect of Marriage on the Surname of the Wife

D is the correct answer. At common law, although wives usually took their husbands' surnames, it was a customary practice rather than a legal requirement. A is incorrect because a married woman who wished to retain her name could do so. B is wrong because even though married women are not required to take their husbands' surnames, they can do so by usage in most jurisdictions, rather than by legal process. C is incorrect because married women did commonly take their husbands' last names at common law; however, it is true that legislation and court decisions requiring women to do so appeared in some U.S. states in the late nineteenth and early twentieth centuries. However, in the absence of such legislation or judicial decision (which might well violate the U.S. Constitution), Debra is, as D says, still named "Parker" after her marriage.

21. Issue: The Shifting Presumption and Burden of Persuasion of Validity of Successive Marriages by One Individual

The correct answer is **D**. The presumption favors finding the last in a series of marriages to be valid, but that presumption is rebuttable by presentation of evidence that the earlier marriage has not been dissolved by death, divorce, or annulment. Once the continuing validity of the first marriage is established, the burden of persuasion is on the second spouse to establish that that marriage has been dissolved. B is erroneous because it applies the presumption to the earlier marriage.

22. Issue: Family Privacy and the Obligation of Support Within Marriage

The correct answer is **D**. Answer A states a principle that is contrary to the law; in general, the principle of B, that the support obligation undertaken in marriage can only be enforced by a spouse who is leaving it, governs. An exception occurs in family support statutes, described in C. These have been enacted by many states to provide an enforcement mechanism when the failure to support by a solvent party to the marriage reduces the other family members to destitution that would endanger them. Thus, D is the best answer.

23. Issue: The Elements of the Doctrine of Necessaries

Answer **D** is correct. Under this doctrine a third party, like the repairman, who has supplied a necessary item to the wife that the husband has failed or refused to supply can recover from the husband. Whether an item is a necessary is determined by whether it is suitable and proper for the wife, considering the husband's income and status. This common law principle has been discarded in some jurisdictions as gender-biased, but most of the jurisdictions that have recently considered the doctrine have retained it in a gender-neutral form.

24. Issue: The Continued Existence and Elements of the Tort of Alienation of Affection

The correct answer is **B**. In most U.S. jurisdictions, the common law tort of alienation of a spouse's affection has been statutorily eliminated, along with most "heart-balm" actions, in the twentieth century. The policy underlying its elimination was that such actions afforded opportunities for blackmail and extortion, were often gender-biased, and were premised on a view of spouses as one another's property. Although another tort action might be available to Wally and/or Brenda on the basis of Pastor Flynn's breach of his professional duties as a counselor, Wally's alienation of affection suit would be dismissed. A is incorrect because, in states where this tort still is recognized (most notably North

Carolina), it does not require that the defendant's actions be the sole cause of the alienation, but an effective cause. C is incorrect because, where the tort exists, it does not require that the marriage of the defendant had previously been perfect, but that it was a marriage with genuine love and affection. D is incorrect because, where the tort is still recognized, the seduction of another's spouse is considered legally wrongful; Pastor Flynn's status as a counselor to Brenda is added evidence that his actions meet the standard of "wrongful and malicious."

25. Issue: The Characteristics of Covenant Marriage Statutes

The correct answer is **A**. Covenant marriage statutes do not seek to enhance flexibility in marriage structure; their goal is to make divorce more difficult to obtain in the interest of reducing its occurrence. B, C, and D state genuine characteristics of covenant marriage statutes.

26. Issue: Whether a State Can Refuse Access to Divorce to Individuals Unable to Pay the Requisite Fees

Answer **A** is correct. In a very limited holding, the Supreme Court held that the state could not deny access to divorce to those genuinely unable to afford state-imposed fees because of both the status of marriage in our society as fundamental, and the state's monopoly on its dissolution. B is incorrect; the Supreme Court did not state that divorce itself is a fundamental right; it is a method of adjusting a fundamental relationship. C is incorrect because the justices explicitly rejected any claim that they were recognizing access for all persons to the courts as a right that a state cannot deny for any reason. Thus, D is incorrect because C is incorrect.

27. Issue: Standard for Finding Cruel Treatment as a Fault Basis for Divorce

The correct answer is **C**. For a finding of cruel treatment, most jurisdictions require evidence of conduct that is harmful to the plaintiff's health so that continued cohabitation is intolerable, unsafe, or improper. The actions alleged to be cruel will be viewed in the context of the length of the marriage. Given the differences in their age and physical condition, Eliza's behavior could seriously injure Frank. The behavior is not something that Frank has condoned throughout a long-term marriage, because it is related to the children, the older of whom is 4. A is not correct because Barbara and Alec appear to be incompatible in their personal habits, rather than Barbara being cruel; mere incompatibility and bickering are not serious enough for most courts to find Barbara at fault, especially because Frank tolerated it for ten years. B is not correct because the allegation is based on a single incident in a long marriage. In general, courts require that a cruelty claim be founded on a continuous course of conduct rather than on a single incident, unless the latter is life-threatening. D is not correct because the behavior itself was tolerated for ten years during which the couple produced three children, indicating that Gene did not find Helen's admittedly ugly behavior intolerable. Rather than meeting the standard for cruel treatment, it appears to be an indication of incompatibility.

28. Issue: Proof Required for a Finding of the Fault of Adultery Prior to the Late Twentieth Century

The correct answer is **A**. The fault of adultery should have been difficult to prove prior to the change in U.S. social mores that occurred beginning in the 1960s, but in fact it was not. The requirements appeared high: First, because adultery was a fault ground for divorce largely because of a lack of a techno-logical means to establish paternity of children born in the marriage, adultery required reproductive intercourse, which was unlikely to have witnesses. Second, the standard for proving adultery was stated by courts to be a high one. However, circumstantial evidence of adultery was accepted. Given the restrictive mores of the period, mere socializing or demonstrations of affection between a man and woman not his wife, followed by a period of privacy (especially at night), was often accepted as proof that the adultery had taken place. Moreover, lawyers and private detectives often willingly arranged a sham performance by one of the parties to the desired divorce of acts that would satisfy this standard of evidence. Hence, B and C are wrong. D is also wrong; the fault provided a ground for the innocent spouse to bring an action against a guilty one. The guilty spouse could not use her own fault to obtain a divorce.

29. Issues: Constructive Abandonment as a Divorce Ground; Condonation as a Defense to a Divorce Ground

The correct answer is **B**. A is incorrect because courts extended the fault ground of abandonment (or desertion) to include constructive abandonment or constructive desertion. This fault consists of conduct by one spouse that makes the marital relationship unendurable, and justifies the departure of the other spouse. See *Lynch v. Lynch*, 616 So. 2d 294 (Miss. 1993). The persistent refusal of one of the spouses to engage in sexual acts with the other where no excusing health condition exists is considered to be such conduct. See *Davis v. Davis*, 889 N.Y.S.2d 611, 612-613 (N.Y. App. Division 2009). C is also incorrect because when Harry said he forgave Ginger and continued to live with her for years despite the evidence of her adultery, he provided her with the defense of *condonation*. Condonation is forgiveness of a ground for divorce, usually signified by resumption of the marital relationship; that ground then becomes unavailable for a divorce in the future. See *Chastain v. Chastain*, 672 S.E.2d 108, 110 (S.C. 2009). In forgiving Ginger's behavior and continuing to live with her as a spouse, Harry forfeited his 1905 adultery ground. D is incorrect because the state, in accepting constructive abandonment as a ground for divorce, has determined that it was a sufficient basis for ending the family, and thus the protection of its family privacy.

30. Issue: Court's Sua Sponte Finding of Collusion of the Parties to Deny a Divorce in Fault-Based Divorce Systems

The correct answer is **D**. Under a fault-based divorce system, courts would scrutinize the evidence for divorce to prevent married couples from receiving a divorce when in fact they had no ground to do so. See *Nelson v. Nelson*, 24

N.W.2d 327, 346–348 (S.D. 1946). Staging a phony scene that supported the ground of adultery was one means of attempting this fraud on the court. Collusion could be raised by the court independently of the parties. A is wrong because the appellate court is more likely to defer to the trial court on issues of fact based on credibility of the parties and the witnesses. B is wrong because the court could not take such social norms, as opposed to legal ones, into consideration. C is wrong because confession to adultery by one of the spouses was not dispositive on the issue where the possibility of collusion existed.

31. Issues: The Effect of a Change in the Grounds on Which a Divorce May Be Granted on Those Who Entered Marriage Prior to the Modification; Who May Receive Alimony

The correct answer is **C**. A is incorrect under the U.S. Supreme Court's determination in *Maynard v. Hill*, 120 U.S. 190, 210-211 (1888), in which it ruled that marriage, although entered by consent, is more than a contract; it is a status governed by state law, which sets the terms, including the requirements for dissolution. Thus, the constitutional provision prohibiting state legislation impairing existing contracts is inapplicable to divorce legislation. The state could have created the sort of exemption Harry was asking for, but it didn't, and it was not required to do so by the U.S. Constitution. The same reasoning applies to B; without a state statutory requirement that the time be accumulated after the statute was passed, there's no legal basis for excluding time accumulated before then. See *Hurry v. Hurry*, 76 So. 160 (La. 1917). As for D, until the late twentieth century, alimony statutes provided support exclusively to the innocent ex-wife, based on the ex-husband's duty to support her within the marriage; he could not terminate this duty through his own wrong behavior. This support duty was not reciprocal. An innocent husband at this time could not obtain an alimony award, but not for the reason stated in D.

32. Issue: Insanity as a Defense to Divorce for Fault in the Traditional Fault System

The correct answer is **A**. Rochester could not divorce Bertha on a fault ground because under the traditional view of divorce, it was a remedy for an innocent spouse against a guilty one. Insanity was a defense to fault provided there was a causal relationship between the insanity and the fault. The insane spouse was considered not to be responsible for her actions that would ordinarily constitute, in this case, cruel treatment; therefore, she was not a guilty spouse. Thus B is incorrect. C is incorrect because there is no indication that either party has left the matrimonial domicile. Rochester could not obtain an annulment for error as to the person, suggested in D. That ground required a mistake on the part of the spouse alleging it as to the actual identity of the other spouse.

33. Issue: Connivance as a Defense to Fault-Based Divorce

The correct answer is **D**. Connivance is defined as consent by one party to the adulterous act of another; it is sometimes treated more expansively as consent by one party to the commission of acts by the other that constitute a ground for divorce. See *Farwell v. Farwell*, 133 P. 958, 959 (Mont. 1913). There is, therefore, no "innocent" spouse who can claim injury from these acts, the basis of a fault system of divorce. In agreeing to the "open marriage," Andrew consented to Barbara's adultery. A is erroneous because it does not take the defense into account. B is erroneous because a prenuptial contract that attempts to waive the obligation of fidelity within marriage would be an unenforceable nullity because it is contrary to public policy; it is not the reason Andrew's request for a divorce for Barbara's adultery would be denied. C is wrong because, although the prenuptial contract is a nullity, Barbara still has the common law defense of connivance to Andrew's charge of adultery.

34. Issue: Recrimination and Unclean Hands as Defenses to Fault-Based Divorce Actions

The correct answer is **C**. The other results are possible in the type of system described. Recrimination and unclean hands were related defenses against divorce actions in common law. Recrimination barred a spouse who was guilty of a fault that was a ground for divorce from obtaining a divorce on the basis of the other spouse's fault. Whereas some courts mechanically applied the rule, others weighed the two faults and, if one was more serious than the other, granted the divorce to the spouse whose fault was less significant. Thus, depending on the jurisdiction, A or B could result. D could result because courts at common law could invoke the doctrine of "unclean hands" to dismiss the divorce action brought by a spouse whose own conduct in the marriage was morally unacceptable. However, C is unlikely to be the result because in recrimination cases, adultery tended to be treated as a more serious fault than almost any other.

35. Issue: The Characteristics of No-Fault Divorce Grounds

The correct answer is **D**. Reconciliation requires the cooperation of both spouses; in accordance with the policies underlying the no-fault divorce regime, the desire of one spouse to reconcile and preserve the marriage will not bar a no-fault divorce if the other spouse desires to obtain one. A, B, and C are wrong because all three state genuine characteristics of no-fault divorce grounds. No-fault divorce statutes were designed to eliminate the traditional guilty spouse vs. innocent spouse paradigm of divorce, and to allow one spouse to terminate the marriage if she or he believes it to be irretrievably broken.

36. Issue: The Domicile Required of the Spouses for Out-of-State Recognition of a State's Judgment of Divorce

The correct answer is **B**. Under the U.S. Supreme Court's ruling in *Williams v. North Carolina (Williams I)*, 317 U.S. 287 (1942), other states must give full faith and credit to a divorce judgment of a state if at least one party to the divorce was domiciled in the granting state. Domicile of one party in the state is both necessary and sufficient to give its courts subject matter jurisdiction over his or her marital status. A is wrong because it imposes a greater requirement, and

C is wrong because it states an earlier Supreme Court ruling that was overruled by *Williams I*. D is wrong; it contains a conflicts of laws test that is inapplicable to divorce.

37. Issue: Challenging the Establishment of Domicile, Needed for Subject Matter Jurisdiction over a Divorce

The correct answer is **B**. Domicile has two elements: physical residence in the state for the statutory period of time, and the intent to make the state one's home indefinitely (sometimes termed "permanently"). Although Phillip has the first element, the activities he undertook in Nevada strongly suggest that he lacks the second. He made no changes in his address to indicate that he had abandoned his domicile in North Carolina; he used a temporary residence, a hotel, in Nevada; he continued to work for his North Carolina business; and he returned to North Carolina as soon as he got his divorce. North Carolina's subject matter jurisdiction for the divorce requires domicile; a judgment from a court without that jurisdiction is null. A is wrong because, under *Williams I*, the fact that an otherwise valid divorce is ex parte does not make it a nullity. C is wrong because it states an overruled requirement of subject matter jurisdiction for divorce. D is wrong because Ellen's due process rights do not require that she participate in the divorce action, but merely that she be sent notice (which Phillip sent her) and an opportunity to be heard.

38. Issue: Recognition in the United States of Foreign Divorces That Are Valid Where Obtained

The correct answer is **C**. A is wrong because the Full Faith and Credit clause applies only to judgments of courts of U.S. states; it does not apply to judgments of a foreign sovereign's courts, as Derrica Isla's court would be. B is wrong because although U.S. states often recognize divorces in foreign countries on the basis of comity, this foreign court lacks subject matter jurisdiction, and thus does not meet U.S. standards of due process so that its judgment in this case would be deferred to. D is wrong because the U.S. Constitution makes no provision placing exclusive power in the federal government to recognize other nations' divorces as valid. States can grant deference to these divorces under the principle of comity. See *Rosentiel v. Rosentiel*, 209 N.E.2d 709 (N.Y. 1965), *cert. denied* 384 U.S. 971 (1966). C is correct because in these circumstances — an extremely short residency period rather than a requirement of domicile, which is needed to confer subject matter jurisdiction for divorce — the due process requirements of the U.S. Constitution would be offended; as a matter of public policy, the divorce will not be recognized. See *De Pena v. De Pena*, 298 N.Y.S. 2d 188 (App. Div. 1969); *Warrender v. Warrender*, 190 A.2d 684 (N.J. App. 1963).

39. Issue: Equitable Bars to Challenging the Validity of a Divorce Obtained by the Challenger

The correct answer is **D**, which means that both A and B accurately state the rationales used in most states that have dealt with the issue. A is accurate because some states would invoke the equitable principle of unclean hands to bar Victor from obtaining an annulment because he procured the invalid divorce in Derrica Isla and benefited from it in marrying Nikki. He would not be heard to deny the validity of the divorce that permitted him to obtain this benefit. B is also accurate because other states would bar Victor in the name of "equitable estoppel." Although this use of the term is somewhat imprecise, courts have invoked this principle when a party takes a position inconsistent with his prior conduct, the other party has relied on it, and the expectations of the other party will be upset if the divorce is held to be invalid. For an examination of the rationales for this version of estoppel, see Homer Clark, The Law of Domestic Relations in the United States, 2d Student Edition, 434-443 (1988). Thus, D is correct. C is incorrect because most states that have addressed the issue utilize equitable principles to avoid granting an annulment.

40. Issue: The Substance of the Doctrine of Divisible Divorce

The correct answer is **B**. In *Vanderbilt v. Vanderbilt*, the Supreme Court determined that, because the economic actions incident to divorce decide property rights, their adjudication requires personal jurisdiction over both spouses. This personal jurisdiction is based on minimum contacts with the state, such as physical presence within the state, purposefully availing oneself of the state's laws, acquiring or owning within the state the property involved in the action, or engaging in tortious acts with effects in the state provided the action is related to that tort. A is wrong because it is the opposite of the correct statement. C and D are fictional rules that have no relation to reality, and are therefore wrong.

41. Issue: The Relationship Between the Fault Ground for Divorce and the Award of Alimony

The correct answer is **B**. Although originally a fault-based divorce meant that the party at fault was barred from receiving alimony from the other ex-spouse, this position has been rejected by almost all the states in the era of no-fault divorce. Only three states retain the ban. In other jurisdictions, fault can be a comparative factor in determining the suitability and amount of alimony, or can be regarded as irrelevant to the financial awards. A is wrong because, although it states the position of the law in the past, that position was rejected in the later twentieth century in most U.S. jurisdictions. C is incorrect because it states the defense of recrimination, used in the past to prevent divorce; it is not a rule concerning awards of alimony. D is erroneous because most states have not abolished alimony; when alimony was found discriminatory in *Orr v. Orr*, 440 U.S. 268 (1979), it became available to either ex-spouse in most states.

42. Issue: Appropriate Circumstances for Awards of Either Permanent Periodic or Rehabilitative Alimony

The correct answer is **B**. Although permanent periodic alimony is no longer favored in almost all jurisdictions, especially for someone as young as Brenda, her illness and lack of skills make it extremely unlikely that she will get a job through which she can support herself. Her speech defect and drooling would make it difficult for her to be hired for a position in which she deals with the public. The fact that she has to wipe the drool from her face using a handkerchief at short intervals means that a low-skilled office job like file clerk or typist would also be difficult for her to obtain. Even a court that subscribes to the rehabilitative notion of alimony will award permanent alimony if the spouse seeking it lacks sufficient income to provide for her reasonable needs and is unable to support herself through suitable employment (UMDA sec. 308). A is incorrect because of the high probability that Brenda will have to return to court within six months to request alimony again; such a decision would protract litigation and cause a waste of judicial resources. C is incorrect for the same reason; the 12-month period is likely too short for Brenda to get enough education or training to begin a new career, and is also unlikely to produce a newly discovered cure. Answer D is wrong because answer A is wrong.

43. **Issue: The Analysis for Determining Whether a Reduction in Alimony Is Warranted When the Change in Circumstances of the Alimony Payor Is Voluntary**

The correct answer is **C**. Courts have not limited themselves to considering financial benefits and burdens in determining whether a reduction in alimony after a voluntary change in circumstances is justified. They have also considered benefits such as physical and emotional health. A and B are steps in the analysis to determine whether a decrease in alimony in the particular case is warranted, and D is a method that the court could use if it so finds.

44. **Issue: Whether Cohabitation with a Same-Sex Partner Will Terminate the Alimony Obligation That a Former Spouse Has to the Cohabitating Recipient**

The correct answer is **D**. Although some states consider cohabitation to be a termination factor like remarriage, others require that support continue to be paid because without remarriage, there is no relationship of mutual support between Bob and another person. A is in error because it takes the original position of fault-based divorce concerning entitlement to alimony, but does so in a context where no fault exists. B suggests one approach taken by some states: to treat cohabitation of any kind as relieving the paying ex-spouse of the obligation to support the recipient. C presents the position of other states, in which termination of alimony payments is triggered by the fact that the alimony recipient has entered a relationship of mutual support with another person, so that the ex-spouse's support is no longer necessary. Thus, D is correct because either B or C is likely to be adopted as the rule in Anna's jurisdiction.

45. **Issue: Differences That Distinguish the Community Property Approach to Marital Property from That Used in Most States**

The correct answer is **C**. Answer C *does not* state a difference between community property and noncommunity property states. In fact, community property regimes also consider property acquired during the marriage by gift or inheritance to be separate, and not subject to distribution. A minority of noncommunity property states consider separate property to be subject to distribution as well. A, B, and D all contain genuine differences between the community property states and those that have not adopted that system.

46. Issue: Classification of Property as Marital or Separate in Most Equitable Distribution States

The correct answer is **D**. In most equitable distribution states, the following property is classified as separate: (1) property acquired from a third party during the marriage by inheritance or gift; (2) property the acquisition of which is directly traceable to separate property; (3) property acquired before the marriage; (4) property excluded from the marital estate by a valid contract between the parties. B is true because the stocks and bonds fall into category (1). C is true because the antiques fall into category (2). Thus D is correct. A is false because the house was acquired by Zelda prior to the marriage, and thus falls into category (3).

47. Issue: Initial Presumption of Equal Division in Most Equitable Distribution States

The correct answer is **A**. In most equitable distribution states, equal distribution of the marital property is presumed to be equitable, and must be rebutted for a different division to take place. B is erroneous because it looks to title as the basis for distribution. Equitable distribution was created to replace reliance on title in property division in divorce. C is erroneous because, although relative contributions can be used to overcome the presumption of equal division, they are not a starting point, and the contributions are not limited to monetary ones. D is erroneous because, although the economically weaker party might well be awarded a larger share of the property to attain certain policy objectives, it is also not a starting point.

48. Issue: Classification of Intangibles as Marital Property

The correct answer is **A**. Although New York has found professional licenses and degrees to be marital property subject to equitable distribution, most states do not because they regard these as personal to the holder. The three other items are all considered to be divisible marital property.

49. Issue: The Distribution of a Pension That Is Earned at Least in Part During the Marriage

A is the correct answer. A portion of the pension benefits of one spouse will be distributed to the other on divorce in proportion to the amount of time during the marriage that the spouse worked at the business in relation to the total time that he worked at the business. B is incorrect because the lack of knowledge as to whether Tom will receive the pension in the future does not affect the fact that it is a marital asset. C is erroneous because the division is not equal, but in the proportion described above: marriage during work years: total work years. D also proposes a factor for division that is not used, whether the spouse with no pension should receive a larger share, and is therefore erroneous.

50. Issue: The Requirements for the Domestic Relations Exception to Federal Diversity Jurisdiction

The correct answer is **B**. Judgments of divorce, awards of alimony or modification of alimony awards, and child custody decrees have been explicitly recognized by the U.S. Supreme Court as under a "domestic relations exception" to federal jurisdiction, even if the requirements for federal diversity jurisdiction are otherwise fulfilled. A is incorrect because in *Ankenbrandt v. Richards*, 504 U.S. 689 (1992), the Court recognized that the exception applies to exempt these three types of domestic cases from diversity jurisdiction because domestic relations are considered peculiarly a matter of state concern and state expertise. C is incorrect because it is narrower than the actual exception, which includes awards of alimony as well. D is incorrect because the exception, which first was announced in the mid-nineteenth century case of *Barber v. Barber*, 21 How. 582 (1859), has never been codified; it is a matter of statutory construction by the Court, based on Congressional acceptance of its interpretation of the diversity jurisdiction provision, according to the *Ankenbrandt* opinion.

51. Issue: The Substantive Limits of the Domestic Relations Exception

The correct answer is **A**. In *Ankenbrandt v. Richards*, 504 U.S. 689 (1992), the U.S. Supreme Court concluded that the domestic relations exception to federal jurisdiction encompasses only cases involving the issuance of a divorce, alimony, or child custody decree. B is incorrect because Mindy's tort case is outside the narrow boundaries established in the *Ankenbrandt* ruling. C is also incorrect not because of the outcome it proposes, but because of the reasoning. It is the type of case, not the legal relationships of the parties, that determines whether it falls within the domestic relations exception; one does not have to be a blood relative of a child to seek to be his or her custodian. D is incorrect because A is correct.

52. Issue: Discriminatory Treatment of Nonmarital Children in Common Law

The correct answer is **D**. None of the inheritance rights listed, all of which would flow to a marital child from his parents and grandparents, were available to Andrew. He would have been treated by the law as *filius nullius*, the child of no one; thus he had no relatives to inherit from. This legal condition was called "illegitimacy," and was imposed on children born of parents who had not contracted the legal bond of matrimony with one another.

53. Issue: The Common Law Evidentiary Rules That Protected the Legitimacy of Children Born to a Married Mother

The correct answer is **C**. Under Lord Mansfield's Rule, neither the husband nor the wife could testify to their lack of access to one another during the time when conception would have taken place. All of the answers describe evidentiary rules in the common law for litigating paternity. Answer A is the basic common law presumption of paternity of the husband, known as the "marital presumption." Answer B describes the very limited possible means of rebutting the presumption. Given the state of medical science until the twentieth century, proving inability to reproduce would be extremely unlikely. If the husband's doubts were based on physical separation from his wife, Lord Mansfield's Rule, stated in C, closed off the most likely way that he could prove it. It thus made the marital presumption almost irrebuttable; until the late twentieth century, it was often labeled "the strongest presumption in law." Answer D provides the outcome of a successful disavowal by the mother's husband. The child was treated as illegitimate because he was not born from married parents. Hence the common law's reluctance to bastardize such children; there were draconian economic consequences for the children, and ultimately for the state.

54. Issue: Court Resolution of Conflicting Presumptions of Paternity

The correct answer is **A**. Because most states allow rebuttal of the presumption of paternity, the appellate court is most likely to remand the case for a trial on the evidence of biological paternity. B is incorrect because the appellate court should not dismiss Gerald's claim, but set the matter for trial. Although Seth has a presumption of paternity in his favor under the UPA, that presumption can be rebutted. C is erroneous because although the time limit for contesting the husband's paternity is usually two years (UPA sec. 204), it is inapplicable where, as here, the mother and her husband were not cohabiting and did not engage in sexual relations at the probable time of conception, and the husband never openly held out the child as his own (UPA sec. 607). D is incorrect because there's no firm policy established to guide the courts to favor marital over nonmarital paternity. States are divided as to whether the legal relationship or the biological one should be decisive.

55. Issue: Status in Most U.S. Jurisdictions of Consenting Husband of the Mother of a Child Conceived by Artificial Insemination

The correct answer is **C**. Most states' statutes on assisted reproduction resolve the question of paternity by providing that the husband who consented to his wife's artificial insemination with another man's sperm is the legal father of the child. See, e.g., *Levin v. Levin*, 645 N.E.2d 601 (Ind. 1994). Permitting Harry to revoke his consent and deny parenthood on the basis of his or Wanda's later actions would undermine the public policy of parental support for children. Thus, Wanda's consent to Harry's divorce request, Harry's suit itself, and the availability of abortion are irrelevant to Harry's status as the child's father, and answer D would be an interference with Wanda's reproductive rights as well.

56. Issue: The Parental Rights and Responsibilities of a Nonspousal Sperm Donor Under Typical State Assisted Reproduction Statutes

The correct answer is **B**. Assisted reproduction statutes usually protect the sperm donor who is not married to the donee from parental responsibilities, notably child support; at the same time, the mother is protected from any claim he might bring for parental rights. A is erroneous because Jason is not recognized as Tom's father, so the court would not reach the issue of the best interest test. C is erroneous because Jason, although aware of Mia's pregnancy, did not in a timely manner take the steps that would entitle him to constitutional protection as Tom's father, such as registering as his putative father or suing for recognition of his paternity. D is erroneous because the common law classification of a nonmarital child as the child of no one is no longer the law anywhere in the United States.

57. Issue: The Right of a Same-Sex Partner to Recognition as the Parent of Her Former Partner's Child

The correct answer is **D**. All of the answers have been used, each in a different state whose courts have confronted the question. Answer A comes from the Oregon case of *Shineovich v. Shineovich*, 214 P.3d 29 (Or. App. 2009), *writ denied as Shineovich v. Kemp*, 222 P.3d 1091 (Or. 2009); the Oregon state constitution recognizes discrimination based on sexual orientation as a trigger of strict scrutiny, which the artificial insemination statute failed. California's Supreme Court used answer B to recognize two women who were former partners as legal parents under the state's version of the Uniform Parentage Act in *Elisa B. v. Superior Court*, 33 Cal. Reptr. 3d 46 (Cal. 2005), and to award child support to the birth mother. Answer C was used in *Allison D. v. Virginia M.*, 572 N.W.2d 27 (New York 1991), to deny visitation to the birth mother's former partner.

58. Issue: Establishing the Maternity of a Child Produced by Reproductive Technology

The correct answer is **C**. The court is most likely to recognize Annette as the child's legal mother because she intended from the outset to procreate and raise the child. See *Johnson v. Calvert*, 851 P.2d 776 (Cal. 1993). A is not correct because the courts tend to look not just at the law of contract, but also at the situation in which the child will be placed, when deciding between the surrogate and the genetic mother. B is not correct because the analogy to an egg donor is imperfect. The gestational mother in true egg donation cases, unlike Barbara, intends to gestate and raise the child, whereas the donor is only supplying her with the means to do so. Compare *McDonald v. McDonald*, 608 N.Y.S.2d 477 (N.Y. App. Div. 1994). D is incorrect because courts have rejected the purely genetic identification of the mother, preferring to decide on the basis of intent.

59. Issue: Factors Used to Determine Custody on the Basis of the Best Interests of the Child

The correct answer is **D**. Although A, B, and C are typical best-interest factors, promoting affection, continuity, and stability, the parents' relative financial resources are not. A significant disparity would normally be corrected by means of the child support order.

60. **Issue: The Inapplicability of Res Judicata to Requests to Modify a Child Custody Judgment**

The correct answer is **B**. The principle of res judicata would be violated if either of the parties to the original custody dispute was permitted to relitigate the same facts in requesting a modification. (But see *Swope v. Swope*, 689 A.2d 264 (Pa. 1997) (court's paramount concern is child's best interest).) Almost all states require such a request to be based on an allegation of a change in circumstances. See *Wade v. Hirschman*, 903 So. 2d 928 (Fla. 2005). A is incorrect because the state's protective duty toward children does not trump res judicata; to permit it to would allow a disgruntled parent to harass the other parent and waste judicial resources in arguing that the original judgment was wrong. C is also incorrect; such a waiver would have the same effect. D is incorrect because B correctly explains the ability of the same parties to relitigate child custody: The facts underlying the question of custodial placement have changed.

61. **Issue: The Role of Racial Identity in Determining the Best Interests of the Child for Custody Purposes**

The correct answer is **A**. The U.S. Supreme Court overturned the state court's award of custody in *Palmore v. Sidoti* on grounds that race was used impermissibly in arriving at the award; however, in that case, race was the sole factor used by the Florida courts, which did not apply other relevant factors to each parent in making its decision. Since then, courts have interpreted *Palmore* not as a blanket prohibition of considering race in child custody decisions as B erroneously suggests, but as prohibiting making it the **sole** or **decisive** factor. See *J.H.H. v. O'Hara*, 878 F.2d 240 (8th Cir. 1989) and *Tallman v. Tabor*, 859 F. Supp. 1078 (E.D. Mich. 1994). Answers C and D are wrong because they rely on rejected gender-biased notions of the best interests of the child.

62. **Issue: Possible Restrictions on Parental Visitation**

The correct answer is **A**. Beatrice has a constitutional right to continued contact with Carlos, and it is unlikely that Alberto can demonstrate that that right has been defeated on these facts. Although courts sometimes deny visitation to a noncustodial parent, they require that that parent pose a serious danger to the child's physical, mental, moral, or emotional health. Examples of conditions that pose such a threat include domestic violence, sexual abuse, and substance abuse. Beatrice's behavior does not pose a serious danger to Carlos's physical health, as she only has him intermittently and feeds him when he tells her to. The mental or emotional damage that might result from her ignoring him during his visits, and from her depressive talk, is not that great, and there is a less restrictive alternative — supervised visitation. The greatest danger is that she might attempt suicide while he is visiting, which supervised visitation would prevent. B is incorrect because, as indicated earlier, an alternative is available that has less impact on her rights as a parent. C is incorrect because terminating parental rights requires a much greater and more intractable threat to the child. D is incorrect, although it proposes only a temporary suspension of her visitation, because it unnecessarily imposes a complete ban for an indefinite time period without regard to the effect of her mental illness on Carlos. If Beatrice's mental illness does not pose the threat contained in the standard that courts have artic-ulated, then she should have the right to continue contact with her child.

63. Issue: The Standard for Modification of a Custody Order

The correct answer is **D**. Which of these two standards governs depends on whether the jurisdiction has adopted the majority or the minority rule for modifying a custody order. A higher standard is usually required to change custody than that to obtain it in the first place because of the danger of parental overuse of motions to modify. B and C both require a substantial change in circumstances, but each contains an additional requirement. B, which states the majority rule, requires Beatrice to prove that as a result of the change, the present custody order is no longer in the child's best interest. C, which states the minority rule, requires Beatrice to prove that the benefit of her replacing Alberto as sole custodian outweighs the change's disruptive effect on Carlos. The facts she presents don't indicate any substantial change in circumstances; occasional lateness and occasional childhood accidents are minor failings, and Carlos's missing his parent is a result of the divorce rather than of Alberto's custody.

64. Issues: Effect of a Parent's Sexual Activity in Modifying or Granting Child Custody

The correct answer is **C**. Although almost all jurisdictions require the substantial change in circumstances that Alberto's sharing his and Carlos's home with Sandi represents, a change is not in itself sufficient for modification. There must be either a negative impact on the present custody from it, or, under the minority rule, the benefits of the noncustodial parent's custody must outweigh the disadvantages of disrupting the child's present way of life. But states exhibit such diverse norms with respect to sexual behavior that it's impossible to state with certainty how Alberto's behavior would be regarded. In addition, gender stereotyping still occasionally crops up when a parent's sexual mores are a factor in a decision concerning custody. In a conservative and traditional community, the relationship could be seen as a sign that Alberto selfishly pursues his own pleasure without regard to the effect on his child's moral and social development, as in answer A, and should marry Sandi if he wants to continue as sole custodian. In a more liberal and diverse community, the relationship could be seen as normal and neutral with respect to the quality of Carlos's care, as in answer B. Thus C is correct, and D cannot be because both A and B are possible results.

65. Issue: Sexual Orientation as a Factor in Parental Custody

The correct answer is **D**. As with the sexual activities in the preceding question, the usual threshold for considering custody modification, a substantial change in circumstances, has been met. However, for Beatrice to prevail, the court must either reach a different conclusion from that in question 64 in the best interest analysis, or, under the minority rule, the benefits of the noncustodial parent's custody must outweigh the disadvantages of disrupting the child's present way of life. States' norms with respect to sexual orientations other than heterosexual, and to the relationships that result, diverge greatly, and can impact both original and modification custody decisions. A minority of jurisdictions would agree with the position in answer B. At present, Alberto's same-sex relationship would not in most jurisdictions be held to be a dispositive factor in Beatrice's favor. However, Carlos's questions and observations might provide courts in more conservative states with a basis for seeing the relationship as a negative factor, and Alberto as selfish in refusing to conceal it. To a court in another state the same facts might indicate that the relationship is a neutral or even a positive factor, providing Carlos with valuable insights into the different forms that families take. Thus, A, B, and C are all possible rulings, depending on the norms of the state.

66. Issue: The Requirements That Must Be Met for a Custodial Parent to Secure a Modification of the Custody Order so That She May Relocate with the Child

The correct answer is **D**. Different states' rules on interstate relocation of the custodial parent with the child differ greatly in many ways; some derive from judicial decisions (e.g., New York and California) and some from detailed statutory law (e.g., Florida). The terminology in which the rules are expressed varies greatly. However, the states for the most part require a significant good-faith justification for the change from the custodial parent, and examine the impact on the child's best interests. Answers A, B, and C, which are the formulations of Connecticut, New Jersey, and New York, are examples of the consistency of these values despite differences in expression.

67. Issue: Determining Jurisdiction over an Initial Award of Child Custody Under the UCCJEA

The correct answer is **C**. The preferred jurisdiction over an initial award of child custody in the UCCJEA is the child's "home state." The home state is identified as one in which (1) the child lived with a parent or a person acting as a parent for at least six consecutive months prior to the commencement of the proceedings; (2) a parent or person acting as a parent continues to live there; and (3) even if the child no longer lives there, it was the home state of the child within six months of the commencement of the custody proceedings. Answer A states the wrong basis for child custody jurisdiction. Answer B references home state jurisdiction, but defines "home state" erroneously. Answer D is wrong because it relies on the "significant connections" test. That test only comes into play in two circumstances: if there is no "home state," or after the home state court declines jurisdiction.

68. Issue: Exclusive Continuing Jurisdiction in the Court Issuing Original Custody Order Under the UCCJEA

The correct answer is **A**. Once an initial custody order in conformity with the UCCJEA has been issued, the issuing court retains exclusive continuing jurisdiction over future custody disputes between the parties. B is wrong because establishing a new home state for the children does not confer jurisdiction on that state; New York's continuing exclusive jurisdiction exists without regard to the length of time that the children and the other parent are absent from the jurisdiction. However, if the further circumstances in answer A occur—neither the children nor either parent retains a significant connection with the original jurisdiction, and substantial evidence concerning the children is not available there—exclusive continuing jurisdiction in the New York court would terminate. Hence, answer C is erroneous. D is wrong because although the New York court could give permission to the California court to hear the case for this reason, a change in jurisdiction does not occur without such permission. None is mentioned in the facts, and because New York is issuing contempt orders, it's not likely under the circumstances.

69. Issue: Limitation on an Action to Challenge Paternity of the Mother's Husband

The correct answer is **D**; see the Uniform Parentage Act sec. 601 *et seq.*, and the California Family Code sec. 7541(a) and (b). Where there is a presumed father, states place a relatively short statute of limitations on challenging paternity to preserve established family relations and responsibilities. Answer A is an exaggerated statement of the common law position; in fact, in common law, it was possible for the husband to disavow his wife's child by establishing that his parenthood was physically impossible. B is erroneous because the biological parent's standing to assert his due process right might be limited by state law; see *Michael H. v. Gerald D.*, 491 U.S. 110 (1989). C is erroneous in this factual context as it states factors only used in finding standing to assert paternity in the face of maternal opposition if no one is presumed to be father under the marital presumption.

70. Issue: The Requirements for a Finding of Equitable Parenthood Status

The correct answer is **B**. The doctrine of equitable parenthood has been used to award the status of father to a man who, within the context of his marriage to the child's mother, developed a parent–child relationship with children who are not biologically his. Because of the mother's cooperation in developing the relationship, she is estopped from denying it now, whether she objects to its continuation or not. The other three answers state three requirements for success under the doctrine.

71. Issue: The Standard for Awarding Child Custody to a Third Party as Against the Natural Parent Who Has Not Been Found Unfit

The correct answer is **D**. This answer states the legal principle governing awards of custody to third parties as against a natural parent; the natural parent has a presumption in favor of his or her custody that prevails unless he or she is unfit, or unless an exceptional circumstance exists presenting the danger of substantial harm to the child from his or her custody. Marla's actions offer no sign of unfitness, such as abuse, neglect, abandonment, or incapacitation, so no unfitness has been found. Her absences are not a circumstance threatening substantial harm or detriment to Derek. They are temporary; she joined the National Guard for her child's benefit and she acted responsibly in arranging competent care for her child during her absences. Therefore, the presumption in her favor has not been overcome. A and B are both incorrect because both rely on the best interests of the child standard, used in custody disputes between parents, where no presumption favoring either exists. A "best interests" determination is irrelevant when the custody contestants are a natural parent and a third party. C, which states a best interest factor, is therefore also incorrect.

72. Issue: The Standing of a Nonparent to Receive Court-Ordered Visitation with Minor Children in a Parent's Custody

The correct answer is **D**. Depending on the jurisdiction, either of the two outcomes in A and B is possible. On the one hand, the court could take the position in answer A: Dismiss Edith's request for lack of standing because the common law does not provide a basis for it to issue an order of visitation with a nonparent over the fit parent's objection, and there is no statute in the jurisdiction permitting such an order. See *Alison D. v. Virginia M.*, N.W.2d 27 (N.Y. 1991). On the other hand, it could take the positions in answer B: That Edith stands in loco parentis to the girls, and although a nonparent, has overcome the presumption that the fit parent's decision was in the children's best interest provided by Betty's constitutional right to rear her children. See *Spells v. Spells*, 378 A.2d 879 (1977). Answer C is erroneous because it treats Edith's request as the equal of Betty's, without giving Betty the benefit of the presumption that the fit mother's decision is in the child's best interest.

73. Issue: The Operation of the Hague Convention on the Civil Aspects of Child Abduction

The correct answer is **A**; the Hague Convention does not provide for a new determination of custody. The Hague Convention has as its primary goal the prompt return of the abducted child to his or her lawful custodian under the custody determination made in the nation-party that is the child's habitual residence. It only permits the court to make a new custody determination if the court has ruled that the child cannot be returned. Some reasons that the child might not be returned appear in answers B, C, and D. In addition, there are other defenses available in the convention; for example, the child is older than the Convention's maximum age, or the other party was not actually exercising custody rights at the time of retention.

74. Issue: The Elements Required to Prove That a Child Was Wrongfully Removed or Retained from His Habitual Residence Under the Hague Convention

The correct answer is **B**. The Hague Convention does not require that a child must be removed or retained from his or her habitual residence by force or threat of force to prove wrongful removal; mere refusal to return the child is sufficient to create a cause of action, provided that the other elements — which appear here as B, C, and D — are met as well.

75. Issue: The Meaning of *State of Habitual Residence* Under the Hague Convention

The correct answer is **D**. The party lawfully exercising custody under the law of the state of the child's habitual residence is entitled to a judgment returning the child when she has been wrongfully removed or retained, but the Hague Convention doesn't define "habitual residence." U.S. courts have interpreted it as requiring "a degree of settled purpose," demonstrated by examining the child's circumstances in that place and the shared intentions of the parents regarding their child's presence there. See *Friedrich v. Friedrich*, 983 F.2d 1396 (6th Cir. 1993). France is Chloe's habitual residence; it has been her residence for her entire life. Her parents married there, worked there, established a home there, and divorced there. Brian continued to live there after the divorce. Those facts reflect the parents' "settled purpose" to establish Chloe's life in France. A is wrong because Annick only gave her consent to Brian take Chloe to New York for a limited period of time; beyond that, he is wrongfully retaining the child. B is wrong because Chloe's stay in New York was not supposed to last indefinitely; there was no settled purpose on the parents' part for her to reside habitually in the United States. C is wrong because Brian can still live in the United States if he wishes, but he must do so at present in accord with the French custody order, which means that he cannot retain Chloe with him. If he is dissatisfied with the order, he must seek its modification in France.

76. Issue: Whether Violation of a Noncustodial Parent's *ne exeat* Right Constitutes a Violation of a Right of Custody Protected by the Hague Convention

The correct answer is **D**. Resolving a split in the Federal Appellate Circuits, the U.S. Supreme Court has determined that the *ne exeat* right, standing alone, constitutes a right of custody, even if the parent does not have other incidents of custody of the child; to rule otherwise would permit an end run around the Hague Convention and defeat its underlying purpose. See *Abbott v. Abbott*, 130 S. Ct. 1983 (2010). Answer A is wrong; although the federal Court of Appeals in *Abbott* refused to recognize *ne exeat* as a custodial right, the Supreme Court reversed that determination, stating the reasons in B and C. Its conclusion is expressed by answer D.

77. Issue: Application of the Requirements for Proving Wrongful Retention of a Child to Facts of a Typical Hague Convention Case

The correct answer is **C**. Although the parent seeking return of her child should file her petition for return of the child within a year under the Hague Convention, if the child is not "well settled" in his new environment, the original custodian is entitled to the child's return. A is incorrect because the custodial parent's delay beyond a year before asking for return only results in the child being given to the other parent if the child has become "well settled" in his new environment. Here, Ben's changes in domicile, lack of friends, and lack of participation in anything other than solitary technological entertainment mitigate against a finding that he's "well settled" in California. B is incorrect because although Sam has violated the custody order in Rachel's favor, the Hague Convention provides several affirmative defenses that can defeat Rachel's claim for Ben's return. Among them are the custodial parent's consent to the retention; delay in seeking redress for it; nonexercise of her custodial rights at the time of the retention; objection of a mature child; return would violate principles of human rights and freedoms in the state asked to return the child; or return poses a grave risk of psychological or physical harm to the child. None of these are evident here. D is incorrect because Rachel was exercising her ne exeat rights as Ben's custodian (see question 76) at the time that Sam retained Ben and ever since that event.

78. Issue: Whether the Parental Kidnapping Prevention Act Implies a Private Federal Cause of Action to Resolve Conflicting Custody Orders

The correct answer is **A**. In *Thompson v. Thompson*, 484 U.S. 174 (1988), the Supreme Court of the United States held that the PKPA did not create an implied private right of relief for child custody litigants in federal court. B is incorrect because, although the PKPA is intended to subject custody determinations to Full Faith and Credit, it does so by requiring the states to enforce properly issued out-of-state custody orders, not by empowering federal courts to evaluate them. C is incorrect because the Oregon court's original order was temporary; Maryland has a continuing duty to enforce Oregon's permanent order once it was properly issued. D is incorrect because the failure to infer a federal cause of action does not undermine the effect of the PKPA. It is addressed to the states, and state courts must resolve custody deadlocks in accordance with it.

79. Issue: Whether the Jurisdictional Provisions of the Parental Kidnapping Prevention Act Apply to Child Protection Actions by the State, or Only to Actions Between Private Parties

The correct answer is **D**. State courts are divided as to whether the jurisdictional rules of the PKPA apply to a child protection case to which the state is a party. Some states have held that the PKPA's requirement that every state not modify "any custody determination" properly made by a court in another state includes modification by a state child protection order. See *In re Pima County Juvenile Action No. J-78632*, 711 P.2d 1200, 1206 (Ariz. Ct. App. 1985), *rev'd on other grounds*, 712 P.2d 431 (Ariz. 1986); *In re E.H.*, 612 N.E.2d 174, 183 (Ind. Ct. App. 1993); *In re Vivian*, 652 N.E.2d 616, 619 (Mass. 1995); *In re D.S.K.*, 792 P.2d 118, 130 (Utah Ct. App. 1990). Thus, New Hampshire's action would have been barred because North Dakota already has established subject matter jurisdiction over this case. A would therefore be accurate. However, other state courts have found that the purpose of the PKPA was to discourage parties from moving the child to another state in the hope of obtaining a more favorable custody order. This purpose is irrelevant to actions in which the state is a party. Thus Congress did not intend child protection actions to be barred by the PKPA, and B is also accurate. See *L.G. v. People*, 890 P.2d 647, 662–63 (Colo. 1995); *In re K.A.K.* 723 N.W.2d 449 (Iowa Ct. App. 2006), *In re L.W.*, 486 N.W.2d 486, 500 (Neb. 1992); *State ex rel. Dep't of Human Servs. v. Avinger*, 720 P.2d 290, 292 (N.M. 1986); *In re Sayeh R.*, 693 N.E.2d 724, 727 (N.Y. 1997); *Williams v. Knott*, 690 S.W.2d 605, 609 (Tex. App. 1985); *In re Higera N.*, 2010 Me. LEXIS 78. Therefore D, which includes both A and B, is the correct answer. C is incorrect because the PKPA's application is not limited to parental kidnapping cases, but applies to civil interstate custody disputes as well.

80. Issue: The Circumstances in Which Tribal Jurisdiction over Child Custody Supplants State Court Jurisdiction Under the Indian Child Welfare Act

The correct answer is **A**. Statement A is *not true* because the ICWA does not apply to child custody determinations arising out of divorce of the Native American child's parents, although it makes possible tribal court jurisdiction over the other four custody proceedings listed in A if they involve a Native American child. B is true; under 25 U.S.C. §1903(4), defining the term "Indian child," the ICWA appears to preclude jurisdiction in cases involving adopted children of Native American parents who are not the biological children of tribe members. C is true; §1911(a) of the Act vests exclusive jurisdiction over the custody of reservation-domiciled children in tribal courts with only a couple of limited exceptions. D is also true. In §1911(b), the Act requires state courts to transfer to tribal court jurisdiction a foster placement or a parental rights termination case involving Native American children who are not domiciled on their tribe's reservation, with the limited exceptions already listed.

81. Issue: Whether the Tribal Court, in Delaying Its Transfer Request, Provided the State with Good Cause to Refuse to Transfer the Case to Tribal Court

The correct answer is **D**. The tribal court's delay while the state sought reunification of the family, and the further delay owing to circumstances not within the tribe's control, do not constitute good cause to deny transfer of the case, for the two reasons stated: the policy of reuniting Native American families and the injustice of permitting the ICWA to be circumvented by delays not of the tribe's making. A is not correct, despite the inclusion of delay as a possible "good cause" under the ICWA, because the delay was not caused by the tribe's lack of diligence, but by the state's attempted reunion of the family and the state's failure to share information with the tribe. B is not correct because the state can share its evidence with the tribal court. C is incorrect because tribal courts do not have exclusive jurisdiction, but only concurrent jurisdiction ("transfer jurisdiction") over tribal families that are not domiciled on tribal lands.

82. Issue: The Extent of the Transfer Jurisdiction of a Tribal Court over Custody of Native American Children Not Domiciled on the Reservation

The correct answer is **C**. Both A and B are true statements, providing the rationales for reading the grant of tribal transfer jurisdiction as including jurisdiction over other types of custody cases involving tribal families. See *In re M.S. (Puyallup Tribe of Indians v. State)*, 2010 OK 46, 2010 LEXIS 50 (Okla. 2010). D is incorrect, for the Oklahoma Supreme Court found that the ICWA 1911(b) contains no language that explicitly precludes tribal court transfer jurisdiction over preadoptive and adoptive proceedings.

83. Issue: The Effect of the Statutory Child Support Guidelines on Judicial Decisions in Child Support Cases

The correct answer is **C**. The federal government ultimately mandated not only guidelines, but that the guidelines be strictly applied; a court that deviates in its award from the amount calculated by means of the guidelines must provide oral or written reasons for doing so. This legislation reflects the effort to make child support consistent across similar cases within each state. Answer A is false; although the initial Congressional statute required only advisory guidelines for each state court, after four years Congress added legislation requiring that the guidelines be the mandatory method for state courts to determine child support awards. Answer B is also false. The award amount arrived at using the guidelines is only rebuttably presumed to be the proper amount. D is also false because in most states the guidelines provide the means to accommodate these two and other extraordinary circumstances (e.g., by allowing judicial deviation from the usual calculations, or by explicit statutes included in the guidelines).

84. Issue: The Most Successful of the Three Different Mechanisms Through Which Courts Arrive at Child Support Awards

The correct answer is **B**, the income shares method, used by roughly two thirds of the states. The flat percentage of income model is the second most popular, but is far behind, and the Melson formula, which requires complex calculations based on individualized analysis, is used by only a handful of states. D is a false statement, as B is the correct answer.

85. Issue: Standards for Modifying a Child Support Order

The correct answer is **C**. The statement made is not a true statement concerning child support modification; in contrast to rule for alimony modification, for child support modification, a substantial increase in the payor parent's income provides the basis for an increase in the child's support. The rationale is that the child's relationship to the payor parent is unchanged by the divorce; by virtue of it, the child is entitled to share in the parent's improved standard of living. Answers A, B, and C are all true statements concerning modification of child support orders. Therefore, they cannot be correct answers to the question.

86. **Issue: Whether a Payor's Subsequent Acquisition of Additional Children Justifies Modification of the Earlier Children's Child Support Award in a Downward Direction**

The correct answer is **D**. States take different approaches to the issue of whether a payor parent can obtain downward modification of an existing support award for children in his first family on the basis of a support obligation for children in a second family. Some states treat children acquired subsequent to the support order as a voluntary change of payor's circumstances (first family first), and reject downward modification. Other states treat additional children as justifying downward modification of the earlier award, analogous to an involuntary change in circumstances; the payor's income would be adjusted by what he requires for their support, and a modified award to the earlier born children calculated. Some state guidelines permit courts to treat additional children as justifying a departure from strict application of the guidelines, allowing the court to take an equitable approach to insuring that all the payor's children benefit fairly from their parents' income.

87. **Issue: Availability of a Noncustodial Parent's New Spouse's Income for Child Support of His or Her Stepchildren**

The correct answer is **C**. A court is most likely to modify the award on the basis that Robert's subsidizing Dorothy's living expenses is a change in circumstances justifying upward modification. The amount of Robert's subsidy would be imputed to Dorothy as income. A is incorrect because even though Robert has not acquired a child support obligation, Dorothy still has one, and Robert's support of her increases the amount she has available for child support. Thus the court is unlikely to deny Alan's motion. B is incorrect because, although this result is not completely unknown — some community property jurisdictions have employed it — it is rare; it is thus not a likely result. D is incorrect because Dorothy's lack of a legal claim on Robert's earnings does not prevent the court from modifying the order. The court can increase the amount of her child support obligation on the basis of the increase in the amount of Dorothy's income available thanks to Robert's shouldering of some of her expenses.

88. **Issue: Effect of a Voluntary or a Bad-Faith Change in the Payor (Obligor's) Parent's Employment on His or Her Modification Request**

The correct answer is **D**. A is wrong because, although Christopher has the right to exercise his religion freely, it cannot trump the state's compelling interest in his children's support; thus the court can refuse to modify his obligation. B contains the position of the states on bad-faith reductions in income; these are universally unsuccessful in obtaining a downward modification. If Bella can convince the court of Christopher's bad faith, she will prevail. C states the position of most courts on voluntary reductions in income; even if done in good faith, a purely voluntary reduction in the payor parent's income usually will not result in a downward modification of child support because of courts' unwillingness to make children take the consequences of a parent's midlife crisis. Thus in this case, in which Christopher's reduction in income not only might be in bad faith but is voluntary as well, either or both of these reasons will justify the likely ruling, a denial of Christopher's request for modification.

89. Issue: Occupational License Suspension as an Enforcement Mechanism Against Nonpaying Child Support Obligors

The correct answer is **B**. Several states have passed statutes allowing suspension of professional licenses for noncompliant child support obligors whose work requires a license from a state or local authority. Lawyers are commonly included in such legislation, along with a variety of licensed professionals, such as doctors, morticians, real estate agents, dentists, and beauticians. Christopher's law firm might dismiss him because of the complaint, but Bella would not seek that method of enforcing the child support order; it would terminate the source of his income, unlike the temporary license suspension. The penalty described in C does not exist. Bar associations do not decide who can run for public office. Because A and C are erroneous, so is D.

90. Issue: Criminal and Civil Contempt as Enforcement Mechanisms Against Nonpaying Child Support Obligors

The correct answer is **C**. Both civil and criminal contempt charges can result in the jailing of the delinquent obligor, so answer C does not state a true difference in the effect of civil and criminal contempt determinations. Whereas a finding of criminal contempt can result in a prison sentence of a determinate length, civil contempt can result in imprisonment until the obligor complies with the court's order. Answer A is true; the two mechanisms have different goals. Answer B is also true, as the federal constitutional protections of rights of the accused, as well as civil rights, are afforded an obligor accused of criminal contempt. Answer D is incorrect because answers A and B state genuine differences between the two types of contempt.

91. Issue: Additional Mechanisms for Enforcement of Child Support Payments by a Delinquent Obligor

The correct answer is **D**: Blocking Christopher's attempt to declare bankruptcy is **not** a mechanism for forcing a delinquent child support obligor to disgorge the payments that he owes. However, Christopher's child support obligation is not dischargeable in bankruptcy, so the bankruptcy proceeding will not affect that debt. Answer A is true; wage assignments or garnishments can be secured by the obligee (payee) to secure payment of the child support before the obligor (payor) receives the money. Answer B is also true. Federal law permits denial or restriction of a passport if an obligor owes $5,000 or more in arrearages. Answer C is also true; states have seized the lottery winnings of a delinquent parent to satisfy his child support obligations.

92. Issue: The Mechanism by Which a Child Support Obligee (Payee) Can Enforce Payment by an Obligor (Payor) Who Lives in a State Other Than the One That Issued the Order

The correct answer is **B**; the New York court does not have to have personal jurisdiction over Mr. Kay at the time of the order's enforcement. At the time of the substantive determination of Mr. Kay's support obligation, the New York court had personal jurisdiction over him. California, which has personal jurisdiction over Mr. Kay at this point, is merely enforcing the New York order in accordance with both the UIFSA (which has been adopted by all the states) and 28 U.S.C. sec. 1738B, the federal Full Faith and Credit for Child Support Orders Act. A and B are incorrect answers because they are true statements of enforcement mechanisms available to Ms. Kay under the UIFSA. This Act provides the originating state with continuing, exclusive subject matter jurisdiction over validly issued child support orders, and creates mechanisms for their enforcement in other states. D is an incorrect answer because it too contains a true statement concerning a similar, although more limited enforcement option available to Ms. Kay under the federal act cited.

93. Issue: The Most Common Basis for Which Court-Ordered Child Support Terminates

The correct answer is **B**. Although all four events provide a basis for terminating child support, it most commonly terminates because the child has reached the age of majority after graduating from high school, or graduates after attaining majority, but before reaching the state-determined age limit after which a full-time high school student is no longer entitled to child support; or attains that state-determined age limit while still a full-time student in high school. Child support can, of course, be terminated after the child has died, but minor children in the United States today commonly live to majority, so A is wrong. C is wrong because only a minority of states — approximately one third — extend the obligation to provide support for children attending college; therefore, this is not the most common basis for termination. D is wrong also because, although active-duty military service emancipates a child in a number of states, and can thus be a basis for terminating support, it is not universal, and only a minority of support recipients will see such service.

94. Issue: Whether the Marriage of a Minor Automatically and Irreversibly Results in the Minor's Emancipation

The correct answer is **D**. Depending on the jurisdiction, Della's marriage might either have effected emancipation for a short period of time and been reversed by the marriage's nullification, or not effected emancipation at all. In some instances, courts have found that a voidable marriage (in contrast to a void one) emancipates the minor for the period of time until it is annulled. If at that time the minor who married would not otherwise have become emancipated, she reverts to unemancipated status, and the parental support obligation is revived. See, e.g., *State v. Demetz*, 130 P.3d 986 (Ariz. Ct. App. 2006) and *Thomas v. Campbell*, 960 So. 2d 694 (Ala. Ct. App. 2006); see also, 1 D. Kramer, Legal Rights of Children §15:1 at 1080 (rev. 2d ed. 2005). On the other hand, the Supreme Court of Illinois has held that a minor may remain unemancipated although married (or despite having experienced some other emancipating life event, such as military service or incarceration in prison). Marriage by itself does not accomplish a minor's emancipation; the minor must as well establish independence of the parent. See *In re Marriage of Baumgartner*, 2010 Ill. LEXIS 671 (Ill. May 20, 2010).

95. Issue: Whether the Unmarried Biological Father of a Child Can Prevent the Child's Adoption Immediately After Birth

The correct answer is **B**. Noah will be able to prevent the adoption provided he timely establishes a relationship with his child. Answer A is wrong because Noah has not been afforded a reasonable amount of time to establish a relationship with his child after indicating by his registration and offer of support that he intends to do so. Answer C is wrong because Noah's fundamental right as a parent is not absolute; he must seek to establish, and ultimately establish, a relationship with the child. See *Lehr v. Robertson*, 463 U.S. 248 (1983). Answer D is wrong because the decision as to Noah's unfitness to parent cannot be made until he has had an opportunity to do so.

96. Issue: Whether the Father of an Unborn Child Has a Right to Prevent the Pregnant Mother from Obtaining an Abortion

The correct answer is **C**. The U.S. Supreme Court, in determining that the father who was the husband of the pregnant woman had no right to be notified of her impending abortion, provided reasoning that would apply *a fortiori* to an unmarried father who seeks to prevent the abortion: The father's interest in the unborn child's welfare does not approach in weight the pregnant woman's liberty interest in her body. See *Planned Parenthood of Southeastern Pennsylvania v. Casey*, 505 U.S. 833 (1972). A is incorrect because any right Noah has to establish a relationship with his child is conditional on his child being carried to term; Queenie's liberty interest in her bodily integrity will trump it until that time. B is incorrect for the same reason. D is incorrect because the reason given is wrong: The father of the unborn child, whether married or not married to the pregnant woman, cannot override her constitutionally protected decision to have an abortion.

97. Issue: The Right of Parents of a Pregnant Minor to an Injunction to Prevent Her from Obtaining an Abortion

The correct answer is **B**. Whether Queenie can obtain an abortion without her parents' permission depends on a court's determination that she is mature enough to make the decision to have an abortion, contrary to her parents' wishes. If the state statute is constitutional, as the parents represented it to be, it will have an adequate judicial bypass procedure to override the parents' decision. If not, the statute would be struck down as unconstitutional. See *Planned Parenthood of Southeastern Pennsylvania v. Casey*, 505 U.S. 833

(1992). A is incorrect because although the interest described is a strong one, it is not absolute, as *Casey* indicates. C is incorrect because the fundamental parental right to the care, custody, and control of their child is not absolute either; Queenie's interest in her bodily integrity outweighs it if she is mature enough to make a reasoned decision to have an abortion. D is incorrect because although a court might find against a pregnant minor who does not have sufficient maturity to make the decision, balancing her parents' interests with hers is not part of that determination.

98. Issue: The Legal Test of Emancipation of One Who Is Still a Minor

The correct answer is **C**. The test of emancipation is whether the minor has moved beyond her parents' sphere of influence and responsibility and obtained independence. Queenie has not done so. Although she has moved out of the family's domicile, she is still living in her mother's residence. Because her unborn child's father is unable to support her and she has not been able to get a job, Queenie is still dependent on a parent, her mother, for support. Moreover, she is still within her mother's sphere of influence; she obeyed her mother when the latter refused to allow her to quit school and take a job. Queenie has not obtained independence, and hence she is not emancipated. Both her parents, not just her mother, owe her support. A is incorrect because many courts in many states have found that a minor's pregnancy, standing alone, does not emancipate the minor. B is incorrect because many courts in many states have found that no longer residing in the family domicile, without the quality of independence, does not emancipate the minor. D is incorrect because, if Queenie had the attributes of independence, she would be emancipated even if she could not find work.

99. Issue: Whether a Minor's Ability to Live Independently of Her Parents Is Sufficient to Emancipate Her

The correct answer is **B**. Although independence is required for a minor to become emancipated, a prerequisite for emancipation is either consent of the custodial parent or parents, or acquiescence in it. Tammy's parents did not explicitly consent to her emancipation on the facts given. Nor did they acquiesce; once they discovered that she was not voluntarily returning to their home, they began searching for her. They have continued to do so. These are not actions that imply parental consent to her moving away and establishing her independence. A is incorrect because it ignores the requirement of parental consent for emancipation. C is incorrect because her parents did not know what her plans were when she left their house, and their actions afterward indicate that no consent was intended. D is wrong because a court order is one method of obtaining emancipation, but is not required for other methods to be effective.

100. Issue: Liability of Parents for the Torts of Their Children

A is the most likely answer. Parents are liable for the reasonably foreseeable damage from the actions of their children; Dennis and Dooley having acquired a reputation as "hell-raisers" for earlier damage they have caused, Henry and Alice are responsible for not preventing the boys from doing further damage. B is wrong because parents at common law are not strictly liable for their children's torts. C is wrong as well because parents are responsible for their children's foreseeable tortious acts even if the children are too young to understand the possible damage to others that might result from those actions. D is wrong because Dennis and Dooley are too young to anticipate the possible consequences of their actions; as a result Henry and Alice have a duty to supervise their children and prevent behavior that is likely to damage their neighbors.

101. Issue: The Standards for Changing the Surnames of Children After Their Parents Have Divorced

D is the correct answer. In many states, courts have adopted a presumption in favor of continuing the present last name of the child to avoid confusion for the children and possible alienation from the parent whose last name they have borne. Answer A is therefore one correct answer. Answer C is also correct, however; in many other states, the courts do not apply a presumption of any sort, but consider only the best interest of the children. Thus D, offering both of these, is correct. B also states a presumption used by courts in deciding whether to permit change of a child's name after his or her parents have divorced, but it is a minority view, and the frequency of joint custody awards limits its use; thus it is not the most likely rule.